SPEAKING OUT IN VIETNAM

Speaking Out in Vietnam

Public Political Criticism in a Communist Party–Ruled Nation

Benedict J. Tria Kerkvliet

Cornell University Press
Ithaca and London

First published 2019 by Cornell University Press

Library of Congress Cataloging-in-Publication Data

Names: Kerkvliet, Benedict J., author.
Title: Speaking out in Vietnam : public political criticism in a communist party-ruled nation / Benedict J. Tria Kerkvliet.
Description: Ithaca : Cornell University Press, 2019. | Includes bibliographical references and index.
Identifiers: LCCN 2018045337 (print) | LCCN 2018048272 (ebook) | ISBN 9781501736384 (pdf) | ISBN 9781501736407 (epub/mobi) | ISBN 9781501736384 | ISBN 9781501736384 (cloth ; alk. paper)
Subjects: LCSH: Freedom of speech—Vietnam. | Political activists—Vietnam. | Dissenters—Vietnam. | Political culture—Vietnam. | Communism and Society—Vietnam. | Vietnam—Politics and government—1975.
Classification: LCC JC599.V5 (ebook) | LCC JC599.V5 .K47 2019 (print) | DDC 323.44/309597—dc23
LC record available at https://lccn.loc.gov/2018045337

To my son and daughter, Brian and Jodie

Contents

Illustrations

Figures

Tables

Acknowledgments

I am most grateful to Phạm Thu Thủy of the Department of Political and Social Change, Australian National University. From 2003 through 2009, she collected and organized many of the materials I used to write this book. Grants from the Australian Research Council during that period paid part of her salary and for some other aspects of my research. Also vital to this book's genesis was collegial, academic, and financial support from the Australian National University, particularly its Research School of Pacific and Asian Studies and Department of Political and Social Change.

The Trung Tâm Nghiên Cứu Việt Nam và Giao Lưu Văn Hóa [Center for Vietnamese Studies and Cultural Exchange] and the Viện Việt Nam Học và Khoa Học Phát Triển [Institute of Vietnamese Studies and Development Sciences], both at the Vietnam National University in Hà Nội, made it possible for my wife, Melinda, and me to stay several times in Vietnam to do research. Especially helpful were those two institutions' directors Phan Huy Lê, Vũ Minh Giang, Nguyễn Quang Ngọc, and Phạm Hồng Tung and office manager Đỗ Kiên. During our stays, Phan Huy Lê, Hoàng

Như Lan, Lê Văn Sinh, Đoàn Thiện Thuật, Trương Thị Hợp, Nguyễn Quang Ngọc, Đặng Vân Chi, and Nguyễn Văn Chính frequently assisted and entertained Melinda and me.

I sincerely thank numerous individuals, whose names should not be revealed, who shared with me their observations, experiences, and opinions about political and other issues in Vietnam.

At various times Nguyễn Điền in Canberra and Lê Văn Sinh in Hà Nội helped me to find relevant material. Also aiding me along the way were staff members at Menzies Library, Australian National University; Hamilton Library, University of Hawai'i; and Vietnam's National Library in Hà Nội.

For their comments on papers that evolved to become parts of this book, I thank Bùi Duyên, Anita Chan, Đặng Đình Trung, Kirsten Endres, Tom Fenton, Roger Haydon, Jason Morris-Jung, Pam Kelley, Ehito Kimura, Jonathan London, Ken MacLean, David Marr, Pam McElwee, Nguyễn Hồng Hải, Nguyễn Quang A, Nguyễn Văn Chính, David Rosenberg, Jim Scott, Drew Smith, Manfred Steger, Philip Taylor, Huong Le Thu, Angie Ngọc Trần, Trần Đình Lâm, Bill Turley, Tuong Vu, Jon Unger, Gwen Walker, and Brantly Womack. I am also indebted to Melinda Tria Kerkvliet, my wife and best friend, who commented on all chapters and was with me throughout the research journey from which this book emerged.

Also helping to improve my analysis were questions and suggestions received during presentations I made at a conference of the Denmark Association of Development Researchers in Copenhagen, May 2009; the Authoritarianism in East Asia conference organized by Jonathan London at City University of Hong Kong in June 2010; a colloquium convened by Shawn McHale at the Sigur Center for Asian Studies, George Washington University in October 2010; a forum organized by Lydia Yu-Jose at the Ateneo Center for Asian Studies, Ateneo de Manila University in November 2012; the Vietnam Update in November 2013 at the Australian National University; a forum arranged by Kirsten Endres at the Max Planck Institute for Social Anthropology, Halle (Saale), Germany, in June 2015; a colloquium at the Center for Southeast Asian Studies, University of Hawai'i, in September 2015; a forum at the Asia Center, University of the Philippines that Ed Tadem convened in October 2015; and seminars at the Australian National University organized by the Department of Political and Social Change and the Vietnam Studies Group in November 2013 and October 2017.

I sincerely thank Roger Haydon at Cornell University Press for his encouragement and advice and for finding two scholars to read the entire manuscript. To both of those readers I am indebted for their numerous useful suggestions. One reader chose not to remain anonymous so I can thank Andrew Wells-Dang by name.

For helping to finalize the manuscript for this book, I thank Pam Kelley for suggesting a title; Quynh H. Vo for scrutinizing all endnotes; Ann Bone for her conscientious copyediting; and Quynh Chi Do, Nicholas Farrelly, Jill Jokisch, Ellen Murphy, Huong Nguyen, Calvin Tran, and Angie Ngọc Trần for advice about photos. For permission to use their photos, I am grateful to Đinh Văn Dũng, Getty Images, Nguyễn Đình Toán, OCI, Giang Vu Hoang Pham, and Ian Timberlake.

Parts of this book draw on four of my previous publications: "Workers' Protests in Contemporary Vietnam (with Some Comparisons to Those in the Pre-1975 South)," *Journal of Vietnamese Studies* 5 (Winter 2010): 162–204; "Protests over Land in Vietnam: Rightful Resistance and More," *Journal of Vietnamese Studies* 9 (Summer 2014): 19–54; "Regime Critics: Democratization Advocates in Vietnam, 1990s–2014," *Critical Asian Studies* 47 (September 2015): 359–87; "Government Repression and Toleration of Dissidents in Contemporary Vietnam," in *Politics in Contemporary Vietnam*, edited by Jonathan London (New York: Palgrave Macmillan, 2014), 100–34.

Abbreviations

APEC	Asia-Pacific Economic Cooperation
BBC	British Broadcasting Corporation
CFRF	Club of Former Resistance Fighters [Câu Lạc Bộ Kháng Chiến Cũ]
DRV	Democratic Republic of Vietnam [Việt Nam Dân Chủ Cộng Hòa], the government of Vietnam headquartered in Hà Nội from 1945 until 1976
HUD	Housing and Urban Development Investment Corporation [Tổng Công Ty Đầu Tư Phát Triển Nhà và Đô Thị]
IDS	Institute for Development Studies [Viện Nghiên cứu Phát triển IDS]
MoLISA	Ministry of Labor, Invalids and Social Affairs [Bộ Lao Động-Thương Binh và Xã Hội]
MoNRE	Ministry of Natural Resources and Environment [Bộ Tài Nguyên và Môi Trường]
NVGP	Nhân Văn Giai Phẩm [Humanity and Masterworks]

RFA	Radio Free Asia
RFI	Radio France International
RVN	Republic of Vietnam [Việt Nam Cộng Hòa], the government in southern Vietnam from 1954 to 1975
UDIC	Việt Hưng Urban Development and Investment Company [Công ty Đầu tư và Phát triển Đô thị Việt Hưng]
VCP	Vietnamese Communist Party [Đảng Cộng Sản Việt Nam]
VGCL	Vietnam General Confederation of Labor [Tổng Liên Đoàn Lao Động Việt Nam]
VOA	Voice of America

Speaking Out in Vietnam

Introduction

Political Criticism and the Party-State

Since 1975, after thirty years of war, people in Vietnam have largely lived in peace under a political system that in several respects has scarcely changed. The Vietnamese Communist Party (VCP) remains the country's only authorized political party. Its Secretariat, Political Bureau, and Central Committee set national policy priorities. The government's prime minister and other top officials are invariably high-ranking VCP leaders. Every five years, nationwide elections select National Assembly delegates to represent the numerous constituencies within the country. Most constituencies have more candidates than the total number of seats, so voters have some choice among persons but not among political parties. Nearly all nominees are VCP members and hence nearly all the delegates elected are too. Similar procedures are used to elect officials at each subnational level of government.

Despite these continuities, however, political life in Vietnam has changed dramatically. Since the late 1980s to early 1990s, the country's political economy has been renovated: markets have replaced the centralized state-run economic system; family farming has displaced collectivized agriculture; and state-owned enterprises no longer dominate all production and services, much of which is now under the sway of private businesses and foreign companies. The state's reach into Vietnamese citizens' lives has receded significantly. For instance, in the 1970s to 1980s, the government enforced tight restrictions on travel, people had little freedom to form their own associations outside of state-authorized organizations and activities, nearly all urban residents lived in government-controlled housing, and citizens had almost no access to information and publications beyond what official agencies provided. Today, Vietnamese citizens travel quite easily and live in private housing. They also form, usually with little interference from authorities, their own groups, clubs, and organizations around such interests and needs as health, environment, religion, sport, commerce, science, education, and politics.[1] Some civic organizations register with government agencies; many do not. Official government and VCP-run organizations are still active but no longer monopolize associational life in the country.

Sources for news and other information have also been diversifying.[2] State-authorized newspapers, radio and television stations, and publications continue and are still censored. But they have become more numerous, and their content, style, format, and funding have expanded enormously. Meanwhile, media beyond the state's control have vaulted from practically nothing in the 1970s and 1980s to virtually countless. Many Vietnamese now readily access international television and radio stations and read—often online—newspapers and publications from around the globe. Social media, especially Facebook, have become extremely popular in Vietnam. Citizens also use—and create—newsletters, magazines, blogs, and websites produced in Vietnam with content ranging from the very personal to the highly political.

The change in Vietnam that most interested me when preparing this book is the rise and range of public political criticism. Until the early 1990s, discontent about the economy, housing, education, employment, land use, government officials, state policies, and practically all other political issues was rarely voiced openly. It was whispered among family and friends, and acted on in surreptitious and quotidian ways out of sight and earshot of untrusted others lest the critic suffer reprimands that could include imprisonment. Such everyday disapproval and resistance is still ubiquitous. In addition, however, Vietnamese people since the mid-1990s have been speaking out publicly and in many ways on numerous political matters. I focus on four clusters of critics: factory workers striking to demand better wages and living conditions, villagers demonstrating and petitioning against corruption and land appropriations, citizens opposing China's encroachments into Vietnam and authorities' reactions, and dissidents criticizing the entire regime and pressing for democratization.[3]

The book argues that public political criticism since the mid-1990s has evolved into a prominent feature of Vietnam's political landscape, and state authorities have dealt with it with a combination of responsiveness, toleration, and repression. Indeed, one important reason why public political criticism has grown is that authorities have been unable and to a degree unwilling to stifle it. A second reason is Vietnamese people from many walks of life and in numerous parts of the nation have pushed, sometimes aggressively, to expand the arena for speaking out on a wide range of issues.

Foreign commentaries have often described Vietnam's Communist Party government as a totalitarian or authoritarian system that countenances little or no criticism. Reports from Freedom House stress that the regime has been "silencing critics" through numerous means and that every year since about 2007 the "intolerance for political dissent" has been "growing" and a "climate for civil liberties and political freedoms" has been "worsening."[4] The only book-length examination of how Vietnamese authorities deal with dissent concludes that the government "tolerates no dissent or opposition."[5] Similar views have been expressed by several members of the U.S. Congress. In recent years, annual reports about Vietnam from Human Rights Watch and the U.S. State Department, while not branding the Vietnamese government as totally repressive, depict it as extremely intolerant of political dissent of any kind.[6]

Several scholars on Vietnam, however, see the country's political life very differently. For instance, one long-time Vietnam researcher has written that since the late 1990s, "political development has entered an extraordinary, if undefined and not yet formally recognized phase. Coercion and repression remain menacing, though not dominant, features of daily social life" and there are forums for "dissent and contentious politics, which are more difficult to deal with than in the past when . . . harassment, arrest, and imprisonment were the hallmarks of the state's repressive capacities."[7] Actually, observed another scholar of Vietnam, the country "has exactly the kind of political system that stimulates dissidence. It is sufficiently open to tolerate a certain degree of dissent, but dissidents do not lose their lives. At the same time, political opposition carries sufficient risk to provide the dissident with an aura of moral courage."[8] Writing about communication facilities in Vietnam, another analyst said, "There is no legal, independent media in Vietnam. Every single publication belongs to part of the state or the Communist Party. But this is not the whole story—if it was, there would be very little dynamism at work in Vietnam and, as we know, it is one of the most dynamic and aspirational societies on the planet. This has been enabled by the strange balance between the [Communist] Party's control, and lack of control."[9] "Political control," argued another scholar, is certainly present in Vietnam "but this does not mean that all criticisms and opposition to the VCP and the government are disallowed."[10]

This book shows with more detail and analysis than any previous study that public criticism in Vietnam ranges from lambasting corrupt authorities to opposing the political system, from condemning repression against bloggers to resisting land confiscations, from protesting working conditions in factories to questioning the state's foreign policies. The citizens speaking out are also diverse: rural villagers, urban workers, religious leaders, intellectuals, students, environmental activists, leaders of professional associations, and former (even some current) government and VCP officials. The extent, variety, and vibrancy of public political debate and dissent in today's Vietnam correspond to the assessments of the scholars just cited rather than to the commentaries noted earlier. Even if one focuses, as chapters 4 and 5 do, on the regime's harshest critics—those advocating the demise of the one-party political system and the rise of a democratic government—the claim that Vietnamese authorities tolerate no dissent or opposition is erroneous.

Common labels applied by scholars, journalists, and diplomats to Vietnam's political system are totalitarian, authoritarian, and dictatorship. Each, however, is problematic because Vietnam under Communist Party rule has never conformed well to long-standing definitions for these terms. For instance, one feature of a dictatorship is "emergency rule that suspends or violates temporarily the constitutional norms" for exercising authority.[11] Communist Party rule in Vietnam, by contrast, is provided for in the country's constitution and it is not a temporary arrangement, having lasted since 1954 in half the nation and since 1975 throughout. Authoritarianism is a political system that, among other features, lacks an "elaborate and guiding ideology" and, if there is a political party, it "is not a well-organized ideological organization."[12] The VCP, however, is ideological and highly organized, even though analysts do debate its abilities to deal with challenges facing the nation.[13] Among the features of totalitarianism that do not conform to Vietnam's system are central control of the economy and a secret police that terrorizes the country.[14]

Because these general labels are inadequate, scholars have proposed alternatives for one-party political systems, particularly those in Vietnam and China. Each of these two countries has a well-organized Communist Party that led successful revolutions for national independence, espouses an ideology based on socialist principles, sets policy agendas for governing, penetrates virtually all levels and institutions of the state (including the military and police), and successfully oversaw the conversion of a centralized and collectivized economic system to a market economy.[15] To summarize these features, Jonathan London has made a strong case to apply the label "market-Leninism" to the regimes in Vietnam and China.[16]

That term, however, does not capture interactions between the governors and the governed—how authorities and citizens relate, how governing is done, and how policies are made and implemented. There may have been a time when such interactions were irrelevant, and maybe even now that could be true for some aspects of governing. But since at least the late 1970s, relations between authorities and citizens have created a significant dynamic in the politics of both China and Vietnam. To reflect that in a summary label for the political system scholars have proposed such terms as soft authoritarianism, consultative Leninism, contentious authoritarianism, deliberative authoritarianism, networked authoritarianism, fragmented authoritarianism, resilient authoritarianism, and responsive authoritarianism.[17]

Proponents of these terms say little to explain the nouns "authoritarianism" and "Leninism" beyond highlighting the prominence of the Communist Party, the absence of competitive elections, and the frequency of repression. What they emphasize is the meaning of the adjectives, which, despite some differences, all try to encapsulate the same phenomena: the political systems in Vietnam and China, in addition to the features summarized above as market-Leninism, also include methods, opportunities, institutions, and organizations through which citizens can advocate changes, criticize policies, and resist government actions; authorities, in turn, often listen, respond, discuss, and even accept citizens' concerns. These aspects help to account for the durability of the regimes in Vietnam and China. And they can be acknowledged without ignoring or downplaying repression, which is also prominent in each country. As two analysts have put it, significant reforms "have fundamentally altered the two states' interactions with their citizens, often for the better. Recognizing that these countries are authoritarian and use coercive policies regularly should not blind us to the significant, well-documented governance changes that are improving people's lives."[18]

Research for this book and studies by others have led me to regard Vietnam's political system as a Communist Party-state that deals with public political criticism in ways ranging from responsiveness and toleration to repression. Responsiveness means to consider, accommodate, or make concessions to the concerns, criticisms, and demands of individuals, groups, and sectors of society. Toleration refers to countenancing criticism and dissent without doing much to stop it or respond positively to it. Repression means to prevent, stifle, or suppress, through force and other methods, citizens saying or doing things objectionable to authorities. My summary label for this system is a "responsive-repressive party-state."[19]

Responsiveness and toleration along with repression have figured in some other analyses of Vietnam and China. An evaluation of the political dynamics in both countries since the 1980s concluded that, although both party-states have some authoritarian and totalitarian features, their form of governance challenges "the assumption that effective political responsiveness requires competitive parliamentary politics."[20] Referring specifically to how Vietnam's Communist Party reacts to political dissent, one study said the party "is well aware that 'hard' repression should only be exercised as a last resort. . . . It has taken certain measures to show that it is responsive to criticisms in a bid to consolidate its power foundations and improve its legitimacy."[21] In China, the regime has reacted to street marches, demonstrations, sit-ins, and other public protests "with a mixture of repression and sympathy."[22] One study showing that Chinese authorities react to labor unrest in both repressive and responsive ways went on to speculate that the "ability of governments like China's to both demonstrate concern for popular grievances and yet erect some parameters on how far protesters can go in pressing their claims may provide a partial explanation for such governments' surprising longevity."[23]

The hyphenated term "party-state" is used in several analyses of Vietnam as well as China. It conveys that the VCP is entwined with the state. The VCP is an organization in its own right, extending from its central offices and leaders in the nation's capital, Hà Nội, to its local offices and officials in virtually every town and village throughout the country. State institutions—

ministries for finance, agriculture, health, education, etc., as well as the military and police—also extend from Hà Nội to every province, city, district, ward, and subdistrict.[24] The principal officials at each of those levels are VCP members. In that way and by setting national and local government agendas, the VCP controls most functions of the state while at the same time deriving much of its income from the state. In addition, VCP members are typically leaders of the sectoral organizations—for peasants, workers, women, youth, artists, journalists, minority groups, and others—authorized and partly funded by the state.

This summary, I recognize, glosses over tension, debate, rivalry, negotiation, corruption, and other complexities within Vietnam's party-state as leaders and agencies at all levels make and implement policies, mobilize resources, and contend with the myriad aspects of governing. I note those dynamics when they influence how authorities deal with public political criticism, but for the most part they are beyond the scope of this book.[25]

Methodology

Just as the Internet and other electronic technology have helped Vietnamese citizens to speak out, journalists and news agencies to disperse their articles, and government agencies to publicize their policies and activities, so too that technology has enabled me to trace and scrutinize the expansion of public political criticisms and the variety in party-state authorities' behavior. Much of this book draws on materials critics themselves wrote, interviews they gave to journalists, video clips they shot, and recordings they made that were circulated on websites, blogs, and social media. It also uses online newsletters and newspapers that critics produced as well as newspapers and magazines published (in printed and electronic formats) by the party-state's media outlets and by several foreign news agencies. Also valuable for this book are reports and documents that government ministries and research centers and the VCP prepared and often posted on their websites.

Realizing the rapid growth and diversification of relevant Internet materials is partly what convinced me in 2002–3 that extensive research on this topic was possible. A research assistant, Phạm Thu Thủy, and I developed a list of topics and subtopics pertaining to political discord and authorities' actions and a list of websites from which we could regularly download pertinent materials. From the outset, I wanted to know what Vietnamese in Vietnam were saying and doing, and hence I focused mainly on information coming from them and paid much less attention to materials from overseas Vietnamese organizations and media. Initially the number of relevant websites was manageable for us to monitor regularly. But soon there were several hundred, far more than we could handle, so I had to focus on those that were most useful. I also reduced the list of topics and subtopics.

Augmenting online resources were my several stays in Vietnam, mostly in Hà Nội and vicinity, between 2006 and 2016. During those trips I met Vietnamese who shared with me their knowledge and experiences. Initially, because political criticism was a delicate subject, I usually described my interests very broadly and I did not attempt to meet critics themselves for fear of getting them or me in trouble with Vietnamese authorities. From about 2012, however, the subject had become less controversial and Vietnamese scholars, journalists, lawyers, and others talked more forthrightly with me. I also met several critics active in issues pertaining to labor, land, Vietnam-China relations, and democratization, the four broad topics I had decided to emphasize. Besides face-to-face discussions with such people, I communicated with some by e-mail. Also while in Hà Nội I located in Vietnam's National Library some newspapers, magazines, and books that I had not been able to find elsewhere.

While collecting and analyzing material from all these sources, I kept in mind five clusters of questions: (1) what are critics saying and what are their rationales and objectives; (2) who are the critics and what are their backgrounds; (3) to what extent do critics emphasizing one issue, such as Vietnam-China relations or land appropriations, interact and collaborate with critics stressing a different matter, such as workers' conditions or democratization; (4) what are the reactions of party-state authorities and how does their behavior affect what critics say and do; and (5) what does the content, form, and range of public political criticisms and authorities' actions reveal about Vietnam's political system?

Throughout my research, I also had a broad conception of "politics" and "political," similar to that articulated by other studies.[26] Politics is about the control, allocation, and use of important resources and the values and ideas underlying those activities. Resources include land, labor, water, money, power, education, among numerous other tangible and intangible assets. Political ways to control, distribute, and use resources can range from cooperation and collaboration, to discussions and debates, to bargains and compromises, to conflicts and violence. Political activity occurs in numerous settings, not just in governments and other state institutions but also in corporations, factories, universities, religious groups, villages, families, and many other entities. And it has numerous forms, not just the behavior of government officials, actions during elections, and efforts to influence public officials, but also often people's activities while they work, study, raise families, and live their lives. Factory employees criticizing their working conditions and pressing employers to improve them are being political; so are employers as they accede to or oppose such efforts. Also political are discussions, disputes, and protests about how land is used and distributed, about fishing in contested waters, about relations between Vietnam and China, and about Vietnam's system of government.

I end my analysis at 2015, roughly twenty years after political criticism became increasingly public in Vietnam, a sufficiently lengthy period to demonstrate its prominence. Public contestation on political issues in the country persists, and hence researching it could continue. But I needed to stop in order to write this book.

Chapter Previews

The book's chapters focus on topics around which considerable public debate and protest emerged, starting in the mid-1990s. The topic in chapter 1 concerns labor. Between 1995 and 2015, Vietnamese workers frequently and publicly criticized the conditions under which they labored in enterprises, some owned entirely by the party-state but most owned partly or fully by private, especially foreign, companies. Workers' foremost ways of speaking out were thousands of strikes, some with thousands of participants each. None of the strikes were legal. Few were highly organized; most erupted with modest preparation. The chapter explains how these protests occurred, what workers wanted in order to improve their conditions, and why authorities did not criminalize the strikes and rarely were repressive. Often government officials were sympathetic to workers' demands.

Chapter 2 is about land. Villagers in numerous parts of Vietnam spoke out against local government officials and property developers who, the protesters claimed, were confiscating their farmlands. The chapter identifies two patterns in how villagers protested: in one, people in the same vicinity peacefully pressed their claims and sought help from higher officials to force local authorities to meet their demands; in the second, villagers from numerous places collaborated and sometimes used force. In both patterns, villagers' reasons for speaking out were similar and their notions of fairness and justice went beyond what the law recognized. They also sought support and advice from Vietnamese in other sectors of society. Authorities' reactions ranged from tolerating, even trying to accommodate, villagers' complaints to violently evicting them from their fields, breaking up demonstrations, and arresting participants.

Public criticism aimed at protecting the nation is the subject of chapter 3. It examines what fishers, students, writers, and citizens from other walks of life did to speak out against Chinese encroachments into Vietnamese territory. These Vietnamese sought to defend their nation's sovereignty and pressure party-state officials to join them. To some extent authorities did, but often they harassed, combated, and occasionally arrested critics, reactions that puzzled many Vietnamese. In trying to understand why party-state authorities were frequently hostile to patriotic citizens while apparently docile toward China, numerous critics came to doubt the regime leaders' commitment to preserving the Vietnamese nation.

Democratization is chapter 4's topic. It analyzes the views and actions of regime critics who wanted to replace the party-state with a democratic political system. Their objective was much more threatening to the regime than those of the critics who briefly emerged in the mid-1950s and the late 1980s, the only previous occasions the party-state faced significant public criticism. Although regime critics in 1995–2015 agreed on their objective and to pursue it nonviolently, they disagreed on how to displace the party-state. They also differed on the VCP's role, if any, in changing the regime and on the relationship between development and democracy.

Chapter 5 continues the topic of democratization by examining how Vietnamese authorities dealt with regime critics. The analysis shows that to some extent party-state officials tolerated dissidents and that repression was not uniform. Some regime critics were not detained; many more were confined for brief periods but never imprisoned. Others were imprisoned but after serving their prison sentences and resuming their political dissent, they were not imprisoned again. Only a few dissidents served additional prison terms. Also, crimes for which dissidents were convicted became less onerous and the length of their imprisonment became shorter. Compared to the past, when the party-state decisively repressed critics of the political system, it was unable to do so in 1995–2015.

Chapter 6 reprises the book's argument and speculates on the future course of public political criticism in Vietnam. The diversity and intensity of speaking out will likely continue and become more pronounced. That, however, may not evolve into a massive movement aimed at replacing the party-state with a multiparty and election-based democratic system, particularly if the present regime effectively combines repression with toleration and responsiveness.

Chapter 1

LABOR

Protesting Working and Living Conditions

In 2005, workers, most of them young women, labored in the hot, poorly ventilated factory of the Keyhing Toy Company, owned by capitalists from Hong Kong and located in the coastal city of Đà Nẵng in central Vietnam. The company had not raised wages in years yet several times had increased the volume of goods it expected each worker to produce. Workers who failed to meet these daily quotas were fined. They toiled from 6:30 in the morning until 8:30 in the evening, and the one hour of rest they were supposed to get at midday was often shorter. Fainting from exhaustion and paint fumes often aroused not sympathy from supervisors but chastisement. A worker had to beg permission to rest, and her pay was docked if she exceeded the allotted recovery time. Supervisors frequently cursed and insulted workers, arbitrarily penalized their pay, and fined anyone who went to the restroom more than twice a day. Workers also suspected that company officials were responsible for the theft of employees' bicycles parked inside the factory compound. Managers raised the prices for meals in the company's canteen and forbade workers who brought their own food to eat it there. For every thousand workers, the company provided only one jug of water.

Seeking relief from these and other oppressive conditions they had been enduring for months, workers frequently sent written complaints to the company's managers and main office but received no positive responses. Many petitions "went astray" or were simply rejected. Ultimately, said one employee, "workers were only able to speak by going on strike," which ten thousand did for a few days in May until a settlement was negotiated.[1]

During 1995–2015, thousands of factory laborers also spoke through protests, especially strikes. This chapter addresses two sets of questions. One is about the protests themselves. What did workers seek and why, and what happened during strikes—where did they occur, were they peaceful or not, and how were they organized? The other set pertains to the consequences. What were the outcomes? What happened to the protesting workers; what did their employers do? What were the reactions of party-state authorities— repressive, tolerant, or responsive?

The answers, as I will show, are that the protesting workers sought, primarily by using peaceful methods, higher wages and humane treatment. In political terms, they wanted a more just distribution of money and other resources where they worked and lived and they pressed factory owners and party-state authorities to do that. To a considerable degree, owners and authorities were responsive.

My evidence comes mainly from over nine hundred Vietnamese news reports written in the 1990s through 2015 about labor conditions, unrest, and related matters.[2] Vietnamese reporters talked to factory managers, local government authorities, and officials in the party-state's unions within the Vietnam General Confederation of Labor (VGCL). Most importantly, journalists interviewed and observed workers where they were employed, where they lived, and while they protested. Thus news stories helped to publicize workers' complaints, amplify their voices, and get the attention of government authorities.[3] I also draw on several studies by scholars who analyzed the labor unrest.

Forms of Public Protest

Strikes have been a common way for Vietnamese workers to voice discontent since the late nineteenth or early twentieth century during French colonial rule. During 1954–75, while the country was politically divided, Republic of Vietnam authorities in the south had to deal with numerous strikes. After reunification in 1975, strikes began in the late 1980s, possibly earlier. From then until the early 1990s, available evidence suggests, strikes were fewer than forty per year. Thereafter, the numbers rose nearly annually through 2011 (see table 1.1).

The increases are broadly in line with the rising number of enterprises that were entirely or partly foreign-owned, located primarily in the nearly three hundred industrial zones created since the late 1990s especially in southern Vietnam. Not all foreign-invested enterprises had labor unrest, but 70–80 percent of the strikes during 1995–2015 occurred in them, even though they employed only 7 percent of the roughly twenty-five million Vietnamese working in economic sectors other than agriculture, fishing, and forestry.[4] The remaining strikes were mostly in Vietnamese privately owned businesses; a few were in state-owned enterprises. The majority of foreign-invested enterprises with strikes were producing garments, textiles, footwear, and electronic components and were wholly or largely owned by Taiwanese and South Koreans.[5] Well over half of the workers in the foreign-invested enterprises were young, mostly women typically 20–35 years old, who migrated from rural areas to do industrial labor.[6] Far from their families, they saved or sent home as much of their wages as possible before they themselves returned to their villages after a dozen or so years of factory work.

Strikes are a small fraction of all labor disputes and conflicts, which in 1995–2000 numbered around fifty thousand and no doubt were far more than that during the next fifteen years.[7] Many disputes were brief quarrels between workers and their immediate supervisors. Others involved workers sending complaints, in writing or through intermediaries, to managers and employers. Occasionally disgusted workers in an enterprise collectively launched a slowdown to production. For example, one day in 2006 at a footwear factory in the Mekong delta owned by the Vĩnh Long provincial government and a foreign investor, company managers announced that each worker's quota would increase from 120 to 160 shoes per day. Sixty shoemakers, instead of working faster, abruptly slowed down.[8] In early January 2013, hundreds of employees at a Japanese-owned eyewear factory slackened their pace of work upon learning that the company would reduce New Year bonuses by half.[9]

Table 1.1. Strikes in Vietnam, 1995–2015

Year	Number
1995	60
1996	59
1997	59
1998	62
1999	67
2000	71
2001	89
2002	100
2003	139
2004	125
2005	147
2006	387
2007	541
2008	762
2009	216
2010	523
2011	978
2012	539
2013	351
2014	293
2015	245
Total	5,813

Sources: Do Quynh Chi and Di van den Broek, "Wildcat Strikes: A Catalyst for Union Reform in Vietnam?," *Journal of Industrial Relations* 55, no. 5 (2013): 788; Quang Dương, "Tất cả các cuộc đình công đều không đúng trình tự pháp luật" [All Strikes Have Been Illegal], February 2, 2015, *Dân Sinh* [People's Livelihood], accessed April 26, 2017, http://baodansinh.vn/tat-ca-cac-cuoc-dinh-cong-deu-khong-dung-trinh-tu-phap-luat-d1962.html; Trần Thị Bích Huệ, "Mâu thuẫn lợi ích giữa chủ doanh nghiệp và người lao động ở Việt Nam hiện nay" [Conflicting Interests between Business Owners and Laborers in Today's Vietnam], January 25, 2016, *Tạp chí Khoa học Xã hội* [Social Science Review], accessed April 26, 2017, http://vssr.vass.gov.vn/noidung/tapchi/Pages/baiviet.aspx?UrlListProcess=/noidung/TapChi/Lists/Baiviet&ItemID=401&page=2&allitem=0; Hà Nam, "Năm 2015, cả nước xảy ra 245 cuộc đình công" [The Nation Had 245 Strikes in 2015], January 1, 2016, Voice of Vietnam, accessed April 12, 2017, http://vov.vn/tin-24h/nam-2015-ca-nuoc-xay-ra-245-cuoc-dinh-cong-464800.vov.

More common than slowdowns were individuals or small groups of laborers taking their complaints to outsiders. Some workers appealed to government officials to help deal with employers. Usually these complainants were government employees or workers in state-owned enterprises or former state-owned enterprises that had been converted into corporations. Due to their employers' links to state authorities, the workers reasoned that higher authorities might be willing to take action, just as villagers often petition higher authorities to punish or remove misbehaving local officials. Employees in various types of enterprises frequently turned to local offices of the VGCL, as Nguyễn Bích Ngọc did when her employer, a foreign-owned property managing company, attempted to dismiss her because she became pregnant. After the union showed little concern, she went to the *Lao Động* [Labor] newspaper. Even though it was an arm of the VGCL, the paper published her story and in the process chastised both her employer and the union for not giving her proper attention.[10]

Sympathetic journalists and newspapers, including those connected to VGCL, were often the first outsiders to whom aggrieved workers turned for assistance.[11] In July 2005, for instance, about ten employees of a private clothing manufacturer went to a *Lao Động* newspaper office with a litany of objections to how the Vietnamese owners treated workers and even failed to pay them. The newspaper's story, which included both the workers' complaints and the owner's response, ended with a plea that workers be paid at least the wages owed to them.[12] Rather than traveling to newspaper offices, some workers, such as hundreds employed at a chain of bookstores, e-mailed or texted their complaints to journalists.[13]

Strikes in contemporary Vietnam, like in most other countries, frequently occurred after other efforts had failed to get a resolution of, or even attention to their concerns. The strike by Keyhing Toy factory workers noted at the beginning of this chapter is an example. Another example started in Hồ Chí Minh City in late December 2007 when three hundred seamstresses in the Japanese-owned Wonderful Saigon Garment company stopped sewing at precisely 11 a.m. For the next several hours the women simply sat at their silent machines. That slowdown occurred because workers had conveyed, as one participant said, "many petitions [for better wages and bonuses] that management just ignored."[14] Only when the seamstresses stopped sewing did managers consent to meet with representatives of the disgruntled employees. Sewing resumed as serious discussions commenced. When an impasse came in early January 2008, the workers launched a strike that lasted three days before the company made concessions.[15]

Workers' Demands and Objectives

Most workers' criticisms and demands concerned wages and how employers treated laborers. Some accounts estimate that wage disputes were central to more than 75 percent of strikes.[16] Workers, unpaid for weeks, sometimes months, such as those in a Korean-owned factory in Hồ Chí Minh City, demanded their wages.[17] Laborers often accused employers of paying less than the hourly and daily rates verbally promised to them or explicitly stated in written contracts. Piecework employees objected to daily production quotas being increased without additional pay; frequently, they claimed, employers underpaid them by incorrectly or deliberately miscalculating how much was produced.[18] Another frequent complaint was that employers did not pay what the law required to social insurance and other worker benefit programs and even kept for themselves the money they deducted from employees' wages that were supposed to be passed to those programs.[19] A regular contentious issue since the early 1990s was the annual bonus workers expected each lunar New Year but which employers, especially foreign ones, often tried to avoid or gave only small amounts.[20]

The most common demand regarding wages was to raise them. This was a claim in some of the first outbreaks of labor discontent in the 1990s and continued to be so in most subsequent years. In the 1990s and early 2000s, workers frequently implored companies to pay at least the minimum wage set by the government. By 2005–6, many strikes were aimed primarily at the government to raise the minimum wage, which had been stagnant since 1999. In response, the government increased it 39 percent for workers in foreign-invested enterprises within metropolitan areas.[21] Although a significant gain, much of it was offset by inflation that exceeded 32 percent between 1999 and 2006. Minimum wages continued to rise each year through 2015, but often the increases were too small to meet rising costs of food, housing, and other essentials. Vietnamese researchers and officials reported in 2011–13 that the minimum wage in foreign-invested and private companies typically met only 50–70 percent of workers' basic necessities.[22] The large gaps between wages and higher living costs contributed significantly

Figure 1.1. Workers strike a Korean-owned factory in Bình Dương province, southern Vietnam, July 29, 2016, one of their several protests from 2014 against low wages, unpaid wages, and abusive treatment. Photo by Đinh Văn Dũng.

to the 3,020 strikes during 2007–11 as workers pressed for larger minimum wages and protested against employers who violated minimum wage laws.[23] Many strikes demanded that employers pay more than the minimum wage, which numerous companies had essentially made the maximum for all but a few employees.

Second only to workers' demands for higher wages were their objections to employers' behavior toward them. They protested against supervisors and managers kicking, slapping, and punching them. One supervisor in a Hà Nội factory owned by Canon Inc., after turning down two workers' requests to take time off for personal reasons, made sure the women did not leave by tying their legs to their work stations.[24] Many company authorities swore at and insulted employees, prohibited them from talking to each other while working, heavily penalized them for being a few minutes late to work or being pregnant, and severely limited workers' trips to the bathroom. Another major complaint was the lousy food served in company canteens, yet several enterprises prohibited workers from eating elsewhere or even bringing their own food.[25] A final common objection was that employers required exorbitantly long hours of labor. According to national laws, an employee should work just eight hours a day, five days a week. But managers often demanded much more, even if employees did not want the overtime. One factory worker recounted a pattern many experienced: "Managers say everyone must make 500 pieces a day. We do that. Then managers raise the quota to 600. If quotas aren't reached, we're forced to work more shifts. If longer hours don't achieve company targets, we have to work the next day even if that's a Sunday and without additional pay." Moreover, "to rest on Sunday, you must get permission. Anyone taking off three Sundays is put on report."[26]

In both sets of major issues—wages and employers' behavior—workers press for proper treatment, dignity, and a decent living.[27] As one close observer said, workers object to employers and supervisors treating them "like slaves."[28] A major cause of strikes, explained a laborer in Hồ Chí Minh City, is that workers toil such long hours every day that "we'll surely die early."[29] Long work days meant many employees had little time for anything else— they started work early, returned home late, slept, then repeated the routine day after day, often more than a week without letup, because they could not get permission to rest or because they did extra shifts to boost their income.

Yet despite working hard, their meager wages meant they lived poorly. Most discontented workers ate primarily vegetables and rice, not by choice but by necessity. Many lived in dingy, cramped quarters, which one worker described as a "rat's nest" and a reporter likened to "chicken coops."[30] Housing was particularly miserable for the workers who migrated from other parts of the country to find employment.[31] "Four sheets of metal roofing and very hot," said one worker about her living quarters. "Whether standing, sitting, or lying down, I'm still not comfortable. I want to run out of the place but don't know where to go. Why is my life so miserable? All day I'm stuck in the factory. I return home worn out. Tears start to fall as I weep silently and think I should die. But then there's my child. Ten years working in the city, my only possession is my daughter, now in third grade, so, despite everything, I must take care of her."[32] Workers wanted enough time and money to enjoy little excursions, read newspapers, see a film, and have nice food. But for most, these were "luxuries" that, one worker said, "we don't dare dream about."[33] What little they managed to save they typically sent home to relatives, set aside for their children's school expenses, and spent on medical care when they became sick.[34]

Workers directed most of their public complaints and demands to their employers. Less frequently, they spoke out against VGCL unions and officials for neither representing their interests nor helping their struggles. Occasionally they specifically criticized and made demands on the party-state.

One instance was a lengthy letter that eleven workers sent to the party-state's top leadership.[35] Writing in early 2006, they blamed the regime for taking their farm lands, thereby forcing them to sell their labor and become "slaves," "servants," and "exploited." They called on the nation's leaders to fulfill the ideals of communism and protect workers, particularly to ensure that laborers are adequately paid—equivalent, they demanded, to the wages that workers get in Singapore, Thailand, South Korea, and elsewhere in the region. Their letter also argued that VGCL unions fail to assist laborers and should be dissolved, and that workers should be free to form their own organizations.

Several strikes targeted the party-state; among them were those in 2005–11, referred to earlier, that pressed authorities to raise minimum wages. Another series of strikes aimed directly at the government occurred in 2015. They started in late March when thousands of employees at the Taiwanese-owned footwear manufacturing company Pou Yuen in Hồ Chí Minh City stopped working on learning that the social insurance system into which employees make monthly payments would, beginning January 2016, no longer allow anyone to receive benefits prior to reaching retirement age. As word spread of that change and of the Pou Yuen strike, more people walked off their jobs. Within a couple of days, strikes over the issue were occurring elsewhere in the city and in several provinces, among them Long An in the south where one factory worker told a reporter that laborers at all companies in the vicinity were also on strike.[36]

To workers, being required to wait until retirement age before retrieving their entitlements from the social insurance fund would be a huge setback. The strikes, explained workers to reporters, "are not the companies' fault but we got so upset when we found out about the new [social insurance] law that we stopped working. Very few factory laborers like us are able to work until reaching retirement age. So, when I can no longer work and return home, what am I going to live on if I must wait until I am old to get my social insurance money?"[37] "I've been working nine years," said another laborer as she conveyed her major objection and that of countless others, "and now I'm 35 years old. When I stop working [in a few years], I want to get then all my social insurance benefits in one lump sum. I can't wait until I'm 55 [the retirement age for women]. Who knows whether I'll even be alive by then."[38] Another large question troubling many laborers was whether the social insurance system would still be operating or solvent by the time they attained retirement age.[39]

As the strikes persisted, party-state officials, in press releases and in meetings with workers, urged them to return to their jobs, saying the change in the social insurance law was actually, in the long term, advantageous to them because on reaching retirement age, they could qualify for monthly pensions. Few strikers were persuaded. Only on the eighth day of strikes did they begin returning to work after reading news reports that the National Assembly would revamp the social insurance law to meet their demands.

Strike Activities

Most strike activities occurred at or near work sites and, with few exceptions, were peaceful. A typical pattern was striking employees congregated outside the factory where they worked, waiting for management's answers to demands that their representatives had conveyed. While waiting, they conversed, exercised, and read newspapers. They also talked to journalists, explaining why they were protesting and what they sought. Sometimes they blocked driveways and gates to stop people and vehicles from entering or leaving the factories.[40] Occasionally they displayed posters, marched in nearby streets, and blocked traffic.

One unusual type of strike occurred in November 2007 at the Tae Kwang Vina footwear factory near Hồ Chí Minh City. Thousands of the company's fourteen thousand workers, nearly all of them women, refused one morning to leave the buses that had transported them to work. The employees remained seated in dozens of buses parked along a street within the Đồng Nai industrial zone while some fellow workers peacefully stood outside the factory gate, hoping to present their demands to the company's managers. The striking workers primarily wanted higher wages. In the face of rapidly rising prices, including the increased fee they were paying the company to bus them to work, they could not "keep their heads above water."[41]

Strikes typically ended after a day or two. In 2010–11, a high point in their frequency, 54 percent of them lasted one day and 37 percent persisted two to five days. The longest was twenty-five days.[42] Newspaper accounts during

1995–2015 indicate a similar pattern. The size of strikes tended to grow over time, probably reflecting enlarged workforces in manufacturing plants. In 1999, the smallest strike as of August that year involved eighteen workers and the largest had five thousand.[43] In 2005, several strikes exceeded ten thousand workers each; one had twenty thousand. In 2006, the average strike in Hồ Chí Minh City had 4,627 participants.[44] In 2007–15, numerous strikes exceeded five thousand workers each; a few had over twenty thousand. The strike noted earlier at the Pou Yuen company in 2015 had over eighty thousand participants.

The few instances of striking workers becoming violent usually involved breaking things belonging to their employers. In the Keyhing strike with which this chapter began, several frustrated workers waiting outside the factory for managers' responses or trying to meet managers lost their tempers and, using their brute strength in numbers, broke through locked gates then smashed windows and other property inside the factory compound. Occasionally, strikers and company officials came to blows. During a strike at the Japanese-owned Mabuchi Motors electronics factory, managerial staff reportedly provoked a fight with some male workers that resulted in police intervention.[45]

The most serious violence involving factory workers occurred on May 13, 2014, but not during strikes. Two days earlier, thousands of Vietnamese from many walks of life, including laborers, had peacefully demonstrated in numerous towns and cities against an oil rig and dozens of ships that China had put in waters claimed by Vietnam (see chapter 3). On May 13, as a continuation of those protests, hundreds of workers in various industrial zones, especially in and around Bình Dương province near Hồ Chí Minh City, demonstrated at factories owned by Chinese corporations and roamed from one company to the next urging more laborers to join them.[46] Soon some nineteen thousand people in Bình Dương were marching while screaming anti-Chinese slogans. As some participants started throwing rocks and bricks, the crowds became increasingly destructive. By the time thousands of police had restored calm and arrested about eight hundred demonstrators, over one hundred enterprises, mostly owned by Chinese, Taiwanese, and Koreans, had been badly damaged. Also on that day, at demonstrations in an industrial zone of Hà Tĩnh province in central Vietnam, fights between Vietnamese and Chinese workers resulted in several deaths.

How and why those demonstrations became violent is not clear. Many participants condemned the destruction; some government authorities and analysts said a few provocateurs who were not laborers had initiated the violence. In any event, fearing more violence, party-state authorities resolutely squashed an attempted nationwide anti-China protest on May 18.

Modest Organizations

Organizations that theoretically could have led and coordinated workers' actions were the VGCL and its several thousand labor unions authorized by the party-state. But as of August 2015, according to VGCL officials, not one strike since 1995 had been led by a union.[47] Until about 2002, most strikes occurred in enterprises without unions; subsequently roughly 70 percent of strikes were in companies with unions.[48] Yet, union representatives were not strike organizers or leaders, largely because they were usually beholden to company owners for their jobs and privileges, often not permitted by company officials to be active, and frequently ineffective communicators of workers' grievances before strikes erupted.[49]

Nor have striking workers had significant support from other sectors of society, except several journalists. Some Vietnamese organizations have helped to convey employees' complaints to employers and serve as mediators, but they reportedly shunned involvement in strikes and other confrontations.[50] Buddhist groups, particularly the large but unauthorized Unified Buddhist Church of Vietnam, publicly expressed solidarity with many strikes, as did a few outspoken critics of Vietnam's political system.[51] It is unclear, however, whether such supporters went beyond words to give material or other assistance.

Most strikes were rather spontaneous or had minimal organization and planning. When they began, the majority had no identifiable spokespersons; only when they were underway did a few individuals emerge, sometimes through a voting process, to become the aggrieved workers' representatives who participated in negotiations to resolve the conflicts.

That hundreds, even thousands, of workers could rapidly protest together is partly due to their shared predicament of experiencing arduous labor conditions and having similar desires for a better life.[52] Reinforcing this are two additional significant factors. One is that workers learned, through their own and their workmates' experiences, that strikes could improve their situations.[53] The second is the strong networks among laborers in the same factory and in nearby enterprises. Besides working together, they often lived in the same neighborhoods, roomed together, and cooked and ate together. Being from the same region, province or even district and village was frequently an additional connection among workmates.[54] Through their networks, laborers rapidly communicated problems that upset them and others near them. Facilitating the speedy spread of such news were mobile phones, which became increasingly common even among low-income Vietnamese. Shared circumstances, knowledge that collective action can be effective, and extensive networks also help to explain why, in a typical strike, most laborers in the enterprise—often more than 80 percent—joined in.

On numerous occasions, employers provoked strikes by suddenly raising production quotas, reducing wages, or in other ways adversely adjusting workers' incomes. For example, at a Taiwanese enterprise in Bình Dương province, nearly all 2,600 factory workers went on strike when they realized the company, by rejigging wage calculations, had reduced their pay 20–40 percent.[55] Many strikes swiftly erupted when employees learned that their employer would not pay an expected New Year bonus or would be greatly reducing it.

Physical abuse of fellow workers also turned smoldering discontent into a walkout. For instance, forty employees in a package-making company in Hồ Chí Minh City instantaneously stopped working after seeing a foreman badly beat a fellow worker.[56] A worker in Bình Dương province wrote that even harder to bear than low wages and other miserable working conditions in a garment factory was vicious treatment. "One time a foreign manager in the company made some employees sit outside under the hot sun. That was their punishment for merely having talked while working. Seeing those women baking in the sun, crying and sobbing, made all of us so angry that we went on strike."[57]

Some strikes began with just a few employees, but as the news spread from one part of a factory to another, more joined, especially if employers further aggravated the situation. An example occurred at Nikkiso, a Japanese-owned medical equipment manufacturing company in Hồ Chí Minh City. In the context of tensions between employees and employer over wages, a group of about twenty workers stopped working one morning in early February 2007. They wanted a pay raise at least equal to the increase received in early 2006 and a proper New Year bonus. As word spread of their action and the company's indifference, more workers joined. Soon all six hundred of the day shift workers went on strike, which forced management to negotiate.[58]

An analogous phenomenon, but on a larger scale, is a strike in one factory prompting strikes in nearby enterprises, which in turn stimulated others. The result, said journalists and workers, were "waves" of walkouts within a short time period. Nearly half of the strikes in Vietnam's industrial zones after the year 2000 occurred in December through February, a time when frustrations over low wages and unfulfilled expectations of pay raises and annual bonuses were widespread in adjacent enterprises.[59] Sometimes positive results of a strike at one enterprise encouraged workers elsewhere to do likewise. Explaining why she joined a strike at the Vietnamese-owned Hải Vinh shoe manufacturer in Hồ Chí Minh city, one woman said, "Workers at the Freetrend company [a nearby Taiwanese-owned shoe factory] fought and got a raise, so we can do the same."[60]

Several strikes after the mid-2000s involved some planning by one or more groups within each troubled enterprise. Organizers were usually experienced older workers who knew employers' history of abuses and violations of labor laws, ably articulated workers' rights, enjoyed the respect of fellow workers, and had well-established networks, including good contacts with journalists.[61] Strike preparations often involved quiet meetings among initiators and with their circles of fellow workers to discuss demands, timing, and tactics. Planning could also include making leaflets to be passed hand-to-hand among employees prior to a walkout and summarized in graffiti on bathroom walls within the enterprise. For example, the strike at Freetrend in late December 2005 demanding that the company pay more and the government raise minimum wages initially had no one who could speak on behalf of workers to convey their demands. Yet some organizing began when rumors spread that wage increases would likely be tiny. Several disgusted employees began to mobilize fellow workers. The day before the strike, a group distributed leaflets that urged fellow workers to unite. The next morning, nearly all of the enterprise's eighteen thousand employees stopped work, forcing negotiations that a couple days later resulted in more substantial pay increases.[62]

Consequences

Strikes during 1995–2015 usually brought positive results for workers in the short run and sometimes in the long term. According to numerous news reports, employers typically addressed workers' demands quickly rather than let work stoppages drag on. Similarly, academic articles citing data from the International Labour Organization reported that 96 percent of sampled enterprises with strikes in 2006–7 had met their employees' demands, and that employers had satisfied workers' complaints in 92 percent of the strikes in 2010–11.[63] Because a high proportion of an enterprise's workforce normally joined any strike, production came to a complete or nearly complete halt, so strikes soon cost employers more than making concessions. Strikes in foreign-invested enterprises also spurred managers to take action on issues that they had ignored even after receiving workers' written complaints. In many such companies, managers had little power to set wages, bonuses, and workday routines. Those decisions were made by their superiors in the enterprises' head offices. Mere complaints from employees were an insufficient basis for managers to get their bosses to reconsider. The pressure of a strike, on the other hand, enabled managers to make headquarters take urgent notice and get involved in negotiations.[64] Often another significant influence came from local government authorities urging a rapid settlement and participating in negotiations, as did VGCL officials even if the company with the strike had no union. These officials frequently sympathized with the protesting workers.[65]

One might expect company managers and owners to have made a big issue of the fact that all the strikes were illegal (see below). Yet few companies publicly used this as a weapon against workers; rarely, for instance, were striking laborers fired for missing work, a recourse employers could lawfully take against absent employees. Companies essentially ignored the strikes' illegality because they themselves frequently violated laws. A primary cause of strikes, wrote the secretariat of the VCP in 2008, "is employers still don't properly implement labor law provisions nor give adequate attention to laborers' legitimate rights and interests."[66] Numerous other party-state officials and studies also blamed strikes on employers who withheld workers' pay for months, paid less than lawful wages, mistreated employees, hired people without giving them proper contracts, embezzled employees' health and social insurance contributions, and breached other laws.[67]

Although most strikes forced employers to make concessions to their employees, frequently the gains were not durable. Conditions improved for a while but then deteriorated, prompting workers to object and even strike again. Hence, some companies, such as a Korean-owned garment factory in Long An province, had multiple walkouts in a single year.[68] More had them every few years. Between 1997 and March 2008, employees at the Taiwanese-owned Huê Phong shoe manufacturer in Hồ Chí Minh City launched at least five strikes demanding better pay, decent food in the company's canteen, and a halt to physical and verbal abuse. Each time Huê Phong owners accepted workers' demands, but later on the maltreatment and bad working conditions resumed. In April 2008, workers walked out a sixth time when the company reneged on promised higher wages. This time the company's owners sat tight. After nearly a month-long strike, most of its four thousand workers returned to the factory with only a modest pay increase. The strikers gave up, wrote a journalist, because they were desperate for an income.[69] Some government officials with experience in trying to resolve Huê Phong's industrial relations problems concluded that the company's only interest was "exhausting and exploiting labor," not managing and having good relations with workers.[70]

Occasionally, company concessions were mixed with adverse repercussions for individual strike participants after work had resumed. Companies found or invented reasons to dismiss employees suspected of instigating labor protests. In January 2006, for instance, a Korean garment factory in Bắc Giang province north of Hà Nội laid off 102 workers for no clear reasons. The only thing the dismissed employees had in common was conspicuous involvement in a strike seven months earlier that had won workers higher wages.[71] In March 2014, managers at the Shilla Bag company threatened to fire six employees for leading a strike that had recently won concessions for workers. The threat provoked a new strike, which lasted three days until the company backed down.[72]

Party-state authorities reacted to workers' protests with some repression but mostly tolerance and responsiveness. The most severe repression was incarcerating people attempting to establish independent labor organizations. In October 2006, a few Vietnamese announced they were forming two labor unions with no connection to the party-state's VGCL. The founders were factory workers and a couple of pro-democracy advocates. Among the workers were Đoàn Huy Chương (also known as Nguyễn Tấn Hoành) and Nguyễn Thị Tuyết, two signers of the highly critical letter discussed earlier that was sent to national authorities in early 2006. A third group, the Vietnam Labor Movement, started in late 2008; it claimed in 2015 to have a dozen organizers helping fellow workers to defend their rights and improve their labor conditions.[73] The little evidence I found about these organizers and their groups suggests they had modest success and suffered severe repression.

In 2006 and 2007, at least five members of these groups were arrested and convicted of joining "reactionary" organizations and "abusing" their democratic rights by spreading "falsehoods" about the regime. Their prison terms ranged from eighteen months to five years.[74] One of them, Đoàn Huy Chương, served his eighteen-month sentence then returned to factory work and joined the Vietnam Labor Movement. In February 2010, police arrested him for exacerbating an ongoing strike at the Taiwanese-Vietnamese shoe factory Mỹ Phong in Trà Vinh province, south of Hồ Chí Minh City; later he and another Vietnam Labor Movement member were tried and each was sentenced to seven years' imprisonment for abusing democratic rights and disturbing the peace during that strike. A third member was sentenced to nine years.[75]

Other repression against striking workers was rare. A few newspaper accounts referred to police stopping fights between workers and management, which occasionally resulted in clashes between police and strikers. Police hardly ever threatened or hit peaceful strike participants.[76] And apart from participants in the nascent independent unions, police seldom, if ever, arrested workers for participating in a strike.[77]

That party-state authorities were not more heavy-handed is remarkable given that all of the strikes were illegal. None followed the process prescribed by law through which aggrieved workers are permitted to strike.[78] In particular, strikes occurred before negotiations between employees and employers had reached an impasse. Indeed, most happened before such negotiations had even commenced.

Perhaps one reason Vietnamese authorities tolerated strikes' transgressions of the law is that most workers confined their concerns to their labor and living conditions. Moreover, they were not well organized, either within a workplace or across different sites. Additionally, workers did not link their protests to other people's causes or to issues beyond their own needs. The exception was joining some demonstrations against China, especially in May 2014.

Another part of the explanation is that authorities saw workers as essential to the party-state's constituency. Workers and peasants, officials have frequently said, are the two main pillars of the VCP.

Of course, national authorities were also eager to develop a market economy and attract entrepreneurs and investors, especially foreign ones, with tax breaks, access to land on which to build manufacturing plants, and other policies. And once capitalists' enterprises were established, authorities often paid modest attention to their violations of laws regarding labor conditions, minimum wages, social insurance payments, and environmental protection. Many officials also knew that business owners and their numerous associations disliked workers' strikes. Periodically, some officials publicly apologized to company owners dealing with labor unrest and said that striking workers should compensate employers for lost production.

Nevertheless, party-state authorities did not criminalize strikes or strike participants despite their nonconformity with the law and pressure by companies to do so.[79] Instead, a prominent reaction among officials was to tolerate, even support, aggrieved workers and to blame strikes primarily on companies, especially foreign-invested ones, for violating labor laws and workers' rights.[80] National Assembly delegates, Ministry of Labor, Invalids and Social Affairs (MoLISA) officials, VGCL leaders, and provincial and district officials generally put the onus of lost production or revenue on the companies themselves for ignoring laws, particularly regarding wages, work hours per week, treatment of employees, and payments to social insurance and medical benefits. Numerous officials often described strikes as workers' "last resort," their "only weapon" to defend themselves, and said strikes resulting from employer violations of the law should not be deemed illegal or illegitimate.

Authorities also responded positively to workers' protests. As noted earlier, numerous strikes in 2005–6 contributed to party-state officials deciding to increase minimum wages then and to raise them annually thereafter.[81] Strikes also influenced revisions in the Labor Code of 2012, which established a National Wage Council to recommend workers' compensation. That measure contributed to minimum wages rising 32 percent in 2013–15, considerably more than the 12 percent inflation during that period.[82] That there were far fewer strikes during those three years was partly due to increased minimum wages and reduced inflation.[83]

Waves of strikes pushed the party-state to amend the social insurance law in 2015. By the sixth day of those huge protests in March and April that year, Prime Minister Nguyễn Tấn Dũng, MoLISA officials, and other authorities were considering changing the law so that workers could withdraw all money due to them before reaching retirement age.[84] A couple of days later, as noted earlier, the promise to make that change caused the strikes to subside. In May, government leaders instructed the National Assembly to revise the social insurance law's provisions regarding how and when employees could collect benefits. The change is needed, they wrote, because "a portion of laborers, particularly in southern provinces and cities, have petitioned to choose a lump sum payment for their social insurance benefits" just as the 2006 version of the law had allowed. Elaborating how workers had "petitioned," officials cited the strikes that had started March 26, 2015 in Hồ Chí Minh City and then spread to several provinces.[85] In June, the National Assembly amended the law to restore to workers the choice to get their benefits paid in a lump sum when no longer employed rather than wait until retirement age.[86]

The party-state also deliberated on ways to bring labor code provisions regarding strikes more in line with, as some national officials put it, "reality" and "life."[87] Rather than trying to get workers to comply with existing laws, many authorities advocated changing the law to better conform with the conditions workers faced.

Before the mid-1990s, there were no legal provisions for strikes. Yet a few dozen walkouts in the late 1980s and nearly six dozen in 1992–93 occurred, and those contributed to pushing party-state authorities to devise a law. After much discussion, little of it in the public domain, they established a new labor code in 1994, which took effect in 1995 and affirmed the right of workers to strike.[88] To be legal, however, a strike had to meet several conditions. From then through 2006, another 1,365 strikes occurred, none of them complying with these conditions. That and other reasons induced authorities in 2006 to reexamine labor code provisions regarding disputes. This time some deliberations, especially several National Assembly sessions, were reported in the mass media. They revealed two aspects of the debates pertinent to my point about workers' criticisms and protests being influential.

One is the role of official unions. A major condition in the 1995 law was that strikes, to be legal, had to be led by a union within the VGCL. Several National Assembly delegates, VGCL leaders, and MoLISA officials favored retaining this provision. But others, including some within the VGCL, stressed that this provision was unrealistic because many enterprises had no union and in those that did the union officers were frequently inattentive to workers' needs or beholden to the companies.[89] Although this view did not prevail entirely, it did so partly. In enterprises without an official union, the revised labor code finalized in 2006 said, workers could choose their own representatives to organize and lead strikes.[90]

The second issue is whether strikes could be about collective "rights" as well as "interests." "Rights," according to national authorities, are entitlements in laws and labor contracts; "interests" are matters not covered in those documents. Previously, the labor code made no such distinction. In 2006, several National Assembly delegates and other officials argued that the distinction was necessary. Strikes should only be about disputes over interests. Disputes over rights should be settled by authorities responsible for resolving conflicting interpretations of laws and contracts. This is necessary, they said, to foster a good environment for investors. Other delegates disagreed. Distinguishing between rights and interests, they argued, is complicated and impracticable. One assembly delegate, for example, said that the two are a pair, and trying to separate them will deprive workers of their right to strike. Another said that workers do not make these distinctions, and legal experts themselves have difficulties doing so.[91] In the end, "rights" and "interests" figured in some provisions regarding disputes but not regarding strikes.[92]

Both of these issues emerged again during deliberations leading to the Labor Code of 2012. This time advocates opposed to those two provisions in the 2006 version prevailed. The new law stipulated that, to be legal, a strike must be led by a union official, even in an enterprise without a union, and must be about "interests."[93]

Whether or not labor codes better accommodated workers' circumstances, no strikes in 1995–2015 met legal requirements. Yet party-state authorities tolerated and often defended them, while employers remained essentially quiet about their illegality. And by not persecuting workers who protested against employers and for better national policies, authorities reinforced their verbal support. Knowing that the party-state was generally sympathetic toward them also helped workers to persist with their collective struggles. Even local officials in the party-state's unions, although not particularly attentive to workers' concerns prior to strikes, often helped to resolve them and emphasized during negotiations with employers the legitimacy of workers' complaints. Authorities frequently publicly chastised employers for abusing workers. Party-state officials also took workers' conditions and concerns into consideration when revamping policies and laws.

The mass media, especially party-state newspapers from which much of the material for this chapter came, played a significant role in this interaction between workers and authorities. Although party-state media coverage was probably restricted, it nonetheless communicated far and wide workers' conditions and protests. Authorities could not ignore them; and they could not repress either the protests or the news accounts, or they chose not to try. Instead, they were often responsive to workers' demands. News coverage also affected employers. By investigating workers' conditions and complaints, reporting their protests, and being a place to which laborers could turn for assistance, major newspapers made employers aware that discontented employees could readily amplify their anger well beyond their workplace.

Through their letters and petitions to employers and party-state officials, work slowdowns, and strikes, workers criticized the distribution of money, time, and power—the political conditions—in the enterprises where they labored. Employers, they said, should pay higher wages to properly compensate workers for their labor and help them afford adequate living and some leisure. Also, they demanded, employees should not have to work twelve- and fourteen-hour days, six, even seven days a week. And, they insisted, enterprise managers and owners should not abuse workers physically or in other ways; workers must be treated respectfully, as human beings, not slapped, sworn at, and demeaned. While speaking out about these conditions, they frequently asked journalists to amplify their voice, VGCL officials to side with them, and party-state authorities to address their criticisms.

Chapter 2

LAND

Defending Farms and Opposing Corruption

From a distance, the park near Hà Nội's West Lake appeared serene—
the shade of tall leafy trees, emerald grass trimmed with flowers, and people
strolling the pathways. Moving closer I saw several sheets of plastic stretched
over park benches and bicycles. I thought it was makeshift housing by homeless people, similar to what one sees in many American city parks.

Not quite. Temporary accommodation, yes, but not made by homeless
people. They were shelters for people, mostly women, from various parts of
Vietnam, some as far as An Giang and Bạc Liêu provinces more than 1,700
kilometers to the south. The people were camping in the park while seeking assistance from the National Assembly, the prime minister, the Political
Bureau of the Communist Party, and other national offices. In the park they
held signs summarizing their criticisms and distributed to passers-by copies
of their petitions, letters, and other materials voicing their arguments and
demands.

The main grievances for most of those I met with my wife and a Vietnamese friend in the Mai Xuân Thưởng park in September and October 2012

concerned land that local authorities had taken from them and their families.[1] Often their complaints alleged corruption that frequently involved officials getting kickbacks from investors and developers. The temporary park residents exemplify droves of Vietnamese since the late 1990s who have spoken out against being pushed off their farms.

For generations the use and distribution of land have often been contentious political issues in Vietnam. Partly in an effort to diminish those problems, Vietnamese in the late 1980s and early 1990s reallocated rather equitably, especially in the nation's central and northern regions, nearly all agricultural land to farming households. Some land controversies, however, still emerged, occasionally contributing to significant unrest. In 1997, local officials' misuse of land, although not the primary cause, was one reason for waves of protesting villagers in the Red River delta province of Thái Bình. In 2001 and 2004, numerous demonstrations related to land occurred in the central highlands. The land disputes featured in this chapter, although not as tumultuous, were more numerous and persistent and involved people in many parts of the country.

According to Vietnam's land laws since the late 1980s, farming households have the right to use, not own, land for twenty to fifty years, depending on location and type of crops. The party-state can cancel those use rights and retrieve the land for the purpose of "national defense, security, national interest, public interest, and economic development."[2] Such retrievals became frequent as the economy diversified, requiring more land area for urban and industrial purposes. In 2001–5, authorities took 366,400 hectares of agricultural land; by 2010 the total had risen to roughly 745,000 hectares, affecting some nine million farming people, or about 10 percent of the country's population.[3] What proportion of those people objected is unknown but the volume of complaints and protests against land being appropriated suggests it was significant.

In the four years from 2008 through 2011, the government received nearly 1.6 million batches of petitions, accusations, and other criticisms from citizens, a 26 percent increase over a previous comparable period. Some complaints come from individual families, but several were signed by numerous households from the same community. So the 1.6 million figure represents at least a few million people. Over 70 percent of the criticisms—some reports say 90 percent—were about land, especially its appropriation and the low compensation paid to those who had the right to use it. About 42 percent of the complaints were reportedly resolved, leaving over half unsettled for years.[4] Frequently people unhappy with a resolution or still trying to get one resorted to public demonstrations, which by about 2010 had become rather common in numerous Vietnam's towns and cities.[5]

The protests I studied occurred in the nation's lowland areas, where most Vietnamese live, between 1999 and 2015.[6] My information about them comes from letters and other documents written by villagers; complaints on their behalf filed by lawyers; interviews demonstrators gave to journalists; articles by Vietnamese journalists and other observers; documents and commentary from Vietnamese authorities; and my discussions in late 2012 with protesters in Hà Nội and Văn Giang district, Hưng Yên province near Hà Nội. Many of the written materials were on websites.

The main questions I sought to answer were why and how people protested, and what were the consequences, especially what the authorities did. For each protest, I synthesized information about its location, the kinds of people and names of individuals involved, people's criticisms, the reasons for and objectives of their demonstrations, authorities' actions, involvement of other people and interests, and outcomes. Many protests extended over a considerable time, and hence I frequently updated my summaries, while also adding new cases as they emerged. By early 2011, my computer file had nearly one hundred protests, some with sparse information, and others with much more. Due to limitations in time and other resources, I cut back on adding new cases so as to gather more information on those I already knew about. The result is considerable material on sixty protests.

How people spoke out against land appropriations had two patterns. In the vast majority of cases, people in the same community peacefully used legal methods to oppose authorities' decisions and actions against them and their farms and to beseech national officials to help them. In the minority pattern, people from different communities protested together and sometimes resorted to violent methods to press their claims. In both patterns, villagers' criticisms and actions had similar political reasons and rationales: they challenged the legality and justness of authorities taking land from them, they disputed the compensations authorities gave them, and they asserted rights that went beyond what officials had recognized.

Toward both patterns of protests, party-state officials initially combined concessions and toleration. As villagers' criticisms, resistance, and demonstrations persisted, however, local authorities often added degrees of repression against particular individuals and families. Eventually, if accommodation, toleration, and intimidation did not succeed, authorities used brute force.

To elaborate, this chapter analyzes three protests within the predominant pattern and two in the minority one, showing their similarities and differences. The three within the predominant group are fairly representative of protests in and near Hồ Chí Minh City and Hà Nội, vicinities where much of the unrest over land appropriation occurred from the late 1990s through 2015. The two outliers, by definition, are unusual in terms of what demonstrators did; but in terms of why, they are similar to land protests both within and outside the predominant pattern.

Cases in the Predominant Pattern

"We are upright and honest-minded families and citizens of the Socialist Republic of Vietnam," began a four-page letter of March 2005 from nearly sixty households in Phú Sơn village in southern Vietnam. The villagers also affirmed their belief in the Vietnamese Communist Party, the state, and Hồ Chí Minh. They addressed their letter to seven national party-state offices, among them the Central Committee of the VCP, the National Assembly, the prime minister, and the president. Copies went to officials in Đồng Nai province, Trảng Bom district, and Bắc Sơn subdistrict, the locale in which Phú Sơn village sits; and to three newspapers. "We write this urgent complaint," the letter continued, "to respectfully request . . . a fair solution that conforms to a State that is of the people, by the people, and for the people," repeating a slogan Vietnamese authorities often proclaim and celebrate. "Our land is being reclaimed, the compensation from the investor is irrational, and local authorities obstruct, scare, and coerce us." "Please . . . look into this matter; please don't be insensitive to our plight."[7]

The "matter" was the taking by provincial and district authorities of nearly five hundred hectares, most of it farmland, from people in Phú Sơn and several other villages in Bắc Sơn and its neighboring subdistrict, in order to create the Hồ Nai industrial zone where foreign and Vietnamese private investors and party-state agencies would build factories. The zone was one of four established in Trảng Bom district between the late 1990s and the 2000s occupying two thousand hectares, most of it previously agricultural land, and displacing nearly three thousand households with about eleven thousand working-age members.[8] National authorities authorized the zones; provincial and especially district officials were the implementers, and they often had incompatible or vague guidelines. The local authorities promised to pay households for their land and relocate them to other farmland, or to urban sites where they would be trained for new jobs, including factory work.

The payment, the promises, and indeed the entire Hồ Nai industrial park project were challenged by Phú Sơn villagers almost immediately after it was initiated in 1998. "The 10,000 *đồng* per square meter compensation for our land," stated their March 2005 letter "will push us into absolute poverty. Some households have but five hundred square meters; the most any household has is ten thousand square meters." Multiplying each square meter by only 10,000 *đồng*, villagers wrote, yields virtually nothing to live on. "We're being intimidated and coerced into indescribable hardship." Meanwhile, just outside the industrial zone area, said their letter, "the real price for land has risen rapidly, fifteen to twenty times what authorities are forcing on us." Bolstering their claim about the market value of their land was a journalist's report that two years earlier in 2003 a Phú Sơn villager had sold her agricultural land-use rights to another villager for 92,000 *đồng* per square meter.[9] It also angered the villagers that despite their numerous written and verbal complaints to local officials, they had not received documentation verifying the project's size and scope or even the authorities' right to evict them. Furthermore, they wrote in 2005, citing statements by the nation's prime minister and directives from the national government, if they had to move they could not be forced to do so until relocation areas with conditions better than those they currently had were fully prepared. Neither new sites for them nor their ancestors' graves, which were also to be moved, were ready.

At the end of their letter, villagers argued they were victims of greed: "Reclaiming our land is being done in order that a company affiliated with the Vietnam Rubber Corporation can build an industrial zone. We see, we know, we are certain that this is not a state-funded project for the benefit and welfare of the public. Instead, the ultimate purpose of its promoters is their own profit and self-interest. Thus they intentionally impede our efforts [to object and get others to help us] and forget that the objective of programs and policies of the state and the Communist Party is, above all else, to uplift the people."

The villagers' several petitions and letters prompted party-state teams that were investigating various protests against land appropriation in the province to meet Trảng Bom district residents in October 2000 and again in August 2005. Although those sessions did not resolve the problems, the investigators did admonish local authorities for not being sufficiently attentive to people's criticisms. The investigators' visits also encouraged residents to persist.[10] On at least one occasion, in August 2009, Phú Sơn villagers and some others whose lands the industrial zone project threatened traveled by bus and by foot about fifty kilometers to demonstrate at national government offices in downtown Hồ Chí Minh City. To reach their destination they had to evade some police who were reportedly trying to stop them.[11]

Between about 2002 and early 2009, many residents of Phú Sơn and neighboring villages abandoned the struggle, accepted compensations that were slightly larger than the amount initially offered, and left the area. Eventually the remaining Phú Sơn villagers also surrendered their land for less money than they had sought; some were able to move to government-designated land. An unreported number of the young people found work in the factories built in Hồ Nai industrial park, which by 2013 had ninety-five enterprises.[12]

Another case in the predominant pattern of speaking out against land appropriations occurred within Hồ Chí Minh City. In late 2002, Vietnam's prime minister approved a request from the city's authorities to plan a high-tech industrial zone in District 9, a sparsely populated part of the metropolis.[13] Authorities expected the zone to attract Vietnamese and foreign research, software, and electronics companies, providing good jobs for educated Vietnamese and new income streams for the city. To construct the zone, authorities needed to reclaim 804 hectares to which some four thousand households held land-use rights. On farms ranging from a couple of hundred square meters to nearly one-half of a hectare, each family raised vegetables, pigs, fish, fowl, and fruit trees. When the land appropriation process started in 2003–4, many residents objected, individually at first and then collectively.

In February 2004, hundreds of households signed an "appeal for justice," one of the first of nearly eight hundred petitions, letters, and pleas from about a quarter of the residents between 2004 and 2008.[14] Initially, people targeted district and city officials. In 2006, frustrated by little response from local officials, people appealed to national offices, particularly the prime minister, the National Assembly, and the Ministry of Natural Resources and Environment (MoNRE, which is in charge of land-use), and the VCP's secretary general and Political Bureau. Some residents even traveled to Hà Nội. In July 2007, for example, eleven men delivered to the national Anti-Corruption Committee in Hà Nội a petition signed by sixty-one affected households.[15]

In 2007, residents demonstrated.[16] In late May, over fifty women and men marched to the District 9 office in charge of retrieving land. The head official there, they said, had agreed to address their questions about compensation, relocation sites, and other matters. Twice before he had failed to keep his promises to meet them. Upon reaching the office this time, the demonstrators were told he had gone to an urgent meeting elsewhere. As the residents lingered, unsure what to do next, they caught sight of the man. As some demonstrators rushed toward him, they and office personnel scuffled until police arrived. That event, other unsuccessful attempts by groups of residents to meet with officials, and mounting anxieties about what was happening to their farms and homes contributed to another demonstration in late November. Hoping to get answers to questions they had raised countless times before, they marched to the district offices waving national flags, carrying portraits of Hồ Chí Minh, and hoisting placards summarizing their grievances. Numerous police shadowed them, shouted at them, and grabbed and destroyed some of their posters and pictures. At the office, where more police confronted them, authorities refused to meet them.

District 9 residents based their protests primarily on four claims. One was that appropriating the land was illegal. Local authorities were taking land without first making the required development plan and obtaining the prime minister's approval for it; they were using the outdated 1993 land law instead of the 2003 land law; and they failed to consult residents, bullied and harassed those who resisted, disrupted demonstrations, and violated democratic procedures in numerous other ways.[17] The explanation for these shortcomings, many residents said, was corruption, the second reason for their protests. They suspected local authorities were rushing to confiscate land as quickly and cheaply as possible, hold it for a while, then sell it at high prices and pocket the difference.[18] Third, compensation payments for their land were so small, protesters claimed, that the government was essentially stealing their land. The payments, they argued, ranged between only one-fifth and one-twenty-fifth of the land's market value; the average compensation was only one-tenth of market value. Residents who either agreed to leave or were forced off their land in 2004–5 received the least; those who managed to hold on longer received somewhat more.[19]

Fourth, residents contended, taking land against people's will was unjust. All the more unjust was appropriating land from people who had sacrificed greatly for the nation—people like Tư Hảo, a VCP member for forty-five years and soldier in the war against the United States; Nguyễn Xuân Ngữ, a veteran who fought for Hồ Chí Minh in the south from 1966 to 1975; Nguyễn Thị Gái, whose grandparents fought against the French and whose father and two uncles died fighting American forces; and Chín Coi, whose two brothers and a sister died in the war for Vietnam's independence. Chín Coi's mother made her promise never to sell the 4,200 square meters they farmed because it "holds the blood and bones of our family." Now, said Chín Coi in 2008, some years after her mother's death, the very government to which her family and many others had given so much was seizing that land.[20]

City and district authorities denied not consulting residents and cited instances of meeting with individuals (though not groups). They claimed they followed the law in all respects, including compensation payments, which they increased in part because of residents' complaints. Officials also defended the arrests they made of ten residents in early 2008 for disturbing the peace during those demonstrations in 2007.[21]

By mid-2008, opposition had been undermined by the arrests, intensified intimidation, and larger compensation payments, which rose to 310,000 *đồng* per square meter from 150,000 *đồng*. Meanwhile, protesters apparently neither sought nor attracted outside support except for a few bloggers, some Vietnamese journalists, and a lawyer who defended those individuals who had been arrested.[22] By April 2009, about 90 percent of the residents had accepted compensation payments and moved away. To evict the few holdouts, officials used bulldozers and police to destroy homes, fish ponds, gardens, and other property. Construction in the zone then accelerated. Still, a few dozen people continued to speak out and demanded that their farms be returned to them. One statement in April 2013, addressed to several national offices and signed by sixty-five District 9 people, castigated "members of the [VCP's] Political Bureau and the entire political system, including the courts and government inspectorate, for protecting the wrongdoings" of Hồ Chí Minh City officials.[23]

Far north, villagers on the outskirts of Hà Nội waged a similar struggle to keep their fields. In September 2007, the Hà Nội city government instructed authorities in Hoàng Mai district to repossess forty-nine hectares of land for transfer to the Housing and Urban Development Investment Corporation (HUD), which was authorized to create a subdivision around Lake Linh Đàm. Forty-four hectares of the land were in Bằng A and farmed by nearly 460 households, who were to be paid 252,000 *đồng* per square meter plus some relocation expenses.[24]

From the outset, most households objected. By December 2009, however, 174 households had agreed to leave. One reason is that HUD added 240,000 *đồng* per square meter to the original amount, a direct result of people's opposition. Another reason was intimidation and coercion by city and district authorities. Yet despite that repression and the increased monetary incentive, 285 households in December 2009 continued to resist.[25]

Public protests began in 2008 with residents writing to and meeting local officials. Getting no relief, they approached city officials and then national authorities. In June 2009, for instance, a petition with over 230 signatures went to the prime minister. The villagers also gave copies of their complaints to journalists, some of whom wrote about the growing controversy. In March 2009, over two hundred households pooled funds to hire an attorney, who filed legal claims on their behalf. Meanwhile, the VCP members among the protesting villagers sought assistance through their networks in official circles.[26]

Bằng A residents protested on three grounds. One was local authorities' bad behavior. At meetings to discuss the project, officials often prevented objecting residents from speaking. City officials publicly ridiculed the lawyer whom protesters had hired, alleging he did not know the law. Authorities periodically cut the water supply and electricity to the fields and homes of those who had signed letters and petitions, and police detained individuals thought to be leading the protest. Such actions, villagers told journalists, "are undemocratic." One resident, a VCP member who had recently retired from the Ministry of Education, said local authorities "don't respect democratic rights." He himself and nine other local VCP members were "disciplined" by higher party officials because their families were among those refusing to leave.[27]

Villagers also objected to the low payment for their land. Even with the additional amount, the compensation would be only 492,000 *đồng* per square meter, which Bằng A villagers described as "paltry." It was but a smidgen of the millions each square meter was worth to HUD. Villagers knew the local real estate market and wanted to negotiate directly with the developers. But authorities forbade that, which was one reason—along with suspected corruption—why protesters said officials were "excessively solicitous and cozy with the investors."[28] Villagers also argued that the compensation equaled but a few years worth of their earnings from the vegetables and herbs they produced on the land. For instance, the household of Trần Thị Quý typically earned 400,000 *đồng* per day selling produce from eight hundred square meters. The proposed compensation for that land would be 393 million *đồng*, which if divided by 400,000 *đồng* per day would equal only 984 days, less than three years of the family's daily earnings. So, without land, she said, "How are we going to live? We don't have other work. If they want to take our land for business purposes, they have to come to terms with us."[29]

Her comment pertains to a third basis for protest. Farming was most households' primary source of livelihood. Twice before, the city government had taken some of their fields and paid them much less for it. Now, it was even worse, despite the larger compensation, because the city would take everything. "Where are we, some thousands of workers, to go?" asked Lưu Thị Sơn rhetorically. "We'll just be standing on the street. How will we eat; how will we live?"[30] "We live or die because of the land," said one of the protesters' petitions. "How are we to live if the state takes all the land without proper compensation to us? We . . . demand justice."[31]

In late December 2009, authorities warned that they would forcibly take the land of Bằng A villagers who had not agreed to leave by January 5, 2010. Those holdouts would also be deprived of the additional 240,000 *đồng* per square meter compensation. Early in the morning on January 5, authorities accompanied bulldozers that razed the fields of over two hundred and fifty households who were still resisting. Prior to the machinery entering the contested fields, soldiers with mine detectors searched for explosive booby traps.[32] They found none.[33]

Explaining the Predominant Pattern

The protests by Phú Sơn, District 9, and Bằng A villagers and by people camped in Hà Nội's Mai Xuân Thưởng park illustrate a pattern for most land protests I studied. One part of that pattern is how they protested. People in the same village or neighborhood collectively complained to local authorities. Getting no relief, they continued to speak out, sometimes for years, by sending letters, petitions, and other documents to higher levels, usually including national offices and leaders. Often a group designated a few members to travel to higher authorities' offices; many of the people in Mai Xuân Thưởng park, for instance, were representing dozens of others in their home villages. When villagers demonstrated, they did so peacefully, often doing little more than quietly sitting and standing while holding signs, photos, and patriotic symbols. The only significant violence by demonstrating villagers in this predominant pattern that I am aware of was the self-immolation by Phạm Thành Sơn in front of a government office building in Đà Nẵng on February 17, 2011.[34] To broadcast their demonstrations, villagers commonly contacted Vietnamese news media; some also reached out to foreign media, the United Nations, Human Rights Watch, and other international entities. Many arranged for their materials to be put on the World Wide Web. Sometimes they asked lawyers to help them file complaints. Journalists and occasionally lawyers were nearly the only individual outsiders whose assistance they sought or attracted; and protesters in one locality did not collaborate with their counterparts elsewhere.

Influencing how villagers protested were their perceptions of Vietnam's political system.[35] To many demonstrators, the main cause of their land problems was local officials who violated national laws and programs. Consequently, people in one place had little incentive to coordinate with people elsewhere because their problems with local authorities were different. Residents of each place went to national authorities not because that was where the problem lay but to pressure top officials to make local ones behave. Another reason for separate rather than collective protests is that collaboration would likely exceed what authorities would countenance. The surveillance infrastructure of the party-state impeded any inclinations people in one place might have had to coordinate their actions with villagers elsewhere. The single organization authorized by the party-state to represent villagers' interests, the Vietnam Peasants' Association [Hội Nông Dân Việt Nam], rarely helped, indeed often hindered, public protests. Even demonstrations by people from the same place could be risky because officials might deem them to have crossed a hazy line between what is allowed and not allowed. This is a major reason why demonstrators were usually peaceful, silent, and prominently displayed Vietnamese flags and Hồ Chí Minh portraits. Surveillance and legal uncertainties also inhibited outsiders such as professors, students, nongovernmental organizations, and even lawyers from aiding, advising, or joining villagers' protests.

A second part to the pattern is what villagers publicly sought and on what grounds. Their overall demand was justice and fairness. The fundamental basis for this claim was having the means to make a decent living.[36] Protesters often demanded to be allowed to retain their farms so that they could support their families. Some agreed to surrender their fields but only for compensation that was fair, for which they had a couple of measures. One was to provide as well for their families in the future as they could now from farming. A second was the purpose for which the land would be used if they were to leave. Villagers in Bằng A and many other places said they would surrender their land for less compensation if the state needed it for the good of the country.[37] But if, as was frequently the situation, the land was for the benefit of companies, investors, home buyers, and so on, then the compensation should be at least what the land was worth in the real estate market, plus, villagers often added, assistance with relocation and finding decent employment. To identify that acceptable compensation, villagers typically wanted to negotiate with those who would get the land; they objected to government authorities imposing an amount on them. They suspected that authorities, after paying them a small amount, would later sell the land for considerably more and keep the difference or in some other way personally benefit. This, plus harsh, even violent actions by authorities, prompted protesting villagers to rest part of their grievance on officials' undemocratic behavior. Rarely, however, did protesters publicly condemn the political system. Often they affirmed their allegiance to the party-state's leadership. One exception is a woman I saw in Mai Xuân Thưởng park in October 2012. Venting her anger about officials taking her family's land, she screamed, "I hate the state, I hate the party, I hate this country, I hate them all."[38]

The predominant pattern has similarities to public protests over land in the late 1980s and early 1990s when collectivized agriculture was being replaced by household farming.[39] Villagers then also went over the heads of local officials to petition higher authorities, a method that Vietnamese peasants have used since at least the nineteenth century. Besides believing local authorities were inattentive or unfair, they also often suspected them to be corrupt. Also as now, journalists then published articles about the controversies. At that time, news reports were nearly the only means villagers had to broadcast their situation; the Internet and even access to photocopy machines were still years away.

One striking difference between then and now is what villagers protested about. Most of the earlier public disputes involved villagers in the south trying to retrieve fields that, in their view, had been illicitly taken from them during land redistributions prior to and after 1975. Other earlier protests, primarily in the Red River delta, were people demanding fields be restored to their village that years earlier local authorities had allocated to neighboring villages. A second major difference is that numerous protests in the late 1980s to early 1990s became violent. Rival claimants physically fought and sometimes killed each other and burned down houses; neighboring villagers attacked, even murdered, each other and authorities who were trying to resolve the disputes.[40]

The predominant pattern for *how* villagers protested land issues in contemporary Vietnam resonates with the rightful resistance scholars have identified in China.[41] In rightful resistance, too, clusters of relatively powerless people living in the same vicinity use nonviolent methods in approved channels to press their claims locally and then entreat higher officials to help. They also seek support from nongovernmental institutions and people, such as journalists, lawyers, and civic organizations. Their protests can stretch over a considerable time until they get relief, are forced to give up, or are exhausted.

However, *what* Vietnamese villagers sought and *why* only partly corresponds to rightful resistance. Rightful resisters affirm their loyalty to the political system and disavow anti-government sentiments or goals. Indeed, they base their claims on existing laws, rules, and regulations and the commitments and promises authorities have made. Vietnamese villagers did so only in part.

Villagers in Phú Sơn, District 9, Bằng A, and the Mai Xuân Thưởng park, and in most cases for which I have evidence, did link their land claims to officials' pronouncements that the political system should serve the people. They frequently claimed that local authorities were abusive, unresponsive to their complaints, ignored the people they were supposed to serve, and thus were undemocratic. They also argued that authorities' actions contravened laws and regulations about land appropriations, compensation, and other matters.

Vietnamese protesters' demand for fairness and justice, however, went beyond applying existing laws, regulations, and official promises, and hence exceeded rightful resistance.[42] One additional claim was that it was wrong to take land against the will of families who had served and died for their country and the very government that was now mistreating them. Such disregard of people's sacrifices was vulgar and immoral. Another claim was that summarily confiscating land greatly favored those who would end up getting it at the expense of those who were currently using it. Even minimal justice requires an equitable outcome for all concerned. This demand has something of a moral economy ring to it. But unlike moral economy claims, these Vietnamese villagers were not just insisting on subsistence. They wanted, were they to give up their fields, at least the same standard of living they had as farming households. Also unlike moral economy claims, the protesters were not harking back to premarket obligations of institutions and wealthier people. Indeed, by insisting on negotiations between themselves and a would-be buyer, they invoked the market as a mechanism for determining fair compensation.

Also beyond rightful resistance, these additional claims about justice and fairness rejected laws authorizing the state to unilaterally reclaim farmland. The demand to negotiate a price included the possibility that a potential seller could ultimately decide not to sell, another stance at odds with national laws. Indeed, according to these claims, a family was entitled to refuse to sell regardless of price, not only because it held use rights but because it needed the land for its livelihood, it simply preferred to farm, or its family had shed blood for the country in order to have land on which to make a living.

Unusual Cases

The reasons just summarized for why villagers in Vietnam opposed land being appropriated apply well to all the cases I studied, including the few whose form and method of protests were different from the predominant pattern.

The first of my two cases outside the predominant form of protests occurred in Hồ Chí Minh City during 2007. Demonstrators there appealed to higher authorities to correct local officials' wrongs, but unlike in the predominant method, villagers from many different places collaborated. Moreover, their demonstrations in Hồ Chí Minh City overlapped with others in Hà Nội at the same time, bringing Vietnam close to having nationwide protests by villagers.

Land was the main issue for the Hồ Chí Minh City protests.[43] A few people were demanding the return of land taken from them decades earlier. Their struggles were carryovers from contentious land claims in the 1970s and 1980s. The most prevalent demand was to stop taking land for new development projects at the expense of people's livelihoods. As one demonstrator from An Giang province in the Mekong delta explained to a BBC reporter, "On land hangs my existence. I must object to losing my land. The Bình Long industrial zone [being built in An Giang] stated a price which we refused. District and provincial authorities then used force, demolished all our possessions, and even removed our ancestors' graves."[44]

During the demonstrations in Hồ Chí Minh City people made additional demands: police must stop harassing protesters, quit intimidating people who give them food or other support, and release the protesters they had detained. After authorities prevented them from using bathrooms in the government buildings near where they had congregated, protesters added that to their complaints.[45]

The Hồ Chí Minh City protests in 2007 peaked in June and July. For twenty-seven days, hundreds and sometimes over a thousand villagers from the Mekong delta camped outside the southern office buildings of the National Assembly and the central government. They pleaded for national authorities—particularly National Assembly delegates, the prime minister, and the president, all of whom were meeting in the city or rumored to be arriving—to resolve their claims. Enduring hunger, hot weather, rain, and weariness, they stood, sat, and slept on sidewalks. They made banners and posters; and they painted slogans and key demands on white T-shirts, which they wore, gave away, and sold to passers-by. Dozens at a time marched in the streets, carrying placards, Vietnamese flags, and portraits of Hồ Chí Minh to television stations and newspaper offices and through downtown and residential areas, advertising their campaign and soliciting support.[46]

Whenever possible they talked to journalists, most from foreign news agencies. Few Vietnamese media outlets would cover the demonstrations. Officials frequently intimidated journalists and other people showing interest in the protests. On at least one occasion protesters themselves rescued local journalists from club-wielding police.[47]

Most demonstrators were women, many of them rather elderly; several of the younger ones had children with them. Most spokespersons were women, as were most of the people who gave food, water, shelter, and money to the protesting villagers.

By late June and early July, concerned citizens, including Buddhist monks and Roman Catholic clergy, were giving food and other assistance and urging others to do the same.[48] Joining the protesters were a few advocates for democratization, notably Bloc 8406 [Khối 8406] members, who, along with several ad hoc groups, also assisted foreign journalists and uploaded to websites interviews, documents, and news reports regarding the protests.[49]

The nearly four weeks of protests involved a degree of organization. One aspect was communication and coordination among villagers in different places who knew each other from previous demonstrations.[50] Periodically since the late 1990s, people from communities in southern Vietnam had protested in Hồ Chí Minh City, typically outside prominent government offices and in public parks. When separate groups happened to converge at the same site, they swapped stories and formed friendships. An early occasion occurred in 2000 when a few hundred villagers from the Mekong delta protested off and on for weeks outside government buildings. Because their criticisms, usually about land, were not satisfactorily addressed, several groups repeatedly protested—in their home districts, in Hồ Chí Minh City, even in Hà Nội where they met peasant demonstrators from northern provinces. Individuals in the various groups kept in touch, often through cell phone calling and texting. One person in this network was Lư Thị Thu Duyên, whose grandfather gave thirty-five years to Vietnam's revolution. She and her sister, protesting the confiscation of their family farm in the city's Gò Vấp district, were among those demonstrators in 2000. Networks like hers spread the news in late June 2007 that victims of industrial zone and road construction in Tiền Giang province were congregating at the National Assembly's building in Hồ Chí Minh City. By July 5, 2007, groups from ten provinces and four city districts had joined them and Lư Thị Thu Duyên had emerged as one of the protesters' spokespersons.[51]

Other aspects of an organization evolved as the demonstrations continued.[52] Participants from different localities took turns marching in streets and doing such tasks as distributing food and water. The demonstrators selected representatives to speak to journalists and government officials. Often those representatives were in the compound of the government building while most demonstrators remained outside. Each group had a system for rotating participants; while several villagers carried on the protest, others returned to their homes to rest, recover, and collect money, food, and other resources to carry back to the demonstration sites.

While protests persisted in Hồ Chí Minh City, demonstrations about land in distant Hà Nội became more frequent. And in early July, dozens of villagers from the southern province of Bình Thuận who had been in the Hồ Chí Minh City demonstrations joined groups of northern villagers at Hà Nội's Mai Xuân Thưởng park. Now the two cities' protests were linked. Participants in both communicated by phone calls, texting, and e-mail. By July 11, about two hundred people from five southern provinces were demonstrating with hundreds of northern villagers at government buildings in Hà Nội. Among the southerners were several elderly women declaring that even though their husbands and sons had died fighting for Vietnam's reunification, local officials had recently stolen their land.[53]

In the few occasions that officials met with protesters' representatives, they urged everyone to return to their home districts. Local authorities, they said, had been ordered to solve all complaints. Few villagers swallowed this. Having done just that several times before with minuscule results, explained spokeswoman Cao Quế Hoa, "we don't believe it now."[54]

As protests in Hồ Chí Minh City persisted and enlarged, authorities became more repressive. By the second week, police had detained several protesters and forcibly transported many others to their home villages. Some of those participants later eluded police to rejoin the demonstrations. By the fourth week, when protesters from nineteen provinces numbered 1,700 in Hồ Chí Minh City, police from around the country augmented that city's force. On the night of July 18, in front of hundreds of onlookers, waves of police swept over the protesters. Initially the police used words to persuade many to leave the city. By 11 p.m., police used tear gas and batons, forcing remaining protesters into buses that took them home. Several people were injured; some were detained.[55]

Demonstrations, however, did not cease. For the rest of the year, numerous groups of villagers periodically protested at government buildings against land appropriations, corruption, and other injustices. But these demonstrations fit the predominant pattern, which for the most part authorities tolerated. Authorities took measures to stifle a repeat of the concentration of protests that had occurred in mid-2007. Occasionally in later years, villagers from a few different areas converged at party-state office buildings in Hồ Chí Minh City, Hà Nội, and other cities to display banners and posters while seeking opportunities to present petitions and convey their criticisms to particular officials. Authorities typically let them be and often met with them, but prevented these crowds from expanding or continuing beyond a few hours.[56]

The second case outside the predominant pattern is the lengthy struggle, starting in 2004, by villagers in Văn Giang district, Hưng Yên province, about twenty kilometers southeast of central Hà Nội. Three differences from the predominant pattern are that Văn Giang protesters had considerable support from outsiders, they occasionally became violent, and they endorsed land protests elsewhere.

In 2003 and 2004, the prime minister's office approved requests from Hưng Yên and Văn Giang officials to build a highway and a residential area called Ecopark. Chosen to do both projects was the newly formed Việt Hưng Urban Development and Investment Company (UDIC). The plan was that Ecopark, then the largest urbanization project in northern Vietnam and expected to cost over eight billion U.S. dollars, would include townhouses, condominium towers, a commercial center, parks, a hospital, and a university. It would consume five hundred hectares, 70 percent of it farmed by 4,876 households, most of them in three Văn Giang subdistricts.[57]

While Ecopark was being planned, residents claimed, officials and the UDIC did not consult the community or seek residents' views. Only when local authorities approached families to surrender their land-use rights in exchange for 60,000 *đồng* per square meter did villagers become aware of the project. Surprised and irritated, households demanded clarification from local officials and insisted on seeing documents authorizing Ecopark. Getting little or no response, groups of families wrote to provincial offices and then to national ones. No satisfactory answers came.

In late August 2006, approximately four thousand Văn Giang villagers, primarily from the three most affected subdistricts, demonstrated at the National Assembly's office building in Hà Nội, an act timed to coincide with National Day (September 2) celebrations. Some demonstrators carried mementos of relatives killed in the wars for national independence and reunification. The demonstrators vowed to remain until National Assembly leaders or the prime minister himself addressed their concerns about Ecopark. Quickly joining them were villagers from other provinces who had been staying in Mai Xuân Thưởng park across town. By August 30, however, menacing warnings from police prompted most protesters to return

Figure 2.1. Văn Giang villagers opposed to the Ecopark project demonstrate outside a National Assembly office in Hà Nội, April 27, 2011. The sign to the left says, "The Ecopark urban area in the subdistricts Cửu Cao, Phụng Công, and Xuân Quang, in Văn Giang district, Hưng Yên province, is robbing the people's land." Photo by Ian Timberlake. Courtesy of Getty Images.

home. Threatened with arrest, the remaining few hundred left the evening prior to National Day with still no response from national authorities.

Starting in August 2006, Văn Giang villagers frequently demonstrated in their district and in Hà Nội. Each Hà Nội demonstration typically lasted only one day, although in 2012 protests were often repeated several times a week. The protesters returned home each evening because the distance was short and to minimize police intimidation.[58] Occasionally district officials talked to the demonstrators.

In August 2012, six years after the villagers' first Hà Nội protest, national officials of MoNRE met publicly, in the presence of journalists, about one hundred representatives of the Văn Giang villagers and their lawyers. Although ending with no solution to the villagers' demands, the lengthy session was a notable consequence of their persistent petitions, demonstrations, and other forms of speaking out.[59] Then in November 2012, dozens of Văn Giang villagers and a couple of lawyers discussed legal questions about Ecopark with Đặng Hùng Võ, a former deputy minister of MoNRE whose briefings in 2003–4 had contributed to prime ministerial approval of the project. Villagers applauded when he acknowledged that he had made some mistakes in those briefings. But because he was already retired,

MoNRE authorities dismissed his views. Besides, in December, Đặng Hùng Võ essentially retracted what he had said the month before.[60]

Some Văn Giang villagers' actions were violent. In January 2009 and April 2012, a few hundred Văn Giang villagers fought with shovels, picks, hoes, bricks, and stones against hundreds of armed police wielding clubs and throwing tear gas canisters, who escorted heavy equipment to flatten planted fields and reclaim several hectares for Ecopark. Although no match for the violence used against them, villagers resorted to force when police waded through the lines of demonstrators. Bludgeoned demonstrators included mothers of war martyrs who had pleaded with police to turn back.[61] Occasionally thereafter, in an effort to thwart the making of Ecopark, some Văn Giang residents assaulted construction workers and vandalized heavy equipment destroying villagers' crops and homes. Following one such incident in October 2014, some villagers were arrested, tried, and sentenced to prison.[62]

Văn Giang villagers' demands resonated with those of other land protesters. If they were obliged to surrender fields, they argued, they wanted to negotiate a fair price, not accept the compensation stipulated by officials and investors. That amount, even after being raised to 139,000 *đồng* per square meter, was far below the land's value, villagers said. Farming households typically netted that much each year, and frequently, because of the ornamental plants and trees they grew, twice or thrice that amount. Moreover, the advertised price for Ecopark's least expensive residence was 151 times that compensation. Even after deducting construction costs, an extremely handsome profit would remain for UDIC and its partners. Essentially, concluded many villagers, authorities and investors were stealing their land.[63] Second, numerous villagers did not want to sell. "It's the land—the farming—people want, not the money," they said. "Land is our body and blood," one explained. Put differently, said another, "Farming is our livelihood and that of our children." People who want to farm, villagers insisted, should be entitled to do so. Furthermore, without land, many could not support themselves; no land meant no viable livelihood.[64] Third, villagers demanded that authorities be democratic. They objected to local officials preventing them from speaking at meetings; they denounced authorities and UDIC for using force and threats against residents; and they demanded transparent decision making involving their farms and homes.[65]

For many villagers, an underlying rationale for their claims were the contributions Văn Giang people, particularly in the three most affected subdistricts, had made to the nation. Their ancestors had joined the Trưng sisters' rebellion against China two thousand years ago.[66] Văn Giang people fought for Vietnam against the French and Americans. Some of the area threatened by Ecopark had housed anti-aircraft guns that shot down American airplanes fifty years earlier.[67] Because Văn Giang villagers had served their country and remained loyal to the VCP government, protesters reasoned, authorities should heed their demands.

To aid their struggle against Ecopark, Văn Giang villagers elected nine representatives, three for each of the most affected subdistricts, who coordinated demonstrations, liaised with outside supporters and journalists, and often spoke for the protesters. The three representatives in each subdistrict regularly met with fellow villagers and with the representatives of the other two subdistricts.[68]

Văn Giang villagers had more outside support than most other land protesters.[69] Several supporters in Hà Nội posted protesters' photos, letters, and other materials on the Internet. Some political reform advocates wrote about the protests, visited Văn Giang villagers, and helped them. Following the April 2012 violent confrontation with police, villagers sought help from attorneys in Hà Nội.[70] In detailed submissions to national offices, these lawyers, particularly Trần Vũ Hải, argued that district, provincial, and national authorities' actions regarding Ecopark violated numerous laws and regulations and treated "the interests of thousands of peasant households . . . as far less important than the interests of UDIC."[71]

Also rare among land protests, Văn Giang villagers reached out to other protesters. They publicly sympathized with the families of Đoàn Văn Vươn and Đoàn Văn Quý in Tiên Lãng, Hải Phòng province in northern Vietnam, who had fought the police taking their fields and fishponds in January 2012. Together with land protesters in Hà Đông, a sector of greater Hà Nội, Văn Giang villagers signed a statement deeming Đoàn Văn Vươn a "hero . . . in the struggle to protect peasants' basic rights." During the April 2013 trial of the two men and others, a delegation from Văn Giang traveled to Hải Phòng, joining hundreds of other villagers as well as many political reform advocates to express solidarity with the accused.[72] Some Văn Giang villagers broadened their activism beyond land confiscation issues. In 2012, several participated in demonstrations against Chinese incursions into Vietnamese territory.[73] In 2014, two Văn Giang villagers were among six members of a "mobilization committee" to establish an Association for

Victims of Injustice that would advocate for citizens whom authorities had mistreated, swindled, or otherwise oppressed. The other four members lived in Hà Nội and Hồ Chí Minh City. The committee petitioned the National Assembly and Ministry of Public Security to approve the association but was turned down.[74]

Văn Giang villagers' protests delayed, but did not halt Ecopark construction. Their protests did make authorities increase the compensation from 60,000 *đồng* per square meter to 139,000. Partly for this reason, more villagers abandoned the struggle. By April 2012, according to district authorities, 79 percent of households had accepted payment to surrender their fields.[75] Protesters and their representatives, however, claimed the figure was only 50 percent in late 2012 and did not reach 70 percent until early 2014. Additional compensation, they said, was one reason people gave up the struggle, but another was intense coercion and harassment by local authorities and UDIC. For instance, officials threatened that anyone refusing to surrender land would not be allowed to sell their produce, use medical clinics, bury their dead in the local cemetery, or send their children to school. Also, unidentifiable persons beat up members of protesting households, broke into their homes, and threw bottles of pesticide into their residences.[76]

The project divided the community, pitting accepters against protesters. Even the local unit of the VCP split and ejected dozens of members who opposed Ecopark. Several subdistrict officials quit because they detested Ecopark or grew weary of being wedged between its advocates and opponents.[77] In December 2008, two village officials siding with the protesters were sentenced to one year's imprisonment for disturbing the peace. Shortly after their trial, a person thought to be hired by Ecopark threw acid on their attorney, burning his neck and chest.[78]

Elucidating Authorities' Actions

In all the cases examined in this chapter—and in most of the protests against land appropriation that I have learned about—party-state authorities' initial actions were toleration and even accommodation. Local authorities in Phú Sơn, District 9, Bằng A, and Văn Giang reacted to letters, petitions, and other forms of complaints with degrees of disregard and indifference but also with conversations and meetings where people questioned the development plans, refused offered compensations, and pleaded to retain their fields. In all four places, as in many others, villagers' arguments and resistance pushed officials and project investors to increase significantly the amount of compensation, a concession that satisfied some villagers to give up their land-use rights. National authorities, too, were often tolerant and responsive when villagers appealed to them for just and fair solutions. When villagers protested outside government buildings, police usually stood by, watching and keeping participants from blocking traffic but not attempting to stop the demonstrations. In Hồ Chí Minh City in mid-2007, even as demonstrations enlarged and persisted, authorities were fairly easygoing for the first couple of weeks. Indeed, those and other protests against land appropriations arguably pushed officials to tolerate public discontent generally.[79] Unimaginable in the 1980s and early 1990s, rural people's demonstrations since then widened the public arena in which Vietnamese from many sectors of society could speak out. Officials' tolerance of public protests did not become boundless but it did greatly expand.

Land protesters took their complaints to national offices expecting favorable reactions there.[80] To an extent, their expectations were realized. Beginning in 2000, national party-state authorities sent several problem-solving teams to places generating persistent opposition to repossessing fields and house lots, low compensation, and other land issues. Meeting with villagers, local officials, and investors, these national teams and sometimes provincial ones resolved numerous contentious cases. They often found merit in villagers' criticisms and demands.[81] So did several national agencies. In July 2007, shortly after the lengthy demonstrations in Hồ Chí Minh City had been dispersed, the MoNRE minister said studies showed that 80 percent of criticisms regarding land were entirely or partly correct. Villagers seeking more compensation, he added, were not being greedy. They mainly wanted fairness, and what greatly upset them was being forced to surrender their land at low prices for the benefit of business interests. In 2012, the Government Inspectorate reported that nearly half of all citizen complaints (70 percent of them concerning land appropriations) between 2008 and 2011 were entirely or partly valid.[82]

Due in part to people's criticisms and demonstrations, national authorities revised regulations regarding land appropriation, compensation, and assistance to affected people.[83] Broadly speaking, the legal and administrative changes gradually provided more opportunity for compensation amounts to approach market values and be determined by negotiations between land-use holders and developers, a process that happened faster in the southern part of the country than in central and northern regions.[84] In 2013, the National Assembly, partly in response to public pressure, wrote a new land law "that effectively addressed some of the issues . . . raised by experts, civil society advocates, and the media, as well as by farmers themselves" and may have contributed to fewer land repossessions in 2014–15.[85]

Besides being responsive and tolerant, party-state authorities were also repressive, even violent toward villagers' protests. Authorities rarely used police or other repressive means against workers' strikes (chapter 1), but they did mobilize police to break up villagers' large demonstrations, even arresting some participants, and on numerous occasions they forcibly evicted villagers from their fields and harassed and intimidated those who refused to quit protesting.

One reason for this difference is the duration of protest. Workers' strikes were usually brief—a few days or weeks, then settlement. Opposition to land confiscation often extended for months, even years, with letters, petitions, meetings, marches to local offices, demonstrations at national offices, and other activities. During that process, authorities made some concessions while also often using bullying tactics, which influenced many villagers to give up. But others continued until a showdown between them and authorities ordering them to leave. When they stood their ground, police used force.

Another reason is the differences between the workers' and villagers' protests. Labor strikes occurred at enterprises whose owners and managers mistreated employees and in other ways violated major laws. Party-state authorities typically blamed them more than the workers for the unrest and thus were more inclined to side with the strikers. In land protests, national authorities often learned that villagers had legitimate criticisms against how they were treated, the compensation packages, and other issues. That realization contributed to national agencies' efforts to resolve many long-lasting disputes, modify regulations, and revise laws. Some protests, however, persisted and national authorities essentially left the problem of finding solutions to local officials, who, together often with land investors, frequently resorted to intimidation, scare tactics, and force.

Party-state authorities did not devise an effective method for resolving persistent land appropriation disputes.[86] National officials often referred such cases back to provincial and district authorities to settle, even though those officials' actions had caused villagers to appeal to national authorities in the first place. Indeed, national authorities themselves frequently said lower-level officials failed to take seriously villagers' complaints, did not follow the law, and misused their authority.[87]

Laws and regulations made provincial and district authorities the party-state's agents responsible for repossessing land and compensating people. Because the rules and regulations governing these actions were complicated, evolving, and often contradictory, these local authorities were frequently ill-informed and confused.[88] At the same time, many officials were eager to attract investors who proposed projects that promised to diversify local economies; a key to getting such investment was low-cost land. This helps to explain why many local authorities, instead of aiding discontented villagers and thereby avoiding protests, minimized compensation payments and ignored or dismissed villagers' demands.[89]

Other considerations, too, motivated officials' behavior. Land acquired from current users at a low price could be sold to investors at a higher price. The difference could augment local government revenues so as to improve public services like healthcare and education; some of it could be stolen by officials. When investors' managers dealt directly with villagers, they too strove to keep compensation low in order to reduce the project's costs. Often district and provincial officials expected, even demanded, payments from those managers. That money could be for community improvements but some could be for authorities themselves, one of the common forms of corruption. Indeed, the numerous opportunities for authorities to benefit personally from land appropriation and compensation arrangements were often reasons why they shunned villagers' claims.

Comparing Villagers' and Workers' Political Criticisms

Villagers who spoke out against land being appropriated claimed that local officials violated laws and regulations, abused their authority at villagers' expense, and were often corrupt. They also said authorities were not consultative and transparent about community affairs, and thus violated the democratic practices that officials were supposed to follow. For factory workers, neither corruption nor democratic procedures were prominent issues, but abusive treatment was one of their major criticisms. Others were that companies paid less than the minimum wages required by law, ignored their contractual obligations to employees, failed to abide by social insurance laws, and violated labor codes.

But workers' and villagers' claims and actions went further. Workers sought more than the minimum wages and other conditions prescribed by law. They wanted fair wages, shorter workdays, a decent standard of living, and enough leisure time to enjoy life a bit. They also ignored laws intended to govern when and how they could go on strike. Villagers rejected laws that authorized the state to unilaterally claim their farmland. Their refusals to surrender land were often based on their notions of fairness and justice. One was that it is unjust to take land against the will of families who had served the Vietnamese nation. Another was that confiscating land against a family's will unfairly harms that family and benefits those who get that land.

Most strikes and other protests by workers involved people employed in the same factory, and their protests occurred in or near that place. Only occasionally did workers at a particular enterprise march to sites further away. Land protests, too, were primarily by people in the same vicinity. But because they often aimed their petitions and demonstrations at authorities in distant towns and cities, villagers often took their protests far beyond their communities.

Some land protests involved villagers from numerous communities converging at a strategic location to create large and sprawling demonstrations lasting days, even weeks. Workers' protests, too, could become large and involve laborers from several different places, but their evolution was usually different. Rather than protests at various enterprises merging together at a specific location, large strikes with workers from various factories typically developed in a wave-like fashion. A strike at one enterprise inspired workers at a nearby factory to rise up to express their own festering grievances, which in turn aroused employees at still another factory to walk out, and so on.

Most protests by workers were aimed primarily at the managers and owners of the enterprises where they worked, and occasionally at official labor unions. Sometimes, however, workers explicitly targeted national party-state authorities and policies. Villagers' protests almost invariably directed their criticism at party-state authorities, initially local ones but soon higher ones.

Although the political actions and justifications of villagers and workers had similarities, the two groups operated separately. Aggrieved workers and villagers did not join together nor reinforce or help each other. Many factory workers were from farming villages; several probably had relatives or friends who participated in protests against land-use rights being abrogated. Some workers possibly had even joined such protests when they were in their home villages. Beyond that, however, striking workers and protesting villagers scarcely overlapped.

Chapter 3

Nation

Protecting Vietnam and Questioning the Party's Patriotism

Kicking soccer balls to each other near a playing field in Hà Nội, a bunch of young and middle-aged men were preparing for one of their Sunday evening practice sessions. It was mid-September 2012, about a month before the group would celebrate its first anniversary of playing and doing other activities together. Most of the players wore jerseys with "No-U FC" printed on them in large letters, as well as a U with a big X scrawled through it. As they warmed up, some of their family members and friends meandered nearby, chatting, nibbling on fruit, and taking photos. One man was busy snapping pictures with his iPad, some of which later appeared on the group's website.

My wife and I were unsure how to approach the players; we did not know any of them. As they walked near us to enter the soccer field, my wife said to one of the smiling players that we know Nguyễn Quang A. Immediately that fellow and everybody near him shook our hands, introduced us to others, and made us feel at ease. To the team, Nguyễn Quang A was an honorary coach, although, he had laughingly told us a few days earlier, he himself plays no soccer.

Figure 3.1. No-U players wearing shirts with anti-China wording and symbols, Hà Nội, September 16, 2012. Photo by author.

This group of Vietnamese was actually more than a soccer team. The No-U FC was an informal organization committed to speaking out to protect Vietnam's territorial integrity. "No-U" means rejecting the nine-dash U-shaped line China's government drew on maps of the South China Sea, which Vietnamese call the East Sea [Biển Đông]. Within that line, Beijing authorities began to insist in 2009, every bit of land, seabed, water, and anything in the water belongs to China. That amounts to about 80 percent of the sea and included territorial waters, atolls, and islands long claimed by Vietnam as well as the Philippines and some other Southeast Asian countries. The "FC" in the group's name, explained one member, means "football club" or "friendship club." But it can also mean, another member whispered to me, "fuck China," which, he added in Vietnamese, better reflects his enthusiasm for the club.[1]

Joining marches several times in Hà Nội in 2011 against China's encroachments into Vietnamese territory is how many No-U members came to know each other. They deliberated additional ways to raise awareness about

China's threats to Vietnam and decided to form a soccer team to compete with other clubs in Hà Nội. By wearing shirts with "No-U," "Hoàng Sa" and "Trường Sa" (the Paracel and Spratly Islands that Vietnam claims but China is taking), and other wording expressing their concerns, they figured other teams and spectators would become more aware of the issues and perhaps get involved as well. Between 2012 and 2106, No-U members also raised money and other resources to improve schools in a village near Vietnam's border with China and aid fishing communities hurt by Chinese activities along Vietnam's central coast, and they co-organized anti-China demonstrations and inspired people elsewhere in the country to form No-U groups.

The Issues

No-U members and thousands of other self-described patriotic Vietnamese see themselves engaged in a struggle to protect their country by opposing China's transgressions and by protesting the Vietnamese government's reactions. In these critics' eyes, China has for years, even decades, been undermining their nation. Just since the late 1990s, many said, the evidence is vast. The border agreement in 1999 signed by Vietnamese and Chinese governments, critics said, ceded 750 square kilometers to China. In 2010, Chinese state-owned corporations and subsidiaries began to mine and process bauxite as well as build roads and other mining-related infrastructure in the central highlands of Vietnam. Chinese manufacturing, engineering, construction, and technology companies became prevalent in numerous parts of Vietnam. In central Vietnam's Hà Tĩnh province, China secured a seventy-year lease to 228 square kilometers for Chinese companies to use. Elsewhere, in northern and central Vietnam, Chinese firms obtained lengthy leases to exploit thousands of hectares of forests. Although these Chinese enterprises hired Vietnamese, they also brought, frequently illegally, large numbers of workers from China. Springing up around their factories, office buildings, and mines were clothing shops, grocery stores, restaurants, and other establishments commonly run by Chinese.[2] In the East Sea, critics contend, Vietnam's losses have been even worse. China has claimed nearly the whole sea. Chinese navy, coast-guard, and other vessels attack Vietnamese fishing boats and oil exploration ships in those waters. China's government has occupied Vietnam's islands and atolls, then enlarged them to make airports and military outposts and has deemed that everything there now composes a new administrative district within China.[3]

Vietnamese also criticized their own government for tolerating, even condoning these Chinese activities. The party-state's top leadership approved the deal that allows Chinese companies to mine bauxite, process it, and export the resulting product, aluminum. Authorities permitted, even encouraged, Chinese companies to come to Vietnam, bring in Chinese employees, pay modest fees for land they lease, and get other benefits at Vietnam's expense. Meanwhile, critics contended, authorities objected only mildly to China taking Vietnam's territorial waters in the East Sea, yet often beat, detained, and incarcerated citizens who publicly condemned China's actions. Trying to understand their government's gentleness toward China and harshness toward patriotic Vietnamese, numerous critics began to doubt the commitment of Vietnamese Communist Party leaders to the nation.

This chapter analyzes critics' arguments, the various ways they have spoken out, and the reactions of party-state authorities. It draws on more than six hundred written accounts in Vietnamese blog sites and news sources as well as my observations and conversations in Vietnam.

Fishers

In early March 2016, fifty-nine-year-old Trần Sinh and his crew were retrieving nets flapping with fish when a Chinese coastguard ship steamed rapidly toward his boat. When very near his wooden craft, Sinh later told a journalist, uniformed men in the much larger steel-hulled vessel shouted something in Chinese through an amplifier.[4] Trần Sinh and his crew didn't understand. Then, in stilted Vietnamese, Sinh said, a Chinese sailor screamed, "These waters belong to China; you and all Vietnamese boats must leave immediately." As Sinh and his crew hurried to bring in their nets, Chinese sailors opened fire, riddling his boat with bullets and injuring one of his crew members. Sinh throttled his boat's engine to leave as speedily as possible. Hours later, he and his crew reached port in his badly damaged boat.

This episode is emblematic of approximately two thousand Chinese attacks between 2005 and 2015 on Vietnamese in waters that the fishers insist belong to Vietnam. Trần Sinh's boat was near the Paracel Islands and well within Vietnam's Exclusive Economic Zone of two hundred nautical miles.

Virtually all other Vietnamese fishing boats assaulted by Chinese vessels were also within this zone; often they were less than fifty nautical miles from Vietnam's shoreline.[5] Yet, according to China, the Vietnamese are trespassers.

"It is totally absurd," exclaimed Tiêu Việt Là, "to say that we Vietnamese are violating Chinese territorial waters. We are fishing in waters belonging to Vietnam that the Chinese have captured and occupied!" He said this to a reporter in July 2010, a few months after Chinese had abducted him and his boat for the fourth time since 2007, each instance costing him huge amounts of money before he and his boat were released.[6] "Even though Chinese boats pounce on us, causing much hardship," Phạm Văn Dũng of the central coastal province of Phú Yên told a reporter in May 2011, "I won't abandon those fishing areas. The waters [near Paracel Islands] belong to my country and I must make a living."[7] Mại Phụng Lưu, a fisher in Quảng Ngãi province on the central coast, recounted how Chinese had seized him and his boat and crew "in Vietnam's waters, waters where my grandfather fished, my father fished, and now I fish. Those waters are our history and our sovereignty."[8]

These men were among the thousands of Vietnamese fishers along their nation's lengthy coastline who regularly since the early 2000s tried to protect their livelihoods, their fishing grounds, and their country's territory in the face of Chinese who stole their equipment, damaged or sank their boats, abducted them, extorted money, and beat them. Chinese even killed an unreported number of Vietnamese fishers. In one instance in January 2005, Chinese coast-guard ships besieged two Vietnamese fishing boats in Vietnam's territorial waters off the coast of Thanh Hóa province in the north.[9] The Chinese rained bullets on the Vietnamese, killing nine men and gravely wounding seven more, then held the survivors and one boat until the fishers' families paid substantial money, which the Chinese called a "penalty" for trespassing but which Vietnamese called a "ransom" to kidnappers.

According to Vietnamese government figures, 7,045 fishers on 1,186 boats were attacked by foreigners, mostly Chinese, between 2006 and March 2010.[10] Comparable figures for subsequent years are unavailable but are likely larger. In 2010, China's government intensified efforts to enforce its claims over the East Sea, targeting especially Vietnamese fishing boats. Between November 2015 and early April 2016, Chinese assaulted twelve fishing boats from just one village, nearly a third of the boats owned by residents in that community on the coast of Thừa Thiên-Huế province in central Vietnam. During

2015, Chinese attacked seventeen boats with two hundred men from the small island Lý Sơn of Quảng Ngãi province in central Vietnam; those numbers amounted to 20 percent of the island's fishers.[11]

Often the attackers were in Chinese coast-guard and navy vessels; sometimes, especially after 2013, they were Chinese fishers reportedly encouraged and even financed by their government.[12] Some of attacking boats showed no flag or other country identifiers. In nearly all those cases, Vietnamese fishers reported that the attackers were Chinese. One such incident occurred in late November 2015 and was recounted to Vietnamese journalists by the victimized fishers. While they fished in waters claimed by Vietnam near the Spratly Islands, two unmarked boats, each with four armed men, came very close to their boat and started shooting, killing on the spot one of their crewmen, forty-two-year-old Trương Đình Bảy. The two vessels and the method of attack used, said the surviving fishers, were like others that Chinese often use against Vietnamese boats.[13]

Until about 2011, Chinese frequently abducted Vietnamese boats and crews deemed to be infringing on China's waterways, and held them captive while taking anything of value from the crew members and their boats and beating and starving them. In subsequent years, fewer Vietnamese fishers were kidnapped. More commonly, armed Chinese boarded fishers' boats; robbed crew members; stripped or destroyed their fishing equipment, navigational instruments, and other mechanisms; took or dumped their catch; and confiscated much of their petrol and fresh water, leaving only enough for the crews and boats to limp back to port. Sometimes the Chinese boats rammed, even sank, Vietnamese fishing boats, leaving the fishers floundering in the ocean.[14]

Vietnamese authorities regularly implored China to stop pursuing Vietnamese fishers and reiterated that the fishers are in Vietnam's territory. Vietnamese officials also used diplomatic channels to get abducted fishers released. In 2009, for example, persistent diplomatic efforts by Vietnam's Ministry of Foreign Affairs and other offices contributed to freeing twenty-five Vietnamese fishers, many of whom Chinese had held for two months on an atoll in the Paracel Islands while demanding large "penalty" payments.[15] Perhaps due to the Vietnamese authorities' intervention, the Chinese dropped their demand for payments; however, they kept two of the fishers' three boats (worth more than the "penalties"). Possibly the Vietnamese officials' persistent condemnation of Chinese seizing Vietnamese fishers contributed to Chinese switching from capturing fishers to robbing them and destroying their boats and equipment.

Fishers criticized their government for providing little or no financial or material assistance to those who were abducted. Numerous local officials, too, urged national authorities to help fishers and their families recover their financial footing after being kidnapped or robbed by Chinese.[16] Fishers also wanted the Vietnamese coast guard and navy to protect them against the Chinese, but officials said they lacked sufficient manpower, ships, and other resources.[17] Even some National Assembly members publicly questioned the claims of national party-state leaders to be protecting the nation's sovereignty and citizens in the face of Chinese hostilities that include, said delegate Lê Văn Lai from Quảng Nam province in April 2016, "squeezing Vietnamese people, stealing from them, even killing them."[18]

Demonstrators

News that Chinese coast guards had killed and abducted Vietnamese fishers in early January 2005 quickly kindled a public outcry. Citizens around the nation contributed money and other assistance to the fishers' families, and by January 20 over five thousand Vietnamese had signed a petition, directed at China's leaders, condemning the murders and kidnappings.[19] Then on Sunday, January 23, 2005, dozens of people demonstrated near China's embassy in Hà Nội and its consulate in Hồ Chí Minh City. Some displayed signs and leaflets bearing Vietnamese words meaning "oppose Beijing" and "immediately release those blameless men." The demonstrations were brief because security police in both cities quickly detained some participants and chased others away. Police also prevented numerous people from reaching the embassy and consulate, and school administrators had barred many students from demonstrating. Prominent party-state newspapers reported nothing about the demonstrations.[20]

On January 20, 2005, Vietnam's Ministry of Foreign Affairs stated that, by "killing innocent people," Chinese coast guards had "seriously violated" international laws and covenants.[21] That was about all Vietnamese authorities said publicly about the matter. Information about the attack had spread mainly through the newspaper articles, word of mouth, and the Internet, which by early 2005 had become more accessible. Monitoring the Internet is also likely how Vietnamese police learned some citizens were planning public protests and thus took preventative action.

The January 2005 demonstrations were the first of hundreds that spoke out against China's hostilities toward the Vietnam nation and its people.[22] I have material on thirty that occurred between then and late December 2015 in Hà Nội and a similar number in Hồ Chí Minh City, usually on the same day—typically a Sunday—and at about the same time—frequently starting at 8 or 9 a.m. Most had a few hundred people each, but they ranged in size from dozens to thousands of citizens in each city. Often smaller protests also occurred simultaneously in Cần Thơ, Đà Nẵng, Huế, Vinh, and Hải Phòng, among other cities across the country.

No single person or group organized the protests. People used their networks to spread the word. Organizations and websites distributed calls to demonstrate that listed the reasons, objectives, dates, and rendezvous locations. An example is an announcement from twenty "independent civic groups in Vietnam" addressed to "all patriotic Vietnamese" to demonstrate peacefully on May 11, 2014, at 9 a.m. in front of China's embassy in Hà Nội and its consulate in Hồ Chí Minh City to oppose China's oil rig within Vietnam's domain and other "aggression by Chinese leaders," demand that party-state authorities "stop China from seizing Vietnam's territorial waters," and insist that authorities release all citizens who have been imprisoned "for expressing their love of country and opposition to Chinese aggression."[23]

Without the Internet, getting the word out would have been much more cumbersome and less effective. With it, beckoning people to join coordinated protests became infinitely easier. In early December 2007, for example, messages on Yahoo Messenger and several blogs urged people to mobilize against China on December 9, outlined reasons, and named places in Hà Nội and Hồ Chí Minh City at which to congregate.[24] In 2011 and 2012, the Facebook page for Nhật ký Yêu nước [Patriotic Diary] and the blogs of Nguyễn Xuân Diện and Mẹ Nấm were popular sites announcing reasons, times, and assembly places for protests on several consecutive Sundays.[25] Often announcements asked people to bring Vietnamese flags and other patriotic symbols, suggested wording for placards and banners, emphasized that protests should be peaceful, and gave advice about how to prepare and behave during protests. Attached to the flyer calling for demonstrations on May 18, 2014 were twenty-one "dos" and twenty-one "don'ts" for participants to observe, among them "Bring enough water and wear a hat—and ladies, apply sun screen to protect your skin from ultraviolet rays"; "Don't litter streets and parks"; "Young people, stand with older people so you can help them and they can help you"; "Don't throw bricks, stones, or anything else at security forces." Other "dos and don'ts" were suggested for security forces and for people watching the protest marches.[26]

What usually ignited the demonstrations were provocative Chinese actions in East Sea areas claimed by Vietnam. In January 2005, it was Chinese forces killing Vietnamese fishers; in December 2007, it was Beijing authorities announcing that the Paracel and Spratly Islands and all the area in-between were now part of China's Hainan province. Setting off a series of demonstrations in June 2011 was a Chinese vessel cutting a seismographic cable of a Vietnamese oil exploration ship well within Vietnam's territorial waters. Several protest marches in July 2012 resulted from China's government soliciting bids from companies to explore for oil and gas in waters near Vietnam's coastline; the demonstrations in December 2012 followed Beijing authorities' decision to embed Chinese passports with a map of China that included the nine-dash line in the East Sea. Demonstrations in May 2014 started almost immediately after China placed an oil drilling rig in Vietnam's Exclusive Economic Zone and over 130 armed ships to protect it.

Specific acts like these were highlighted in announcements calling citizens to protest and in posters at the demonstrations themselves. "China, get that putrid, filthy oil rig out of the Vietnam homeland's luxuriant sea," said some placards in Vietnamese at the May 11, 2014 demonstration in Hồ Chí Minh City.[27] Even more prominent in announcements, posters, and banners were condemnations of China's overall behavior in, and sweeping claims to, the East Sea. Signs at numerous demonstrations read in Vietnamese, "The Paracels and the Spratlys are Vietnam's" and "Oppose the illegal cow's tongue path," a reference to China's nine-dash line on its maps of the East Sea. Common slogans included "Down with Chinese aggression," "Oppose China's provocative hostility," and "Justice and peace in the East Sea."

The protests were also directed at the party-state. Early ones urged authorities to resolutely oppose China's hostilities against Vietnam, protect Vietnamese fishers, and support demonstrators. On December 9, 2007, for instance, demonstrators in Hồ Chí Minh City cried out, "Officials, join us" and shouted to their government, "No need to be weak; Don't let Vietnam fall into China's hands." Later protests made similar demands but in addition frequently criticized authorities for accommodating China. In June 2011,

Figure 3.2. Anti-China protesters in Hồ Chí Minh City, May 11, 2014. The banner says, "Paracel and Spratly Islands Are Inviolable Territory Belonging to the Vietnam Homeland." Photo by Giang Vu Hoang Pham. Courtesy of Getty Images.

signs aimed at Vietnam's policies toward China read, "After sacrificing so much blood and bones for this country, why now protect and defend the invaders?" A call to demonstrate in December 2012 said, "Our own state has given in to China, yet the more it concedes, the more China prevails."[28] Some demonstrators questioned authorities' commitment to the nation. A scowling security policeman confronted two students protesting in Hà Nội in 2007: "You say you're patriotic? What about us [in the police force]? Aren't we patriotic?" The students replied softly, "Yes, sir. You're patriotic but only by loving the [communist] party and socialism do you love your country."[29]

Young Vietnamese, especially high school and university students, were among the most numerous participants in the January 2005 demonstrations and many subsequent ones. On June 12, 2011, for instance, students reportedly constituted half the demonstrators in Hồ Chí Minh City and 70 percent in Hà Nội.[30] In November 2015, students were prominent in the demonstrations when China's president Xi Jinping visited Hà Nội.[31] Hồ Chí Minh City student protesters frequently came from the Economics University, College of Architecture, and Hồng Bàng University; in Hà Nội, many were from the University of Science and Technology and the Economics University.

Although only a small fraction of all students joined these demonstrations, their participation altered the perceptions of many observers inside Vietnam who doubted urban youths, particularly students, were interested in such matters; they were said to be "preoccupied with money and their own lives and indifferent to current affairs and political issues."[32] Possible punishments by parents, school administrators, the police, and other authorities also precluded young people from publicly expressing political views.

No doubt many students were engrossed with their own lives and feared running afoul of elders and government officials. Nevertheless, thousands demonstrated. What propelled them, many said, was their love of country and anger at China's aggression. "Even if I'm alone," one student told a journalist shortly after demonstrating on June 5, 2011, as he and others pondered whether to join future protests, "I'll still stand at that [Chinese] embassy, unfurl my banner, and express myself. If someone arrests me, so be it. I'm expressing my love of country. . . . Because of patriotism I shall take to the streets to speak up, whether there's one, two, or a hundred people" with me.[33] Sharing that attitude were hundreds of demonstrators converging on Hồ Chí Minh City's opera house on December 9, 2012.[34] As they came face to face with police blocking their way, tension filled the air. The crowd grew quiet. Suddenly a young man dashed toward the opera house waving the nation's flag over his head and shouting "Long live Vietnam." The crowd then surged through the police lines, chanting "Paracels, Spratlys, Vietnam! Paracels, Spratlys, Vietnam!"

Besides students, protesters included numerous writers, artists, musicians, researchers, teachers, public intellectuals, office workers, retired soldiers, and retired government and VCP officials. Some active VCP members demonstrated. Also among the protesters were a few villagers and factory workers, the latter being most pronounced during May 2014 protests against China.[35] Anti-China activists, however, made no concerted efforts, so far as I can tell, to urge villagers and industrial laborers to join their demonstrations.

All protesters focused on China's actions against Vietnam, the Vietnamese party-state's responses, and the threat China posed to the nation. As one statement put it, demonstrators were "protecting their flesh and blood—the wealth and territorial sovereignty they inherited from their forefathers" against China's "hegemonic" actions.[36] Some participants voiced additional complaints by waving signs opposing land appropriations, advocating political reform, and demanding the release of political prisoners.

Usually Vietnamese authorities knew ahead of time, from their monitoring of Internet sites and surveillance, when and where demonstrations would occur and prepared accordingly. In some cases, protesters informed officials directly and invited them to join. After all, their invitations stressed, the demonstrations were expressions of patriotism to Vietnam.

Party-state organizations joined protests on May 11, 2014, shortly after China had placed an oil rig in Vietnam's waters. Members of the Communist Youth League and other groups in the party-state's Homeland Front demonstrated in several cities, although they avoided merging with other protesters.[37] Their placards did not condemn China's actions; instead they replicated mild and familiar official slogans such as "Great unity, great unity" and "Peaceful and stable justice."[38] That official organizations flashed a green light to demonstrate did embolden many otherwise hesitant citizens to also speak out, making those May 11 demonstrations among the largest and most widespread beyond Hồ Chí Minh City and Hà Nội. For instance, in Cần Thơ, a city in the Mekong delta, about two thousand people protested, and Đà Nẵng, a city along the central coast, had about three thousand demonstrators.[39]

Toward virtually all other demonstrations, authorities' actions ranged from toleration to repression. Similarly, party-state press coverage of anti-China protests ranged from blackouts to occasional reports, some of which praised the expressions of patriotism while others said that protesters were paid to demonstrate or that overseas groups hostile to Vietnam had instigated the marches.

To prevent people from even reaching protest sites, authorities frequently ordered neighborhood police to go to the homes of likely participants and instruct them not to join demonstrations and block their passageway. At protest locations, security forces, usually unarmed except for batons, used loudspeakers, overwhelming numbers of uniformed and plain-clothed officers, barricades, and force to disperse most protesters and cart others away to police stations and detention centers and hold them for hours, if not longer. Using these repressive tactics, police smothered some demonstrations so quickly, such as those in January 2005, December 2008, and June 2013, that protesters were scarcely able to assemble and hoist their placards.[40]

Often, however, officials countenanced a degree of protest, perhaps to signal their objection to an outlandish Chinese action, but then stopped the demonstrations so as to prevent them from snowballing and possibly becoming demonstrations about other issues. On December 9, 2007, for instance, a few hundred people marched through downtown Hồ Chí Minh City and Hà Nội for about three hours with only modest police interference; officials in Hồ Chí Minh City even had discussions with several students who were heading to join the protest. A week later, more people rallied in each city, reportedly numbering about one thousand in Hà Nội, but greater police interference forced demonstrators to disperse early. Police promptly stifled attempted follow-up demonstrations on December 23 and January 9 and 19, 2008.[41] On December 9, 2012, a few hundred people marched in downtown Hồ Chí Minh City and Hà Nội for about an hour while police mostly just watched. Then, suddenly, massive numbers of police appeared, scattered the crowds, and detained dozens of protesters. That repression deterred follow-up demonstrations, except for the colorful dolls, holding signs condemning Chinese aggression, that early the next Sunday had been stealthily placed near China's embassy in Hà Nội.[42] Soon after the May 11, 2014 demonstrations that authorities had allowed, calls circulated through the Internet for nationwide protests against China the following Sunday, May 18. But massive police operations, reportedly ordered by Prime Minister Nguyễn Tấn Dũng, prior to and during that day prevented all except a few short-lived rallies.[43]

The large exception to this pattern was the eleven, almost weekly demonstrations, primarily in Hà Nội and Hồ Chí Minh City, between June 5 and August 21, 2011, made possible by authorities' vacillating reactions and demonstrators' resolve. What provoked the protests was a surge in Chinese attacks on Vietnamese fishers and news that Chinese ships had cut cables of Vietnamese oil exploration vessels in the East Sea, transgressions that the Vietnamese government sternly condemned. Toward the demonstrations on Sunday, June 5, which the Vice Minister of Defense Nguyễn Chí Vịnh described as "peaceful, orderly" and without "incendiary placards," authorities took a relaxed attitude. Police even allowed some of the thousands of marchers to reach China's embassy in Hà Nội and its consulate in Hồ Chí Minh City.[44] During subsequent Sunday protests, police prevented demonstrators from going there and became stricter, even violent, often detaining dozens of people. Behind the scenes, as Vietnamese officials complained to their Chinese counterparts about China's transgressions, Chinese leaders objected to the demonstrations in Vietnam. The two sides agreed in late June that both should "steer public opinion in the correct direction" so as not to harm their friendship.[45]

Yet protests continued, and repression was uneven—most severe in such smaller cities as Đà Nẵng and Vinh, both in central Vietnam, and Hải Phòng in the north; less severe in Hồ Chí Minh City; and least severe in Hà Nội.[46] That difference, quipped one protester, suggests that, in the eyes of the regime, "patriots here [in Hồ Chí Minh City] are reactionaries while patriots in Hà Nội are genuine." Another explanation, said a Vietnamese journalist, is that authorities are heavy-handed in Hồ Chí Minh City to show China that they can maintain order but they "distribute bread and water" to protesters in Hà Nội to convey their discontent with China's actions.[47] Prior to demonstrations in Hà Nội on June 19, July 24, and August 7 and 14, city officials there even said that peaceful rallies would be allowed.[48] On August 18, however, city authorities announced that no further demonstrations would be permitted. Several Vietnamese spoke out against that announcement; among them were twenty-five prominent citizens who vigorously stated their position in a petition to city officials.[49] The officials remained firm, and the following Sunday, August 21, police dispersed and detained protesters in Hà Nội and elsewhere who defied that warning.[50] No demonstration was attempted the next Sunday, August 28.

Other Protesters and Critics

Besides marching in city streets and fishing in the East Sea, Vietnamese spoke out in other ways to oppose China and criticize their government's relations with it. At least one citizen committed suicide: Sixty-seven-year-old Lê Thị Tuyết Mai, long distressed about China's actions against her country and extremely upset when China placed its oil rig in Vietnamese waters in early May 2014, immolated herself on May 23 that year in front of Unification Hall, a prominent national landmark in Hồ Chí Minh City. Prior to reaching the site of death she had selected, she penned a list summarizing her desires, three of which read "Support Vietnam's fishers and coast guard"; "Demand China leave Vietnam's sea"; and "Return ocean and islands to Vietnam."[51] In another form of protest, several VCP members quit the organization in disgust at the leadership's tepid responses to China. For instance, Phạm Đình Trọng, a VCP member for nearly forty years, left the party in November 2009. One major reason, he wrote, was that VCP leaders "have intentionally forgotten" all of China's hostilities against Vietnam "in order to align and win favor with China's leadership so as to preserve their own seats of power."[52] Boycotting Chinese products was another protest method. One Vietnamese vendor established a website selling only products made in Vietnam.[53] No-U and other groups made, sold, and gave away T-shirts, cups, headbands, and other useful items featuring anti-China designs.

Some of the blogs with information about protest marches also posted bloggers' own statements and other people's writings about China's transgressions against Vietnam. One well-known blog was Điếu Cày, created in 2007 by Nguyễn Văn Hải, an army veteran and computer technician in Hồ Chí Minh City who had co-organized a club for independent journalists. What particularly spurred his blog site and his participation in anti-China demonstrations were Beijing's heightened claims to the Paracel and Spratly Islands.[54] Two other favorite blogs about Vietnam-China relations were Tễu and Mẹ Nấm. Tễu's founder was Nguyễn Xuân Diện, a researcher in Hà Nội specializing in early Chinese and Vietnamese history and a frequent participant in anti-China protests. Mẹ Nấm's creator, Nguyễn Ngọc Như Quỳnh in the coastal city of Nha Trang, started blogging about social injustices in 2006 at the age of twenty-seven; by 2009 her blog also had much material about China and her own and others' actions in speaking out to defend Vietnam's territory.[55]

On numerous occasions, dozens of citizens in Hà Nội, Hồ Chí Minh City, and elsewhere publicly assembled to commemorate Vietnamese soldiers killed in conflicts with China, particularly in 1974 when Chinese troops overran parts of the Paracel Islands, in 1979 during a border war between China and Vietnam, and in 1988 when Chinese forces invaded some of the Spratly Islands. The party-state had previously paid annual tribute to soldiers killed in the 1979 war, but stopped after 1990. Since then, party-state offices and nearly all their media ignored that war, the soldiers who fought it, and the thousands who died. The reason, said Tương Lai, one of the organizers of the assemblies commemorating those soldiers, is that Vietnamese authorities have "pledged to maintain friendship" with, and want to avoid "offending the feelings" of their fellow communists in China.[56] Many other commemorators agreed.

Tương Lai, who chaired the Sociology Institute of the Academy of Social Sciences in Hà Nội before retiring to Hồ Chí Minh City, had joined the

VCP in 1959. Beginning about 2006, he frequently urged the party to embark on major political reforms to foster open and frank dialogue between authorities and citizens.[57] He also wrote and demonstrated against China's encroachments into Vietnamese territory and pondered why Vietnamese authorities were reticent in vigorously opposing China's actions. The explanation, he concluded, was that the VCP leadership depended heavily on China's government, which in turn was keen to prolong VCP rule in Vietnam. A fundamental link between the two countries' leaders was their shared ideology of socialism and "arrogant communism." This ideology and reliance on China, Tương Lai argued, impedes Vietnam's leaders from reforming the political system. It also means Vietnamese authorities put their relationship with China and their socialist-communist ideology ahead of the Vietnamese nation. Hence, they tolerate Chinese actions at Vietnam's expense. That stance angers many Vietnamese and widens the distance between the party-state and the people, which accentuates the regime's dependence on China. The circle becomes vicious.[58]

Another way to speak out against China's aggression and the party-state's actions was to send to authorities letters, petitions, and other statements signed by numerous Vietnamese. Usually a small group drafted each statement and then signatures were solicited from colleagues and friends or by posting the document on Internet sites to invite signatures from anyone interested. Various groups drafted the documents, although several individuals were in more than one group.

I am aware of fifteen such statements sent to authorities between 2008 and late 2015. Eleven of them are particularly detailed about signers' apprehensions about China and their own government and about actions that should be taken. (Table 3.1 lists each statement and the number of initial signatures.) Together, the documents show an increasingly dire assessment of China's intentions and party-state authorities' priorities. Before elaborating on that, let us look at people who were especially active in preparing and circulating the eleven statements.

The total number of signatures on the eleven statements is 748 (counting only the first "wave" of signatures on those documents that eventually attracted more signers). Besides their names, nearly everyone stated where they lived and their present or former occupations and affiliations; several indicated they were VCP members. Removing the 118 signatures by people residing abroad left 630 names of Vietnamese in Vietnam. By combining alphabetized

Table 3.1. Eleven public statements regarding Vietnam-China relations signed by Vietnamese citizens between April 2008 and April 2015

Title of statement	Date	Signatures	
		Initially	Later
Bản Kiến nghị ngỏ [An open petition][1]	April 23, 2008	11	
Kiến nghị về vụ khai thác bauxite ở Tây Nguyên [Petition regarding exploiting bauxite in the central highlands][2]	April 12, 2009	132	2,746
Tuyên cáo về việc nhà cầm quyền Trung Quốc liên tục có những hành động gây hấn, xâm phạm nghiêm trọng chủ quyền và toàn vẹn lãnh thổ Việt Nam trên Biển Đông [Declaration regarding Chinese authorities' continuous provocative actions, seriously violating Vietnam's sovereignty and territory in the East Sea][3]	June 25, 2011	95	1,045
Kiến nghị về bảo vệ và phát triển đất nước trong tình hình hiện nay [Petition regarding defending and developing the country in the present situation][4]	July 10, 2011	20	1,219
Kính gửi: Đề nghị tổ chức cuộc biểu tình tuần hành phản đối nhà cầm quyền Trung Quốc liên tục có những hành động gây hấn, mưu toan xâm chiếm vùng lãnh hải và đặc quyền kinh tế của Việt Nam ở Biển Đông [Respectfully sending (to Hồ Chí Minh City Communist Party leaders and others): Suggestion to organize a demonstration and march to oppose Chinese authorities' continuous provocative actions and intentional aggression against Vietnam's economic prerogatives and territory in the East Sea][5]	July 27, 2012	42	
Thư ngỏ [Open letter, addressed to the National Assembly, National President, and Government of Vietnam][6]	August 6, 2012	71	
Tuyên bố phản đối nhà cầm quyền Trung Quốc in hình "lưỡi bò" lên hộ chiếu công dân [Declaration opposing Chinese authorities printing the "cow's tongue" figure (nine-dash line) in Chinese passports][7]	November 27, 2012	139	700+
Kính gửi đồng bào Việt Nam ở trong nước và nước ngoài, cùng toàn thể các đảng viên Đảng Cộng sản Việt Nam [Dear Vietnamese compatriots inside and outside the country including all members of the Vietnamese Communist Party][8]	May 29, 2014	115	
Thư ngỏ: Kính gửi: Ban Chấp hành Trung ương và toàn thể đảng viên Đảng Cộng sản Việt Nam [Open letter: Dear Central Executive Committee and all members of the Vietnamese Communist Party][9]	July 28, 2014	61	

	September 2, 2014	20
Kiến nghị của một số cựu sĩ quan Lực lượng vũ trang nhân dân gửi Lãnh đạo Nhà nước và Chính phủ CHXHCN Việt Nam [Petition from some former officers of the people's Armed Forces to Leaders of the State and Government of the Socialist Republic of Vietnam][10]		
Thư gửi Bộ Chính trị, Ban Chấp hành trung ương Đảng Cộng sản Việt Nam [Letter to the Political Bureau, Central Executive Committee of the Vietnamese Communist Party][11]	April 18, 2015	42

[1] Accessed March 17, 2016, https://tiengnoitudo.wordpress.com/2008/04/25/olympics-hs-ts-b%E1%BA%A2n-ki%E1%BA%BEn-ngh%E1%BB%8A-ng%E1%BB%8E/.

[2] The petition was accessed April 23, 2009, http://www.thongluan.org/vn/modules.php?name=Content&pa=showpage&pid=1275; the list of the first wave of signatures was accessed May 11, 2015, http://boxitvn.blogspot.com/2009/04/danh-sach-chu-ky-ot-1.html; the final list of signers was accessed September 21, 2016, http://boxitvn.wordpress.com/kien-nghi/danh-sach-9/.

[3] Accessed November 25, 2014, http://xuandienhannom.blogspot.com/2011/06/ban-tuyen-cao-ac-biet-cua-gioi-nhan-si.html. The eventual number of signatures is cited in *Tự Do Ngôn Luận* [Free Speech], July 1, 2011, 5.

[4] Accessed November 24, 2012, http://xuandienhannom.blogspot.com/2011/07/toan-van-kien-nghi-khan-cap-ve-bao-ve.html. The number of signatures that the statement had later is cited in Mặc Lâm, "Những ảnh hưởng ngầm phía sau những kiến nghị" [Petitions' Behind-the-Scenes Influences], November 3, 2012, RFA, accessed November 12, 2012, http://www.rfa.org/vietnamese/in_depth/the-undergrrnd-impacts-of-petition-ltrs-ml-11032012145748.html.

[5] Accessed April 19, 2014, http://huynhngocchenh.blogspot.com/2012/07/e-nghi-to-chuc-bieu-tinh-phan-oi-trung.html.

[6] Accessed November 24, 2012, http://xuandienhannom.blogspot.com/2012/08/toan-van-thu-ngo-cua-cac-nhan-si-tri.html.

[7] "Cow's tongue" is another term used for the "nine-dash line." Accessed November 28, 2012, http://www.webdoithoai.net/index.php?option=com_content&view=article&id=9070:tuyen-b-phn-i-nha-cm-quyn-trung-quc-v-h-chiu-li-boಸcatid=105:blongnguyenxuandien&Itemid=69. The list of initial signers has 143 names but four are duplicates, thus 139 people initially signed. The later number of signatures is reported in "GS Tương Lai: Đảng 'nên đặt Tổ quốc lên trên hết'" [Professor Trương Lai: The Party "Should Put the Homeland above Everything Else"], December 7, 2012, BBC, accessed December 9, 2012, http://anhbasam.wordpress.com/2012/12/07/1445-gs-tuong-lai-dang-nen-dat-to-quoc-len-tren-het/#more-84462.

[8] Accessed November 25, 2014, http://xuandienhannom.blogspot.com/2014/05/thu-ngo-ve-tinh-hinh-khan-cap-cua-at.html.

[9] Accessed November 5, 2015, https://anhbasam.wordpress.com/2014/07/29/thu-ngo-gui-bch-trung-uong-va-toan-the-dang-vien-dang-csvn/.

[10] Accessed November 25, 2014, http://boxitvn.blogspot.com/2014/09/kien-nghi-cua-mot-so-cuu-si-quan-luc.html.

[11] Accessed February 4, 2016, http://vanviet.info/van-de-hom-nay/thu-gui-bo-chinh-tri-ban-chap-hanh-trung-uong-dang-cong-san-viet-nam/.

lists of these people's names, I found that the 630 signatures came from 361 individuals. About 45 percent of them were in Hồ Chí Minh City, 38 percent were in Hà Nội, and the remaining 17 percent were spread among other locations, especially Huế, Đà Nẵng, and the upland province of Lâm Đồng (mainly the city of Đà Lạt).

Further examination of the 361 names showed that 62 people signed three or more statements.[59] Their prevalence suggests they were often in the groups that drafted the statements and solicited other people's endorsements. Also indicative of their prominence in generating the petitions and letters is that 51 of these 62 individuals were among the first twenty signers on the ten statements in which signatures appeared in the order in which each was penned. (Signatures on the July 28, 2014 letter were listed according to the year each signer had joined the VCP.)

Of these 62 signers, 44 percent were in Hồ Chí Minh City, 39 percent were in Hà Nội, and 17 percent elsewhere in the country. All 62 were prominent citizens. Over half were former government officials and advisers, VCP officials, and officers in the military or police; several others were still serving in government offices, universities, and research units. At least half were VCP members, not counting two former party members. Nearly half of those in Hồ Chí Minh City were veterans of pre-1975 organizations that had opposed the South Vietnamese regime. In other words, nearly two-thirds of the 62 came to their critical stances regarding China-Vietnam relations as people with close and, for many, long attachments to Vietnam's party-state.

Two examples are Tương Lai and Phạm Đình Trọng, discussed earlier in this chapter. Two more examples are Huỳnh Tấn Mẫm and Nguyễn Trọng Vĩnh. While studying medicine in Sài Gòn in the mid-1960s and early 1970s, Huỳnh Tấn Mẫm became a prominent leader of students protesting against the authoritarian methods of the Republic of Vietnam in the south and against the United States government supporting it. For this he was imprisoned. In 1971 he joined the VCP. After Vietnam's reunification, he was a physician and served the government and the VCP in various capacities, including being the general editor of *Thanh Niên*, a newspaper of the party-state's Youth Union, and a member of the country's National Assembly. Deeply angered by China's intensifying aggressions against Vietnam in the 2000s and inspired by youths protesting against China, he joined numerous demonstrations and entreated party-state authorities to do the same. When told by authorities that the demonstrations were unlawful, he and others with whom he often wrote to officials refused to desist, even, he stated in 2012, if that meant "being expelled from the [Communist] Party."[60]

Nguyễn Trọng Vĩnh, a VCP member since 1937, fought in wars against France and to reunify Vietnam, rose to be major-general in the army, and later was Vietnam's ambassador to China from 1974 to 1987. While remaining proud of the VCP's many accomplishments, he began in the 1990s, within the confines of the party, to criticize what he saw as corruption and decadence spreading through the organization. He also warned party-state leaders about China's widening ambitions. Seeing little evidence that officials listened to his criticisms or those of others, he went public with his concerns, especially regarding China. In 2012, he wrote that since 1990, when China and Vietnam normalized relations (after over a decade of intermittent hostilities), China "has continued to encroach" on Vietnam, "intervene in our ministerial offices, buy forests and land, exploit bauxite in the central highlands, do much to sabotage our economy, act perversely in the East Sea, spread tens of thousands of Chinese around our country, and deliberately force us into its orbit."[61]

Three of the eleven statements emphasized specific issues. The April 12, 2009 petition stressed environmental, economic, cultural, and national security objections to the prime minister of Vietnam's plan to allow Chinese companies to mine and process bauxite in Vietnam's central highlands.[62] That project, pleaded the petitioners, must be suspended, in-depth research must be done by experts, and the National Assembly, not just the prime minister, must decide on all matters pertaining to it. The July 27, 2012 letter urged Hồ Chí Minh City officials to organize demonstrations to oppose Chinese transgressions against the nation and its citizens, particularly fishers. If authorities would not mobilize protests, the petitioners said they would and they asked city officials to protect all demonstrators. The November 27, 2012 pronouncement strenuously objected to the new map in Chinese passports showing that all the area within the "nine-dash line" belonged to China. That November 27 statement also applauded the Ministry of Foreign Affairs for condemning China's violations of Vietnam's sovereignty.

These three statements located their particular concerns in the context of China's recent hostilities against Vietnam. The additional eight statements delved deeper into the reasons for China's behavior and Vietnam's official responses. Two early ones, dated April 23, 2008 and June 25, 2011, argued that China's recent forms of "encroachment," "hostility," and "transgression"—

attacking many Vietnamese fishers, creating a new district that included the Paracel and Spratly Islands, cutting seismic cables of Vietnamese oil exploratory ships—were part of ongoing aggression against Vietnam since the 1950s and evidence of China's "expansionism." Subsequent statements used that history and additional evidence to go further. China, said the July 10, 2011 statement, "aspires to be a superpower" and had already "accomplished important steps in its plan to dominate Vietnam." Among those steps, it stated, were that Vietnam now relied heavily on Chinese imports, Chinese firms had 90 percent of construction and engineering contracts to develop key industries in Vietnam, and China had dams upstream of two of Vietnam's large rivers. China's next big step, the statement said, was to "monopolize the East Sea." Later statements contended that China was seeking to absorb Vietnam. The August 6, 2012 letter insisted that China "is implementing a hegemonic strategic plan to weaken and overpower Vietnam or make it a dependent of China." Two years later, the July 28, 2014 letter prepared by sixty-one elderly and middle-aged party members said that China intended to make Vietnam its "new type of vassal" to "serve China's interests." That intention, suggested the statement, began after the two countries renewed relations at a meeting in Chengdu, China, in September 1990.

Although none of the eleven statements advocated war, nearly all urged party-state authorities to take more decisive and firm measures to counter China. Use naval and coast guard ships, said some, to protect Vietnamese fishers and oil explorations against Chinese interference. Protect, even join, Vietnamese citizens who oppose China's aggression. Do not, insisted the September 2, 2014 petition signed by former military and police officers, use soldiers and security police against "the people, such as . . . preventing peaceful patriotic demonstrations." Supporting demonstrators, rather than repressing them, statements contended, would show China that the Vietnamese nation was united in defending its independence and sovereignty. The April 23, 2008 and August 6, 2012 statements urged national leaders to publicly refute China's claims and, said the latter document, make clear to "the Vietnamese people, the Chinese people, and people around the world" the "historical and legal evidence authenticating Vietnam's sovereignty within the East Sea."

China, most statements claimed, flagrantly violates international agreements, particularly the United Nations Convention on the Law of the Sea that it itself had signed. So, implored the July 28, 2014 letter, Vietnam should "immediately file a case against China in an international court." This plea reinforced what numerous Vietnamese had voiced the previous May when more than 3,700 people signed an open letter, posted on the Internet, urging national authorities to file a court case against China for violating the international law of the sea and formally request China to use the International Court of Justice to resolve competing claims to the Paracel Islands.[63]

Several of the eleven statements pressed Vietnamese authorities to collaborate with other Asian countries, especially the Philippines and other fellow members of the Association of Southeast Asian Nations, to pressure China to fulfill its claims to wanting friendship, peace, and stability in the region.[64] The September 2, 2014 petition and the April 18, 2015 letter advised closer relations with the United States. This is necessary, argued the April 18 statement, in order to "more powerfully oppose the bandit assaulting our house."

Yet, the statements often lamented, Vietnam's national leaders appeared reluctant to condemn and resist China's aggression. It is "very hard to understand," said the April 23, 2008 petition, why until now, months after China declared [in December 2007] that the Paracel and Spratly Islands were part of its new district, "all top leaders and the highest offices" in the nation, including the National Assembly and the central government, "have yet to officially and clearly express a stance regarding China's invasion of our homeland." Later statements expressed similar misgivings about party-state reactions to China. The "Central Executive Committee of Vietnam's Communist Party, above all the party's secretary general and Political Bureau," said the May 29, 2014 letter addressed to all VCP members in Vietnam, "failed in its responsibilities to the country and the people" by "not condemning, analyzing, and opposing" in mid-May, a few days after the Chinese oil rig was placed in Vietnam's waters, China's latest "invasive action" against Vietnam.

Why, wondered many Vietnamese, was their government acting so meekly? The answer from several No-U members and anti-China demonstrators was that "national leaders have sold the country to China."[65] Similarly, Hà Nội artist Nguyễn Thị Kim Chi told a reporter in July 2014 that "Everybody knows, including motorcycle-taxi drivers and vegetable vendors, that we're on the verge of losing the nation" on account of China, "yet leaders remain mute" because that's in their interest.[66] The answer that began to emerge in the statements written in mid-2011 and that became more direct by those in 2014 was that Vietnam's leaders were giving higher priority to maintaining good relations with their Chinese counterparts and preserving their political power than to defending the Vietnamese nation. The July 10, 2011 petition called on leaders of the VCP, the country's "sole ruling party," to "put national interests above everything else," hinting that party leaders were losing sight of the nation's needs. "The party and government," it said, "are confused and detached from the might of the people." The nation's leaders, it continued, "have not made public and explicit the actual relationship between Vietnam and China," a concern echoed in other statements in 2011–14. Vietnamese people, insisted the July 28, 2014 letter, "have a right to know, and must know, the truth about Vietnam-China relations and things signed with China, particularly the Chengdu agreement in 1990, the border agreement [in 1999], and various economic agreements." Chinese sources, said the September 2, 2014 petition, claim that Vietnam and China's leaders agreed at the Chengdu conference that by 2020 Vietnam will become an autonomous region under Chinese rule. "We don't know whether this is true or false," said the petitioners, but the "president and prime minister [of Vietnam] should make very clear" what that meeting decided.

Besides those who signed these statements, other Vietnamese also wondered whether national leaders had secretly committed Vietnam to join China by 2020. In 2014, the matter was vigorously discussed in blogs, Facebook, and elsewhere on the Internet. In October, a group named "Chúng tôi muốn biết" [We want to know], composed mostly of young people, went to National Assembly offices in Hà Nội and Hồ Chí Minh City seeking answers about what had happened at the 1990 Chengdu meeting. They were turned away.[67]

Some of the eleven statements, in addition to suggesting that the VCP might have an unpatriotic relationship with the Chinese regime, linked the party-state leadership's timidity toward China to Vietnam's political system. The July 28, 2014 letter argued that "following an erroneous path to build a Soviet-style socialism" and "preserving a single-party totalitarian system that impedes freedom and democracy" also figured in the weak ability of "party and state leaders" to deal with China. This system, being like China's, said the letter, draws together the Communist Party leaders in both countries and inhibits Vietnam from opposing China even as it encroaches on Vietnamese territory. Vietnam's "entire Communist Party, including ourselves," the party members' statement said, "are responsible for this situation," but most responsible "are the Central Executive Committee and the Political Bureau."

"Leaders at the central and other levels [of the party-state], especially those having shady relations with Chinese rulers," claimed the May 29, 2014 letter, "are more worried about losing their positions of authority than losing the nation."

Preserving the nation requires political reform, argued the statements of July 10, 2011 and August 6, 2012, beginning with actually protecting the freedoms of speech, press, association, and demonstration, rights already specified in Vietnam's constitution. Statements in 2014 went further. Change Vietnam in a "peaceful way," insisted the May 29 letter, "from a "totalitarian system to a democracy." Vietnam's patriotic party members and other citizens, said the July 28 statement, must "abandon the mistaken path to building socialism," set the country "firmly on the path of nation and democracy," and "create a state system of laws and real democracy."

Vietnam's officials brushed off these suggested political changes. And they dismissed allegations that Vietnamese authorities had pledged to make Vietnam become part of China by 2020. They insisted, as the VCP's Propaganda and Education Board explained in materials circulated to party members in October 2014, that the 1990 meeting in Chengdu between Vietnamese and Chinese leaders helped to normalize relations between the two countries. The claim that the meeting agreed that Vietnam would be subsumed under China was a "fabrication designed to incite and agitate party members, cadres, and sectors of the people."[68] It was one of many "falsehoods," said an article in Prime Minister Nguyễn Tấn Dũng's unofficial website in December 2014, used by people "seeking ways to disturb . . . [and adversely] affect the country's prestige."[69]

Authorities also defended their method for addressing issues with China, a mixture of public condemnations and persistent diplomacy. Vietnam's prime minister, minister of foreign affairs, and other national officials frequently denounced China's incursions into Vietnam's territory in the East Sea (including the Paracel and Spratly Islands), interference with Vietnamese fishing boats and exploration vessels, and other violations of international laws and agreements at Vietnam's expense.[70] But simultaneously, they stressed, Vietnam needed to resolve tensions and disagreements with China through dialogue and other nonprovocative ways in the spirit of practicing what they and their Chinese counterparts labeled the "four goods": being good neighbors, good friends, good comrades, and good partners.[71]

A prominent analyst of Vietnam's international relations described the country's stance toward China from the early 1990s as a combination of co-operation and struggle. Within that approach are several strategies, summarized by another scholar as ranging from bolstering Vietnam's presence in the East Sea, involving other countries in measures to resolve disputes with China, having bilateral discussions with China, exercising self-restraint, and showing deference to China due to its more powerful position in a hierarchy of states.[72] Vietnamese authorities' overall objective, wrote these and other scholars, is to avoid military conflict with China and enhance beneficial political and economic relations between the two countries while preserving Vietnam's territory and advancing its interests.[73]

Maintaining this delicate relationship with China, according to Vietnamese authorities, requires the skills and knowledge of experienced officials. Critics and protesters, stressed party-state authorities, lack these abilities, have inadequate information, and, worse, jeopardize the Vietnam-China relationship. "Anti-China demonstrations," argued Vice Minister of Defense Nguyễn Chí Vịnh while justifying the party-state's actions against critics, "give China a pretext to misrepresent Vietnam's good will and distort Vietnam's policy of resolving disputes through peaceful means."[74] Concerns about impeding Vietnam's diplomatic efforts and upsetting China contributed to Vietnamese officials attacking some detractors. In mid-2009, for example, complaints from China's ambassador in Hà Nội and other Chinese officials were one reason why Vietnamese authorities harassed, interrogated, and detained Nguyễn Ngọc Như Quỳnh and several other bloggers who wrote forcefully against China's actions in the East Sea and condemned Vietnamese authorities' responses for being too timid. A related reason was that Vietnamese officials claimed the writers disrupted national security.[75] In 2012, when sentencing anti-China blogger and protester Nguyễn Văn Hải for "spreading propaganda against the state," judges declared that he and two fellow bloggers had "adversely affected [Vietnam's] national security as well as Vietnam's international image."[76]

Authorities imprisoned few other opponents of China's actions and Vietnam's responses. For instance, none of the sixty-two people who signed three or more of the eleven statements I analyzed were arrested. More commonly, authorities ignored critics, alleged they were in league with or being used by overseas Vietnamese who despise the regime, and tormented them. Common harassment, usually against relatively unknown critics of Vietnam-

China relations, included stalking, detaining, and interrogating them; hacking their email accounts and websites; preventing them from joining demonstrations and meeting fellow critics; pressuring proprietors to refuse their business; hiring thugs to beat them up; and spreading false rumors about them. No-U members, for instance, told me in 2012 and 2016 that police frequently interfered with their soccer practices; compelled soccer field managers to turn the group away; blocked members from leaving their homes to go to No-U gatherings; harassed members' spouses and adult children; and disrupted, sometimes violently, meetings and dinners members had in coffee shops and restaurants. Police also physically assaulted and seriously injured several No-U participants.[77]

Yet now and again authorities sat down with representatives of petitioners and other critics to discuss their disagreements regarding China. For example, Hà Nội City officials met with some of the twenty-five people who signed a petition against the city's August 18, 2011 order that forbade further protest marches. According to informants, the meeting had a vigorous but well-mannered argument over whether demonstrations are legal or not.[78] Another instance is when Hồ Chí Minh City officials talked with some who signed the July 27, 2012 letter (table 3.1) and acknowledged the justness of struggling against Chinese aggression. But, the officials argued, anti-China marches are illegal and are being used by enemies of Vietnam.[79]

Some officials also took into account critics' arguments. Influenced by open letters, petitions, and other public discontent, some National Assembly delegates sharply questioned the bauxite mining project with China and claims by the prime minister and other government ministers that they were protecting Vietnam's sovereignty.[80] In September 2009, some bloggers vigorously criticized an article from China reprinted without comment in the VCP's online newspaper that stated the Paracel and Spratly Islands belonged to China. The criticisms pushed Vietnamese authorities to remove the article and dismiss the paper's editor.[81] In November 2011, Prime Minister Nguyễn Tấn Dũng publicly acknowledged that China took the Paracel Islands in 1974 by force, the first time a top party-state official had said that. Partly provoking his statement was the widening doubt among many Vietnamese that the government was defending Vietnam's sovereignty.[82] The upsurge in anti-China public discourse and numerous protests by students, workers, and others in May 2014, when the Chinese put an oil rig in Vietnamese waters, also likely contributed to Prime Minister Nguyễn Tấn Dũng publicly threatening legal action against China. That threat figured in the decision by Beijing's leaders to remove the oil rig and the flotilla guarding it.[83]

By late 2015, Vietnamese citizens speaking out against China's behavior toward their nation was a prominent feature in the country's political landscape that party-state authorities frequently tolerated. Poor fishers defied as best they could Chinese gunboats and appealed to national officials for protection. Their plight and Chinese authorities' violence against them contributed to students and other citizens marching in the nation's cities. Chinese actions in Vietnam incited numerous additional nationalistic and anti-China demonstrations and stimulated bloggers, journalists, scholars, teachers, and others to criticize China and Vietnam-China relations. Thousands of citizens signed petitions, letters, and other public statements condemning what they saw as Chinese aggression and they urged party-state leaders to join protesters, vigorously oppose China, and vigilantly protect the Vietnamese nation.

Critics of China and Vietnam-China relations were puzzled as to why officials often opposed, harassed, and arrested citizens for expressing their patriotism. They wondered why authorities seemed so reluctant to stand up to China, not through war but by using stronger diplomatic measures, joining other Asian governments' opposition to Chinese hostilities, and filing cases against China in international tribunals. Many citizens digging into such questions began to doubt that their country's leaders and the VCP itself were committed to preserving Vietnam's independence. Several concluded that, in order to save the Vietnamese nation, the political system must be replaced with a robust democracy.

Chapter 4

Democratization

Advocating Regime Change

One vocal critic of the party-state's relations with China who also advocates democratization is Nguyễn Thanh Giang. His critique of the regime
preceded his growing doubts about the VCP's commitment to preserving
Vietnam's independence from China. He had been a scientist for over thirty
years in the government's General Directorate of Geology and had for
decades, he acknowledged, "enthusiastically contributed actively to building
the present system of authority."[1] But some years before retiring in 1996 at
the age of sixty, he started writing essays and sending letters to national
authorities criticizing certain state institutions. By the early 2000s, his views
had moved from reforming parts of the government to democratizing the
entire political system. Vietnam must have, he wrote in 2003, "a democratic
and free press, freedom of speech, and freedom to debate affairs of the state.
Democracy [is required] in order to fight corruption and to mobilize the
country's internal forces. Only then can strong, healthy development be as-
sured."[2] During the next ten years, he published, in websites, magazines,
and books, hundreds of articles, essays, letters, and poems pertaining to

political, cultural, and economic conditions in Vietnam. He planned to write a history of "Democratization in Vietnam" but instead produced a six-hundred-page book featuring over forty-five Vietnamese whose writings and activities in recent years he deemed highly relevant to the democratization process in today's Vietnam.[3]

Beginning with a few people like Nguyễn Thanh Giang in the mid-1990s, speaking out against the political system evolved into a substantial drive to replace it with a democracy. Within a few years, Vietnam had numerous networks, organizations, Internet sites, and publications, composing what many participants called "*phong trào dân chủ*," a democracy movement.[4] Its evolution was organic; it had no center or dominant organization, clearly identified and accepted leader, or even a single set of leaders. Although many critics and their organizations were in Hà Nội and Hồ Chí Minh City, several lived elsewhere in the country. They objected to the party-state regime, which many called authoritarian or dictatorial. They wanted Vietnam to have a democratic political system.

I refer to them as regime critics or dissidents, people who disagree "with the basic principles of the political system" and "express such disagreement in public."[5] The English equivalents for terms individuals often used for themselves include "resister," "democracy and human rights activist," "fighter for democracy," and "dissident."[6] My analysis is based primarily on these critics' writings and actions. Such material comes mainly from Internet locations; it comes secondarily from printed publications and my conversations and observations in Vietnam.

The Expansion

Four periods demarcate the democratization movement's expansion between 1995 and 2015.[7] In the mid to late 1990s, a few dozen individuals wrote letters to authorities and circulated essays condemning corruption and restrictions on speech and advocating an open political system.[8] Their writings, which included their names and frequently their addresses and other information identifying them, circulated from hand to hand, photocopy by photocopy, and were occasionally published, not in Vietnam but abroad. As the Internet grew in the late 1990s, that became the frequent way to disseminate their views. Some early critics knew each other, but they usually wrote individually; seldom did any speak out jointly.

In 2001–3, a second phase, collaborative activism, emerged, beginning a prominent feature of contemporary political dissent. In September 2001, for instance, Phạm Quế Dương of Hà Nội and Trần Khuê of Hồ Chí Minh City circulated a letter about forming an association to fight corruption. Quickly other people added their names, despite some being detained by security police.[9] In April 2003, the Club for Democracy, formed in 2001, circulated via the Internet its first issue of *Điện Thư* [Electronic Letter]. The Club regularly published the magazine for the next four years.[10] Its articles championed democratization, critiqued regime policies and institutions, and accused party-state leaders of accommodating China at Vietnam's expense. Most authors gave their names, addresses, and phone numbers, unlike a short-lived opposition publication in Vietnam during 1996–97 whose contributors were anonymous.[11]

In the third period, during 2006, a flurry of overtly political organizations emerged as critics took advantage of authorities' widened tolerance because that year Vietnam, for the first time, was the host for the Asia-Pacific Economic Cooperation (APEC) meetings. Some of the critics' organizations emphasized civil rights and democratization: the Alliance for Democracy and Human Rights, Association of Former Political and Religious Prisoners, and Committee for Human Rights.[12] Two others announced themselves as political parties: the Vietnamese Progressive Party and Vietnamese Democratic Party. Together with the People's Democratic Party, secretly formed in 2003 but becoming public in January 2005, three political parties based in Vietnam now openly opposed the VCP.[13] Additional Internet-based magazines began as well in 2006; the English meaning of their names were Homeland, Free Speech, Freedom and Democracy, and Democracy.[14] The first three were independent of other organizations. The fourth, Democracy, was an organ of the Vietnamese Democratic Party. (The Electronic Letter, together with the Club that produced it, merged in July with the People's Democratic Party.)

Also formed in 2006 was Bloc 8406. It pressed for the political liberties advocated in the Declaration on Freedom and Democracy, which started to circulate on April 8 and was the first major use of the Internet by dissidents to solicit support across the country.[15] Initially endorsed by 118 individuals, the Declaration had 424 signatures a month later, all providing their names and locations in Vietnam. By late 2006 more than a 1,400 Vietnamese had signed. According to the list of 424 names, 38 percent of the signers were in the south, especially Bến Tre and Sài Gòn; 34 percent in the central region, primarily Huế and Đà Nẵng; and 28 percent in the north, largely Hà Nội, Hải Phòng, and Thái Bình. Nearly a quarter of the signers referred to themselves simply as citizens; others indicated their occupations, the two most numerous of which were peasants and teachers, 17 percent each; followed by monks, priests, and pastors, 10 percent cumulatively; business people, medical professionals, and office staff members, 7 percent each; engineers and technicians, 6 percent; and a tiny number of professors, lawyers, writers, architects, and retired military officers.[16]

Sixty to seventy people were prominent in the organizations created in 2006. Seventeen of them were in more than one of these organizations, indicative of networks and personal connections among the regime critics. Ages for the seventeen ranged between twenty-seven and eighty-seven; most were between thirty and fifty-nine. Two of them were women. Eight of the seventeen lived in Hà Nội, four in Hồ Chí Minh City, three in Huế, and one each in Thái Bình and Hải Phòng provinces. Six of the seventeen were veterans of war against France or the war for reunification or both; at least two of them had been VCP members. In terms of their occupations, five were writers, scholars, and researchers; the remaining dozen were distributed nearly equally among employment in businesses, engineering, law, the Catholic Church, government, and military.[17]

Two examples of these seventeen individuals are Nguyễn Chính Kết and Lê Thị Công Nhân. Born near Hà Nội in 1952, Nguyễn Chính Kết studied in Đà Lạt in the central highlands before living in Hồ Chí Minh City with his wife, their two children, and his parents.[18] In 2001, he began to speak out in favor of greater religious freedom. This stance, he later claimed, prevented him from getting steady employment, which forced him to work as a freelance translator. By 2005, he was championing other human rights and had friends in the emerging democratization movement. In 2006, he helped to draft the Declaration on Freedom and Democracy, was prominent in Bloc 8406, became one of the founders of the Alliance for Democracy and Human Rights, and was on the editorial board of the new publication, Homeland.

Lê Thị Công Nhân was born in 1979 in the southern province of Tiền Giang but when still young moved to northern Vietnam with her parents, both of whom were teachers.[19] In 2001, she graduated from the Law

University in Hà Nội, then studied an additional two years to become a certified lawyer with a specialization in international and economic law. While employed as a lawyer, she became very concerned about factory workers' conditions and human rights issues and began to work with Nguyễn Văn Đài, another Hà Nội lawyer with similar interests. In August 2006, she joined Bloc 8406; not long thereafter she also entered the recently formed Progressive Party; and in November she, along with Nguyễn Chính Kết and twenty-six others in Vietnam, signed an open letter demanding democracy for Vietnam. The letter was sent to United States president George W. Bush, who was participating in the APEC meetings in Hà Nội.

Nguyễn Chính Kết, Lê Thị Công Nhân, and many others involved in the political organizations of 2006 suffered for their activism. Security police raided their homes and offices and harassed, detained, and interrogated them, sometimes for days. Several were eventually arrested, among them Lê Thị Công Nhân, who was sentenced in 2007 to four years' imprisonment for spreading propaganda against the state. Repression caused some of the 2006 organizations to fade, even disappear. Others persisted, among them the Vietnamese Democratic Party and Bloc 8406. In October 2007, Nguyễn Chính Kết, living by then in the United States after fleeing Vietnam in December 2006, became the Bloc's overseas representative.[20] The magazines Homeland and Free Speech continued to publish twice a month, each issue containing over thirty pages of articles written explicitly for them as well as essays and reports from elsewhere, especially blogs.[21]

Marking the fourth phase in the growth of the democratization movement was the surge in politically oriented blogs and other websites. Websites criticizing the country's government date from the 1990s, but those were by people not living in Vietnam. In 2006–7, a few blogs emphasizing political issues developed in Vietnam itself.[22] Besides posting essays and news, such sites helped to mobilize hundreds of citizens in December 2007 to demonstrate against China's encroachment into Vietnam's territorial waters.[23] The big leap in politically critical websites within Vietnam occurred between late 2008 and late 2010.[24] Some of the new sites, such as Bauxite Việt Nam, began with a particular issue but later broadened to carry material on many political topics. Other new ones, like Dân Luận [People Discuss] and Dân Làm Báo [Citizen Journalist], featured from the outset articles on numerous subjects written primarily by people not directly involved in creating and maintaining the websites. Also during this period, Anh Ba Sàm [the Gossiper], which had started earlier, became a highly popular site for its articles culled from many bloggers as well as such mainstream sources as the BBC, RFA, and party-state news outlets.[25] Despite authorities' efforts to destroy them, most sites survived. And after 2010, additional political bloggers emerged, even as others were arrested and imprisoned. In July 2013, over a hundred bloggers, mostly in Hà Nội and Hồ Chí Minh City but about one-third spread among fourteen other provinces, jointly, defiantly, and publicly condemned such arrests.[26]

By 2015, public political life in Vietnam was teeming with bloggers, websites, petitioners, networks, and organizations criticizing major public policies, key institutions of the party-state, and the entire political system. These individuals and groups had become a prominent part of the country's expanding and diversifying civil society.

Why the Expansion?

Reasons explaining the spread of public political dissent from the mid-1990s can be summarized as expanding opportunities and mounting discontent. Both are partly traceable to the market economy that displaced the centralized economy starting in the 1980s. That change contributed to better living conditions for virtually all Vietnamese. Citizens also became freer to decide where to live, work, and study; what to buy and sell; and how to produce. Communication technologies and their widening availability enhanced opportunities for people to learn, form networks, and monitor party-state authorities. In the early 1990s, few Vietnamese had a television, and a tinier number had a telephone; by 2012, the majority of households had both. And 40 percent of Vietnamese in 2012–14 had access to the Internet.[27] These technologies significantly improved Vietnamese people's exposure to and awareness of events far beyond their immediate vicinity.

The technologies also made it much easier for critics to spread materials questioning the government and its policies and more difficult for authorities to stop them.[28] Previously, circulating unauthorized materials in Vietnam was not only complicated and risky, but also often failed. In 1988–90, for instance, a veterans' organization that sought political reforms encountered immense difficulty reproducing its magazines due to the party-state's tight control over printing facilities. Just getting a duplicating machine was problematic. And the multiple copies that the veterans produced had to be distributed surreptitiously. Even with all this effort, they succeeded in producing only three issues.[29] Contrast that to Free Speech and Homeland, which Vietnamese dissidents produced and circulated to readers near and far through the Internet twice a month starting in 2006, and to the numerous statements condemning government policies and actions that critics have disseminated through the Internet and thousands of Vietnamese have endorsed.[30]

That Vietnamese authorities did not stop online publications and petitions is indicative of another reason alternative political views spread: the Vietnamese party-state became less able or willing to maintain a tight grip on society. The market economy, having improved living conditions of Vietnamese citizens, boosted the party-state's legitimacy. Yet it reduced authorities' hold over people's lives and contributed to an increasingly varied civil society.[31]

While opportunities to publicly criticize widened, discontent with the country's regime swelled. Much of the criticism pertained to three topics: corruption, national pride, and democracy. Corruption is what prompted many Vietnamese dissidents to start questioning the political system, particularly the VCP's domination. One writer in Hồ Chí Minh City likened the VCP to a "gluttonous monster" sucking life out of the people and the country.[32] Corruption is so entrenched, numerous dissidents concluded, that only fundamental changes in the political system can expunge it. The root cause of corruption, they argued, is "dictatorship" and the "mother" of that system is the VCP.[33]

The second theme is national pride, a term I use to include assessments of Vietnam's level of development, its standing compared to other Asian countries, and its relations with China. Besides a strong economy, contended many regime critics, a developed country has high-quality education, wide opportunities for people to innovate, a robust civil society, and democracy. Vietnam, dissidents said, falls far short of these standards.[34] Despite economic improvements, a large percentage of citizens live hand to mouth while a few are exceedingly rich. Some critics blamed this inequality on Vietnam's wholesale move into a capitalism in which foreign-owned factories pay miserable wages to people desperate for work.[35] Others said the opposite: Vietnamese authorities have yet to embrace capitalism fully to rid the country of all vestiges of a socialist economy.[36]

Meanwhile, compared to its neighbors, Vietnam was embarrassingly underdeveloped, according to regime critics. Look, they frequently said, at the enormous economic progress in South Korea, Japan, Singapore, Malaysia, Thailand, and Indonesia. Even in terms of democracy, several dissidents argued, these countries are more advanced than Vietnam. That Vietnam had a long war does not explain its laggard position; South Korea and Japan, too, critics stressed, had major wars yet they greatly improved economically and politically.[37]

Vietnam's relationship with China became a huge aggravation to numerous dissidents. China, many contended, had become Vietnam's gravest external threat. Yet, instead of standing up to China, authorities made concessions to its claims to the Spratly and Paracel Islands, ceded it territory along the China-Vietnam border, opened roadways to accommodate Chinese traders and companies, let numerous Chinese people live and work in Vietnam without visas, and allowed Chinese companies to exploit natural resources. This situation, regime critics argued, irreparably damages Vietnam's economy and greatly compromises its national security.[38]

The absence of democracy is a third prominent theme in regime dissidents' statements and activities. They often cited the United Nations Universal Declaration of Human Rights as the standard which Vietnam should follow. Especially crucial, they argued, are freedom of the press, speech, association, religion, and trade union formation.[39] Essential democratic political institutions, critics insisted, are the rule of law; separation of executive, legislative, and judicial functions of government; fair trials; and competitive elections.[40]

Twice before some Vietnamese had criticized the corruption and lack of democracy under VCP rule. During 1956–58, in what became known as the Nhân Văn Giai Phẩm (NVGP) affair, a few dozen poets, writers, artists, and scholars openly opposed restrictions on intellectual pursuits, the opaque legal system, arbitrary treatment by authorities, and spreading corruption.[41] In 1988–90, several veterans of wars against France and the United States formed the Club of Former Resistance Fighters (CFRF) that, along with some writers and students, publicly advocated procedures to democratize parts of the political system.[42] The differences, however, between these two groups and the democratization movement today are large.

The NVGP participants, with one or two exceptions, accepted, often enthusiastically, the VCP regime. What they disliked was the shape it was taking in those early years following the war for independence against France. The corruption they criticized was partly the maleficence by some officials but mostly the rules and policies that they saw distorting and undermining the VCP and its ideals. Their criticisms were aimed at improving VCP rule so as to realize its stated goals, not at democratizing the political system, the objective of today's regime critics. The CFRF and others in the late 1980s were more critical of the regime than were NVGP supporters but they, too, did not champion regime change.

Two additional major differences are that the NVGP affair and the CFRF were geographically confined and short-lived. NVGP participants' publications and views scarcely reached citizens beyond Hà Nội, and the CFRF's activities were primarily in Hồ Chí Minh City. Authorities moved rather resolutely in 1956–58 to squash NVGP journals and magazines. Similarly, in 1989–90 officials took decisive measures to stifle the CFRF and other emerging nodes of public discontent. Dissidents today, by contrast, reside in many parts of Vietnam, their views have spread widely across society, their actions are varied, and for two decades they have become numerous. The party-state did not stop them.[43]

Alternative Analyses and Approaches

Although corruption, national pride, and democratization are their shared concerns, regime critics have differences about how to change the political system, the role of the VCP in that process, and the relationship between development and democracy. I discern four approaches. One stresses VCP leadership in order to convert the present system into one leading to democracy. A second emphasizes building organizations to confront and dismantle the VCP so as to quickly establish a democratic system, which must come first, insists this confrontational approach, before development can occur. A third approach urges engagement with party-state authorities at all levels in order to press for socioeconomic advancement. From there, democratization will follow. The fourth stresses democratizing society by expanding and strengthening civic, social, and community organizations.

Even though these approaches are identifiable, their boundaries overlap somewhat. Individual critics' views do not always fit within just one approach; and some people's positions changed, initially corresponding to one approach but later to another. Also important is that people applying the different approaches often had good relations and mutual respect. And none of the four approaches and none of the dissidents whose words and actions I have studied advocated violent means to change the political system. All of these dissidents implicitly and often explicitly endorsed nonviolence.

Party-Led Approach

Several regime critics said the VCP was a major cause of Vietnam's laggard development, yet implored it to lead the country to a democracy, which, they argued, would not require wiping away all current political institutions. Vietnam already has, they stressed, several democratic aspects. Sovereignty resides with the people, and the constitution provides for human rights and elections. The major problem is that these key elements of democracy are not practiced or are implemented very poorly. The principal reason, these critics said, is the VCP's excessive power. But the VCP itself can fix these problems by setting the country on a path to democratization and social economic development. In so doing, the VCP will enhance its flagging prestige, thus saving itself from demise, and preventing the grave national hardship and turmoil that otherwise will come.

Trần Độ exemplifies this position. Born in the northern province of Thái Bình in about 1924, this son of a civil servant became a VCP member in 1940, and soon thereafter joined the army fighting for the nation's independence.[44] He was an officer in battles at Điện Biên Phủ, where Vietnamese forces decisively defeated the French in 1954.[45] For much of the war against the United States, he was in southern Vietnam, where he fought in numerous battles. He later became a senior government and VCP official. He was the vice-chair of the National Assembly when he retired in 1991.

One reason for retiring was his growing disillusionment with political trends in Vietnam. Particularly appalling, he wrote often, starting in 1995, was corruption, a consequence of a political system that "lacks mechanisms for restraining and checking authorities."[46] This in turn resulted from the VCP's domination. During the wars, he said, the VCP's commanding rule over the nation was crucial for winning independence from France in 1954 and reuniting the country in 1975. But since then, the VCP's control had become a major liability for Vietnam.[47]

Vietnam's economy, although still pitiful compared to many others in Asia, improved significantly after the 1980s, he said. How this happened is evidence, he suggested, for his argument about the VCP's role in changing the political system. The party in the 1980s wisely listened to the people, who were weary of the state trying to control production and distribution. By allowing markets to flourish, the VCP released people's pent-up creativity and energy.[48] These same steps—listen to the people and let them speak and innovate—Trần Độ insisted, must now be taken in order for Vietnam to develop further and catch up with its neighbors. Otherwise, he warned, the party will have undermined itself and, implying massive unrest, "the people will hasten the party's complete removal."[49]

Trần Độ wrote these views in numerous articles and letters, often addressed to the state's highest officials and circulated through the Internet, between the mid-1990s and his death in August 2002. By 1998, he had so unnerved top authorities that they debated how to shut him up. His prominence probably saved him from being arrested, although police detained him once and frequently harassed him and his family. In early 1999 the VCP's national leadership booted him out of the party.[50]

His views, coupled with his illustrious career, made Trần Độ one of the most prominent early dissidents in contemporary Vietnam. He remains one of the most admired. Unlike numerous other regime critics, however, he maintained that the most promising route to democratization was through the VCP itself.

His contention has three main parts.[51] First, Vietnam already has numerous democratic features that, if properly used, can set the country on a course for further democratization and simultaneously accelerate development. The immediate task, then, is to close the gap between how the political system is supposed to work and how it actually works. Second, the VCP is the organization best placed to lead that process. It brought about a democratic system in 1945–46, before war against France engulfed the country. Many VCP members favor democratization and believe that the party is responsible for the political system's major shortcomings. Moreover, the party has a long tradition of doing what is best for the people. Party leaders can and should draw on its own history, ideals, and power to "renovate itself" and thereby transform the country's political system.[52] Third, VCP leaders can quickly start democratization by implementing human rights provisions in the constitution, opening elections to many political parties, removing the passage in the constitution that privileges the VCP, separating the party from the state, and democratizing the party's own internal procedures.

A similar stance was taken by Trần Huỳnh Duy Thức, a much younger man than Trần Độ and from a very different background. Born in November 1966 in Sài Gòn to a mother from the countryside and an English-teacher father, he studied at a science and technology university in Hồ Chí Minh City in the mid-1980s. Starting in the early 1990s, he and business partners created successful computer and telecommunications companies in the course of which he saw much government corruption.[53] Wondering how to counter corruption, he and a few friends read considerable social science scholarship, mostly in English. He concluded that a multiparty political system is no sure remedy; numerous countries with multiple parties suffer extensive corruption. Also, democracies in many nations are "bogus"; they serve only a small minority of citizens. Creating an authentic democracy, he concluded by late 2008, does not start by having numerous political parties. Rather, democracy emerges over time through improved living conditions, citizens using their human rights, and state authorities being "resolved to building substantive democracy and securing conditions enabling people to be the masters."[54]

His study and business experience also led Trần Huỳnh Duy Thức to tell authorities that the narrow space Vietnamese private enterprises were allowed in the economy and the state's reliance on foreign investors endangered Vietnam's sovereignty.[55] Indeed, he wrote in blogs and to authorities during 2006–10 and in a précis for a book he planned, Vietnam's "market economy with socialist orientations" is prone to collapse. Although it allows more economic freedom than before and has improved people's lives, its limits are near. For further development, people need political freedom. Otherwise, he warned, Vietnam will hit a huge crisis caused by the economy's instability and limitations, opportunists using government offices for their own selfish ends, and authorities ignoring critics like himself who seek not to overturn the political system but improve it.[56] Another major cause is the wide discrepancy between the ideals of equality, democracy, and justice championed by the VCP and promised in the nation's constitution and the realities of pervasive corruption, favoritism, and repression.[57]

To avoid calamity, Trần Huỳnh Duy Thức urged national authorities to rise to the occasion, as they did in the 1980s when they averted disaster by jettisoning the centrally planned economy. Now, he argued, party-state leaders should embrace a market economy in which Vietnamese private enterprises

Figure 4.1. Trần Huỳnh Duy Thức speaking at the Saigon Sofitel Plaza in Hồ Chí Minh City, April 3, 2008. Courtesy of OCI.

could flourish with state guidance based on social democratic ideals and they should "initiate a transfer of political power to the people."[58] The latter effort, he said, should include bringing into the government intellectuals who are not VCP members but can enhance its capacity to deal with a crisis, and breathing life into democratic features already in Vietnam's constitution, particularly the National Assembly, elections, and freedom of speech, assembly, and the press. Doing these things will give people confidence to exercise their rights, expand civil society, and push the country to a Vietnamese-style democracy.[59]

Without these measures, he feared, a major crisis will occur. Then domestic opportunists will "join hands with foreign countries to crush the nation's interests." Or people will rise up and attempt to seize the power and rights that are nominally theirs.[60] Such an uprising, he worried, could release lingering rancor between losers and victors of the last war, making conditions even worse for the nation but better for self-serving opportunists. To avoid these outcomes, people's anger must be channeled constructively. Opposition organizations in Vietnam, he assessed, are too immature to do this. The VCP, however, even though weakened, retains both the ability and responsibility to act positively; it remains the "only force possibly able to concentrate the might of the people."[61]

In May 2009, a month after he and his friend Lê Công Định, another regime dissident, had been to Thailand and met a Vietnamese-American opposed to Vietnam's government, authorities arrested him. In June, they also arrested Lê Công Định along with two others, Lê Thăng Long and Nguyễn Tiến Trung. In January 2010, all four men were convicted of plotting to overthrow the government. Not allowed to defend himself in court, Trần Huỳnh Duy Thức wrote an appeal, trying to prove his innocence.[62] The appellate court, however, upheld the verdict and the sentence: sixteen years' imprisonment, much longer than sentences for the other three men.

Confrontational Approach

Dissidents favoring confrontation stressed direct opposition to the regime. The VCP, they argued, cannot convert the political system into a democracy. And without democratic institutions, especially multiparty elections and basic human rights, Vietnam cannot develop economically, educationally, culturally, or politically to catch up to other Asian countries.[63]

Violent revolution is not a viable way; the only way, these regime critics argued, is straightforward, open advocacy for a multiparty system that protects human rights.[64] This requires organizations, including political parties, to challenge the VCP and propose better policies and programs. Organizations will also give the democratization movement continuity and sustainability when the regime imprisons activists. Whether to have many organizations or to consolidate them is a question these dissidents discussed.[65] Another issue is the role of overseas Vietnamese and foreigners. Some dissidents with a confrontational orientation saw overseas supporters as vital. A few even said that leaders should be outside Vietnam until a strong democratization movement exists inside.[66] Others argued that the movement must rely on domestic resources and leadership.

The Declaration on Freedom and Democracy is a prominent example of direct confrontation. As mentioned earlier, it was written in April 2006 and initially signed by over one hundred Vietnamese, then circulated for more endorsements. It demanded a pluralistic political system; freedom of the press, association, religion, and other human rights; and an end to VCP rule. The present system, it declared, is "incapable of being renovated bit by bit or modified" and should be "completely replaced."[67]

One of its principal writers was Đỗ Nam Hải.[68] Born in 1959 and residing in Hồ Chí Minh City, he is the son of VCP members and veterans of wars against France and for reunification. He studied at universities in Vietnam and Australia, where in the early 2000s he began to circulate through the Internet his criticisms of Vietnam's one-party system. He continued doing so after returning to Vietnam in 2002. In 2005 his political views cost him his job in a bank.[69]

Living in Australia, he wrote, taught him that competition is a compelling advantage of a multiparty political system over a single-party system.[70] With several parties, each one is motivated to learn what people need so as to compete in elections for votes. It is analogous, he said, to business. If there is but one company providing a crucial service, over time that company's attentiveness to customers is likely to degenerate. Two or more such companies, however, will compete; as a result, customers benefit. The same is true for a political system. Single-party rule, he argued, provides abysmal government. Vietnam, he said, is one of the poorest countries in the world, has massive corruption, and faces other serious challenges. The single-party system, Đỗ Nam Hải concluded by late 2004, "has been, is, and will be the problem of all problems, the reason of all reasons for the nation's many painful disasters and shameful laggard status."[71] Replacing it with multiple political parties will not solve all difficulties but doing so is needed in order to tackle them.[72] The present "dictatorial, single-party system," he argued in 2008, "will never be able to build a Vietnam with well-off citizens, a strong country, and a fair, democratic, and civilized society."[73]

To change the system, he insisted, citizens across the country, especially intellectuals, must organize to intensify pressure to force, nonviolently, the VCP to step aside. His models were the masses of protesting citizens who brought down authoritarian regimes in recent decades in Poland, Czechoslovakia, Hungary, East Germany, the Philippines, and Indonesia.[74] Unlike Trần Độ and Trần Huỳnh Duy Thức, Đỗ Nam Hải did not seem worried about such public outrage getting out of hand.[75] Nor, unlike them, did he write to authorities urging them to embrace democracy. That, he seemed to think, would be futile; the VCP must be pushed aside by organized citizens.

Active in several pro-democracy groups, Đỗ Nam Hải was one of Bloc 8406's founders in April 2006 and frequently one of its spokespersons. Together with other organizations, the Bloc aimed to "pressure and force" the VCP's leaders to abandon power.[76] As steps to create that pressure, it advocated boycotts against elections unless opposition parties could run candidates; urged demonstrations against the regime, for multiparty elections, and against bauxite mining by Chinese companies; and implored pro-democracy people to wear white clothing on the first and fifteenth days of each month.[77] With the possible exception of the anti-bauxite mining campaign, these measures generated little enthusiasm among Vietnamese citizens. Nevertheless, Đỗ Nam Hải and other Bloc 8406 supporters saw tremendous progress in the democratization movement since 2006. They were particularly pleased that Vietnamese became less afraid to openly criticize the regime and join pro-democracy organizations.[78]

To silence Đỗ Nam Hải, authorities tried nearly everything short of imprisonment. They frequently raided his house, interrogated him, and harassed his family.[79] In March 2007, security police threatened to arrest him if he continued with Bloc 8406 and other activism; and they persuaded his father, an elderly VCP member, and other relatives to beg him to stop.[80] He did, but only briefly.

Another critic taking a confrontational approach is Nguyễn Văn Đài, who in 2006–7 was active in Bloc 8406, the Committee for Democracy and Human Rights, the periodical Free Speech, and other pro-democracy organizations. Born in 1969, he grew up in Hưng Yên province near Hà Nội, the son of a VCP member. He was a guest worker electrician in East Germany when the regime there collapsed in 1989. After returning to Hà Nội, he earned a law degree in 1995 and established his own law office in 2003. By then he had run unsuccessfully as an independent for a seat in the National Assembly, had defended clients persecuted for their religious beliefs, and had joined an evangelical church. In 2004, he was a founding member of For Justice, a small group of lawyers offering free services to people contesting court judgments against them. The Hà Nội Bar Association and the government quickly squashed the group. Nguyễn Văn Đài continued on his own to represent several clients in legal trouble because of their religious and political beliefs.[81]

To bring about a free, democratic, and equitable society, argued Nguyễn Văn Đài in 2006, the democratization movement needs political parties to challenge the VCP's policies and domination.[82] Vietnamese people, he wrote, are knowledgeable and capable enough to participate in a multiparty political system. Vietnam had several political parties in the nationalist movement of the 1930s, in the initial years of independence from France (1945–46), and in South Vietnam during the 1960s to 1975. Establishing opposition political parties is even allowed under Vietnamese law, according to his interpretation of the nation's constitution.

Vietnamese authorities, claiming his views and pro-democracy activism violated laws forbidding propaganda against the state, arrested and sentenced him in 2007 to five years' imprisonment.[83] The term was later reduced to four years. In 2011 he returned home to his family.

Soon thereafter, Nguyễn Văn Đài resumed his activism. Massive pressure, he urged in late 2011, must be put on the VCP regime. Needed were "thousands, tens of thousands of brave, daring people to stand up and fight for democracy."[84] For that, he wrote in 2014, "We need to create a united movement." Each of, say, ten civil society organizations should train and educate five members intensively for one month. Then, each of the fifty newly emboldened members should train five more, resulting after the second month in two hundred and fifty additional inspired members. Then each of those people should train five more, and so on in subsequent months. After one year, thousands of people across the country would thereby be prepared to "speak out together, take to the streets, and do other things to make authorities respond to demands. If authorities don't, then a street revolution might emerge, like what has happened in north Africa, the Middle East, and elsewhere."[85]

Such views and the actions he took in line with them prompted party-state authorities to rearrest him in December 2015, charging him with spreading propaganda against the state.[86]

Engagement Approach

Rather than organized confrontation, several prominent regime critics advocated remaking the system by actively engaging with it. The urgent task, they argued, is neither to remove the VCP nor to create a multiparty political system. Rather it is to stop policies and actions that hurt people and retard the nation's development. Democratization, they said, is about improving people's lives. It emerges as the country develops economically and socially. Democracy, wrote a critic favoring this approach, "doesn't exist by itself; it is combined with other very important objectives" such as political equality, freedom, and socioeconomic development.[87] A multiparty system does not ensure these qualities, an observation regime critics favoring the VCP-led approach also made, as noted earlier.

Engagement advocates favor interacting and arguing with party-state authorities at all levels, opposing harmful programs and officials, and promoting better ones.[88] Engagement, according to these critics, will further Vietnam's economic and social development and gradually and cumulatively contribute to political improvement and democracy. Indeed, there is no need "to be political or carry a flag for democracy" during struggles about people's livelihood and welfare, otherwise authorities are apt to be repressive rather than responsive.[89] For this reason and because some of these critics suspected certain organizations, especially Bloc 8406, of being heavily influenced by interests outside the country, the engagement approach eschews organizations, demonstrations, and petitions against the government.[90]

Struggles for better living conditions, these critics argued, have already been influential. The VCP, they said, had to endorse family farming in the 1980s due to persistent, yet unorganized peasant discontent with collective farming. Widening dissatisfaction with poverty also forced the VCP to re-place its centrally planned economic system with a market economy. "Communism" and "socialism" have become meaningless to most Vietnamese, another reality to which the VCP has had to adjust.[91]

Thus, wrote Lê Hồng Hà in 2007, "in the last thirty years the people de-feated the [Communist] party on economic and ideological fronts, although not yet victorious politically."[92] A prominent proponent of the engagement approach, Lê Hồng Hà was in the anti-French nationalist movement, which he joined in 1939 at the age of thirteen; a VCP member from 1946 to 1995; and a ranking government official, particularly in the security police and the Ministry of Labor, until retirement in 1991. A couple of years later, he and another VCP member concluded from their research that hundreds of people had been falsely purged from the party in the 1960s. Their report was dis-missed by the VCP's leaders, who then ejected both men from the party. In late 1995, a court sentenced Lê Hồng Hà to two years in prison for reveal-ing state secrets, a charge he strenuously denied.[93]

Before this bitter experience, he had begun to question the VCP's pre-dominance over Vietnam, a line of thinking he pursued after imprison-ment while also studying how to change the system.[94] The system, he found, had already progressed economically and ideologically due largely to Vietnamese citizens' efforts to improve their lives. He also concluded that Vietnam's single-party state socialist system is unsustainable and will likely "self-disintegrate" because it is "anti-development," is run by "cor-rupt and depraved" officials, and "consequently, has lost all prestige" in the people's eyes. As the regime continues this course of self-destruction and citizens press for further improvements, the system will "progressively, step by step" crumble. Think of the struggle that way, he urged pro-democracy supporters, rather than aiming to demolish the system in one fell swoop.[95] Specific tasks he recommended include separating the National Assembly and judicial system from the VCP, creating laws to protect associations and a free press, and making the police and military defend the nation and its citizens, not the VCP.[96]

Cù Huy Hà Vũ, a legal specialist in Hà Nội born in 1957, may not have openly endorsed the engagement approach but his actions beginning in 2005 were in line with it. Also, like several engagement advocates, he avoided join-ing organizations pressing to eliminate the VCP regime.[97] He tried to change officials' behavior and the political system by using existing laws.

He earned a doctorate in law at Sorbonne University in France, where he studied and worked for several years.[98] Before that he had graduated from Hà Nội's Foreign Language University and worked in the Ministry of Foreign Affairs. His mother was a nurse; his father, a famous poet, had held several prominent government positions, including minister of agriculture. After returning to Hà Nội from France, Cù Huy Hà Vũ and his wife, Nguyễn Thị Dương Hà, established a law firm. She was a member of the bar association. He is not a lawyer, but his legal education helped the couple to expand their practice.

Cù Huy Hà Vũ's political actions emphasized trying to protect people from officials' unlawful behavior, hold authorities accountable, and exercise his own legal rights. For example, in 2005, he sued the People's Committee of Thừa Thiên-Huế province in central Vietnam, arguing that the Committee's approval of a plan to build a resort on a heritage site violated laws protecting that area. Already a controversial plan locally, it received national attention because of Cù Huy Hà Vũ's suit. The suit itself, according to newspaper accounts, was a novelty.[99] In 2008–10 he publicly defended Lieutenant Colonel Dương Tiến and others who had been tried and sentenced to prison for "injuring the state"; Dương Tiến had also been fired from his job and purged from the VCP. Yet, argued Cù Huy Hà Vũ, the colonel and his co-accused had committed no crime. They were victims of Đà Nẵng authorities' revenge after they publicized reports detailing corruption by top provincial leaders.[100] Another example of Cù Huy Hà Vũ's engagement is when he sought in 2007 to be a candidate for his home district's National Assembly seat. He pursued the nomination as an independent, a rarity in Vietnam's candidacy selection process. He received one-third of the nominators' votes, insufficient to be nominated but he was pleased with his effort.[101]

He also tried twice to sue the prime minister, something no one had done before. His first attempt, in June 2009, argued that the prime minister had illegally allowed Chinese companies to mine and process bauxite in Vietnam. Both the Hà Nội People's Court and the nation's Supreme Court rejected his suit, declaring that courts have no authority to judge the prime minister.[102] The outcome was the same when he tried to sue the prime minister in October 2010 for prohibiting petitions and complaints signed by several people.[103]

After this second suit, police detained him in November 2010 and then raided his home and law office. They confiscated material they deemed unlawful and charged him with spreading propaganda against the state. He was convicted in April 2011 and sentenced to seven years' imprisonment. His family's prominence, vigorous publicity by his wife and other relatives, and substantial public protests brought his case to national and international attention.[104] His hunger strikes in prison, to protest his and other inmates' mistreatment, were also widely reported.[105] In April 2014, authorities released him "temporarily," they said, because he was ill. But they required him to leave Vietnam. They whisked him from prison to Hà Nội's international airport and put him and his wife on a plane to the United States.[106] There he continued to criticize Vietnamese officials' actions and policies.

Civil Society Approach

A fourth approach links expanding civil society to democratization. It shares with engagement advocates the idea that democracy is more than the multiparty system with elections that the confrontation approach stresses. Both engagement and civil society approaches also see a role for the VCP in Vietnam's democratization, not as its leader, which the VCP-led approach favors, but as one of many participants. Also like the engagement approach, civil society advocates urge people to use lawful means to criticize bad policies and officials.

But engaging government authorities is not primary in the civil society approach. Its emphasis is getting citizens to discuss and tackle political issues through organizations they create.[107] By organizing, people can assist each other, advance shared interests, and enhance civil society, which these critics deem essential for democratization. Civil society, as broadly understood among many dissidents, means organized activities outside the government, family, and economy. Such activity need not be explicitly political, yet because the organizations belong to its members, often bear on public policy issues, and are separate from the state, they enrich the political environment.

And they contribute to democratization. Democratic governance, civil society advocates contended, does not emerge on its own; people need to struggle for it, albeit peacefully and without causing havoc to society and the economy. That struggle includes civil society organizations making their case and interacting with others with whom they agree and disagree. Democracy, civil society advocates insisted, requires citizens knowing how to express themselves yet also listen to others, negotiate, and compromise. By participating in civil society organizations, people learn these practices. Citizens in a democratic society also need to be well-informed about their interests, other people's concerns, and national issues. For this, the civil society approach stressed, citizens need access to wide-ranging sources of knowledge.

The main goal, civil society advocate Nguyễn Quang A explained, is to make Vietnam "a wealthy people, a strong nation, and a society that is democratic, fair, and civilized."[108] To be democratic does not mean starting with a multiparty political system, which would likely cause havoc in today's Vietnam. Political pluralism, he said, "comes at the end of, is a result of, a [democratization] process."[109] That process includes evolving a political culture in which citizens know how to debate, take seriously other views, find information, and be observant. It requires "people understanding their rights, knowing how to use those rights, and continuously pressuring officials to improve an environment in which their rights can be readily put into effect." Learning to live democratically takes time and practice, which is where "civil society organizations play a huge role."[110] Also crucial are a free press and reliable information.[111]

Beginning in 2006, if not earlier, Nguyễn Quang A publicly advocated democratizing Vietnam's political system, a process in which the VCP itself, he said, should participate if it is wise and wants to serve the people and the nation.[112] His political views emerged from diverse experiences. He was born in northern Vietnam in 1946, the year fighting began between Vietnamese nationalists, including his father, and French colonial forces.[113] His father was killed in that war. In 1965 the government sent him to study in Hungary, where he earned a doctorate in information science in 1975. After returning to Vietnam in 1976, he entered the Vietnamese military. In 1983, he went back to Hungary, where he was a research scientist and professor. In Vietnam by 1987, he left the military, worked briefly in the government's General Office of Informatics, then moved from Hà Nội to Hồ Chí Minh City, where he started a software outsourcing business. In 1989, he established with others one of the country's earliest computer equipment companies; and in 1993, the year he returned to Hà Nội, he and other entrepreneurs founded a private bank, one of the first in post-1975 Vietnam. Besides his business, research, military, and government experience, he was also a member of the VCP (1978–93). And he read widely, including books in Hungarian and

Figure 4.2. Nguyễn Quang A speaking at an Institute for Development Studies seminar in Hà Nội, August 22, 2008. Photo by Nguyễn Đình Toán.

English on economics and political science, some of which he translated into Vietnamese.

The first major foray of Nguyễn Quang A into civil society organizations was the Institute for Development Studies (IDS). Established in September 2007, IDS was based on the idea that intellectuals should contribute to public debates about policy issues. Its mission was to do research, discuss, and publicize recommendations on the economy, education, healthcare, rural development, and other topics. Nguyễn Quang A led the institute, which he described as the first independent policy research organization in Vietnam.[114] Some observers called it Vietnam's first "think tank." Governed by a board of prominent scholars, IDS organized public seminars where specialists presented papers that were debated and posted on its website. These activities often criticized government policies. By early 2009, some officials accused IDS of opposing the state; and in July the prime minister forbade researchers from publicizing material disparaging the "direction, thinking, or policy of the [Communist] Party or the State." Such criticisms could only be given privately to specified authorities.[115] IDS members strenuously objected but to no avail. Rather than operate within this constraint, the organization dissolved itself in September 2009.[116]

Subsequently, Nguyễn Quang A was prominent in several collective efforts to bend Vietnam toward democracy. One was boosting public discussion in 2013 about the nation's constitution. When the National Assembly publicly circulated a draft revision of the constitution in late 2012, he and about a dozen others, many former IDS members, saw an opportunity for citizens to discuss the kind of government they would like. The group wrote a critique of the National Assembly's draft constitution, sought input from others, revamped their document several times, and then obtained endorsements. The document became known as Petition 72, after the number of people who initially signed it. Its main point was that the National Assembly's revision was not "firmly, fundamentally a democratic constitution" with distinct branches of government and "premised on rights to freedom of speech, press, association, assembly, and demonstration."[117] In mid-January 2013, Petition 72, including the names, affiliations, and locations of the signatories, was circulated through the Internet together with a possible constitution for a democratic government. By May, over 14,400 Vietnamese inside and outside Vietnam had signed the statement, which had also stimulated numerous others to circulate ideas about how the nation should be governed. Although the public discussion ultimately had little impact on the final revised constitution, Nguyễn Quang A was delighted that his group had helped to provoke widespread debate. Never before in Vietnam, he thought, "had there been such vigorous, lively discussion about a constitution; many people started to have ideas about the constitution, about people's rights, about how the state is organized, etc."[118]

A second major collaborative activity of his was the Civil Society Forum, which he and others started in September 2013. The Forum's objective is to "assemble and debate views that contribute to transforming peacefully our country's political system from a dictatorship to a democracy." For that and to help develop the "civil society required for a democracy," the Forum created a website where "the ideas of all organizations, groups, and individuals sharing this objective" can be expressed.[119] The Forum also collaborated with other organizations for causes such as opposing the arrests of critics and supporting demonstrations against China.[120] Members also sought to run the Forum democratically.[121]

Police never arrested Nguyễn Quang A, but they often beleaguered him. A civil society advocate who was arrested is Phạm Chí Dũng, a journalist born in 1966, a resident of Hồ Chí Minh City, and an economist. Beginning in the late 1980s, he wrote literary works as well as newspaper articles. In 2011–12, while still a government employee, he published, under aliases in online newspapers, articles about corruption in party-state institutions. He was arrested in 2012 for allegedly distributing subversive materials and consorting with overseas opposition groups. Police held him for six months, apparently without making formal charges, then released him. Afterwards, they often harassed him.[122] In mid-2013 he left the VCP, saying it "no longer served and represented the people's interests."[123]

In an article celebrating Vietnam's expanding civil society, Phạm Chí Dũng also noted shortcomings.[124] He applauded the growing number of civil society organizations that are "independent"—formed without seeking official approval or registering with the government. An early example, he said, is the Bauxite Việt Nam group that started in 2009. A more recent one is the Petition 72 group, which he deemed as important for Vietnam as Charter 77 was for Czechoslovakia in the late 1970s to 1980s.[125] He was also excited by the founding in 2014 of the Vietnam Association of Former Prisoners of Conscience.[126] The rising number of independent civil society organizations signals, he conjectured, that "the era" in which people are afraid to express political views contrary to the regime "is gradually drifting away" and the country's "autocratic system is changing to a pluralistic one." On the negative side, however, he wrote that the quality of many civil society organizations is low: they are not terribly active and they have the same, usually older, people. The "struggle for democracy," he argued, needs new faces, civil society organizations with members from different generations, and collaboration among the groups.

These concerns influenced him as he and others established the Independent Journalists Association of Vietnam in July 2014. He became the association's president. Two of its purposes are to protect journalists who are "harassed, arrested, imprisoned, or terrorized" and to oppose laws "used to oppress freedom of the press."[127] One of its activities is publishing a daily online newspaper *Việt Nam Thời Báo* [Vietnam Times], which has articles about economic, social, and political events in Vietnam not reported by party-state media. The association's initial forty-two members, men and women, came from diverse age groups and several parts of the country. Soon after it began, it collaborated with other organizations. In August 2014 it was one of twenty-one signing a statement protesting the arrest of three pro-democracy activists in Đồng Tháp province in southern Vietnam; and in November the association and twenty-four other groups jointly condemned the security police's "violent and torturous" actions against citizens across the country.[128]

Interactions

Phạm Chí Dũng's discussion of shortcomings did not include one that some other regime critics occasionally highlighted: minimal interaction between themselves and factory workers pressing for better employment and living conditions and villagers struggling to retain their land-use rights and oppose corrupt local officials. Some workers and peasants occasionally signed pro-democracy statements and participated in rallies supporting democratization advocates who had been detained or imprisoned. And several individual activists in each of the four democratization approaches periodically joined villagers' demonstrations, helped striking laborers, and circulated essays endorsing their causes. But regime critics had no organized, systematic engagement with workers or villagers. Developing meaningful, ongoing relations with them, said various democratization advocates, needed to be done.[129] That party-state authorities quickly squashed modest steps in that direction, however, made the task very difficult.[130]

Far more prominent was interaction between democratization activists and critics of China and Vietnam-China relations. No overarching organization linked the two clusters of public political criticism, but several individuals, including some of the people named in this chapter, were prominent in both.

Meanwhile, within the democratization movement there were indications of possible convergence among the approaches to regime change. Beginning about 2012–13, some advocates of the confrontation and engagement approaches gravitated to the civil society one. In 2008, Nguyễn Vũ Bình, then a prominent confrontation advocate, argued that, in order to compel the regime to capitulate, the democratic movement needed to have "the strength to attack the VCP and the state's weaknesses." A "necessity for that is one public organization of people fighting for democracy." This, he concluded, "is a basic precondition" for success that everyone in the movement needed to acknowledge.[131] By 2014, his position had shifted. "We don't yet have an organization" leading the movement, he wrote, "nor know when there will be one." And even if one existed, he implied, the outcome is highly uncertain. The regime, he stressed, has "eighty years of experience in political struggle" and it "has the army, the police, the security force, and the power of thirty to forty million people who benefit from the present system." Given these circumstances, he concluded, the better approach now is to embrace the civil society direction that the "movement itself has been creating in recent years." He urged "developing civil society in many aspects of life," directing such organizations "toward political tendencies," and creating linkages "between civil society groups and progressives within the VCP and the state."[132]

Some favoring the engagement approach, which is leery of organizations, demonstrations, and petitions against the government, decided to support certain collective actions. Lê Hồng Hà, for instance, said in 2012 that "within the last couple of years, the movement" to improve the country "has accelerated and strengthened." He cited approvingly the demonstrations supporting Cù Huy Hà Vũ, protests against China's encroachments into Vietnam, petitions against bauxite mining, and other concerted political activities. "Overall, progressive forces in various forms and shapes and with different viewpoints are rising."[133] Similarly, by 2013 Lữ Phương, another engagement advocate, was pleased with the spread and strengthening of political diversity. The people involved, he said, "are sowing seeds in order that, at an opportune time, the country will change."[134] Among the immediate tasks to help this process, wrote Lê Hồng Hà in 2014, is "to encourage and support the establishment of civic associations."[135]

Whether a consensus will emerge is unknown. Notable, however, is some collaboration among regime critics who have favored different approaches to democratization. In August 2013, for instance, Lữ Phương and Hà Sĩ Phu, who have been engagement advocates, joined such civil society activists as Nguyễn Quang A and Phạm Chí Dũng to sign a statement opposing new government restrictions on Internet usage and blogging. In November 2014, Nguyễn Văn Đài, Nguyễn Đan Quế, and Đỗ Nam Hải—three confrontation proponents—signed, along with Nguyễn Quang A, Phạm Chí Dũng, and other civil society approach advocates, a widely circulated letter speaking out against security police abuses.[136]

In any event, regime critics and their democratization movement have already made an indelible mark on Vietnam's history. While doing so, they encountered diverse reactions of party-state authorities, as the next chapter explains.

Chapter 5

Party-State Authorities

Treatment of Regime Critics

Because regime critics seek to replace the party-state with a democratic political system, their criticisms and objectives are the most sweeping in Vietnam. Consequently, they are the party-state's most troublesome and threatening critics. Yet, as indicated by experiences of some of the people discussed in chapter 4, authorities' treatment of these dissidents was not uniformly repressive in 1995–2015. This chapter looks more closely at this matter.

Although the number of regime critics in Vietnam by 2015 is unknown, one indicator is that in 2006 and 2013 several hundred Vietnamese in the country signed statements calling for multiparty elections, free speech, and other democratic institutions.[1] Also indicative are the few hundred Vietnamese in Vietnam between the late 1990s and 2015 who, through their writings, pronouncements, and prominence in organizations defying authorities, publicly spoke out against the regime and in favor of democratization.

Among those few hundred are the sixty-eight individuals emphasized in this chapter for whom, by late 2015, I had collected reliable information regarding their residence, occupation, political activities and stances, and how authorities treated them, especially whether officials had detained them, arrested them, brought them to trial, or sentenced them to prison. The information comes mainly from material that these dissidents themselves and their sympathizers provided, mostly on Internet sites and in publications.

Nineteen of the sixty-eight were born before 1946; ten were born in 1946–54, the years of war against the French; thirty-two were born in 1955–75, when the country was geographically divided and also at war; and seven were born after 1975. Nearly half of those born prior to 1955 had careers in the government and military; only 10 percent of those born later did so. Occupations of those born after 1954 are scattered among several categories—telecommunications, journalism and writing, teaching, medicine, manual labor, and engineering; the two most numerous are business people (seven) and lawyers (six). All but eleven of these sixty-eight dissidents are men. Not including six who died between 2001 and 2014, the ages of these regime critics as of 2015 ranged from the early thirties to the mid-nineties; their average age was about fifty-seven; the median was fifty-six. One-third of the sixty-eight regime critics lived in Hà Nội, a little less than a third were in Hồ Chí Minh City, and the remainder resided in other parts of the country, especially Hải Phòng and Thái Bình in the north; Huế, Đà Nẵng, and Quảng Nam in the center; and Đà Lạt and Đồng Nai in the south.

What all these individuals have in common is that they publicly spoke out to criticize the party-state and to advocate replacing it with a democratic political system.

Authorities' Perceptions of Regime Critics

At one level, these regime critics and party-state authorities have much in common. Development, democracy, and nationalism—themes championed by the dissidents—are also ideals that the VCP and its government celebrate and subscribe to. "Independence—Freedom—Happiness" forms the header on official documents. Vietnam's constitution provides for freedom of the press, speech, association, religion, and numerous other human rights.[2] Party-state leaders regularly talk about democracy and how it should be strengthened in Vietnam. Authorities also frequently condemn corruption and wage campaigns against it that often result in arrests and imprisonment of offenders, usually local officials but occasionally national ones.

Major differences between regime critics and party-state authorities are the meanings of democracy, development, and freedom and how to counter corruption. So large are these differences that authorities frequently have deemed these dissidents to be violators of the nation's laws and the constitution as well as threats to the VCP, its government, and Vietnamese society.

Regime critics' objectives regarded as especially dangerous are multiple political parties, elections in which more than one political party has candidates, and wide latitude for civil liberties. Political systems with those features, party-state leaders have insisted, are "bourgeois" or "capitalist" democracies run for and by rich people, giant companies, and other privileged interests.[3] They are not democracies for all sectors of society. Indeed, in those political systems, workers and peasants are typically suppressed and exploited. Authorities also have contended that a bourgeois or capitalist democracy would gravely threaten Vietnam's stability and unity by pitting wealthy and business interests against workers, peasants, small merchants, and the poor.

According to party-state officials, Vietnam is on a path to a "socialist democracy," which they regard as far more inclusive and substantial than bourgeois democracy.[4] Reaching this objective is the priority, not multiple political parties and extensive individual liberties. Those things, they have argued, would derail progress toward socialist democracy. Hallmark features of a socialist democracy include economic, political, cultural, and social equality for all citizens and a government for and by working classes. Required to reach a socialist democracy is Vietnam's Communist Party, the "leading force of society and the state."[5] Authorities have readily acknowledged that the VCP has significant deficiencies; chief among them is corruption. They have also said that much remains to be done in order for the country to become a socialist democracy. This includes improving the means by which people of all kinds can convey their complaints and preferences to authorities and make officials more responsive to citizens. The measures in that direction thus far, according to authorities, include nurturing "grassroots democracy" in which villagers are supposed to be directly involved in local government policy decisions, budget making, and development projects; giving voters more candidates from which to choose during elections; and expanding the space in which people can publicly speak and organize. Incremental changes like these, all under the direction of the VCP, improve the system, authorities have claimed, but drastic changes like allowing opposition political parties would bring chaos.

Authorities' Responses to Critics in the Past

In the second half of the 1950s, faced with public criticism by writers, scholars, and other intellectuals in the Nhân Văn Giai Phẩm (NVGP) affair discussed in chapter 4, the then newly established VCP government in northern Vietnam initially reacted with a "vacillating admixture of official repression and tolerance."[6] By late 1959 to early 1960, however, authorities had decisively suppressed these critics. The pattern was similar in the party-state's reactions to the Club of Former Resistance Fighters (CFRF) and others in 1988–90, also noted in chapter 4, who advocated reforms to allow freedom of expression and elections. A closer look at what party-state authorities did in those two periods is instructive for examining how they dealt with dissidents in 1995–2015.

In those earlier cases, authorities countenanced the critics to a degree. Although they recalled all the copies of *Giai Phẩm* magazine's first issue in February 1956 and arrested its editor, authorities released the editor in May and between August and December allowed the publication to resume and produce four more issues. Meanwhile, authorities watched as another magazine with similar critical content, *Nhân Văn*, began and published five issues. Additional independent magazines also published materials criticizing various governmental measures. Greatly helping these publications to blossom briefly were authorities' decisions in mid-1956 to ease restrictions in the direction taken by the Communist Party of the Soviet Union in February and the launch by China's Communist Party in May of its "Hundred Flowers" campaign encouraging citizens to speak more freely. Three decades later, the CFRF began with support from Hồ Chí Minh City's officials; many CFRF members were friends of prominent party-state officials. Moreover, beginning in 1987, many authorities took a somewhat relaxed attitude toward writers and other intellectuals who published critiques of the VCP, its government, the country's economy, and constraints on individual creativity.[7]

Soon, however, party-state officials were debating how much latitude to allow critics. While some officials favored continued toleration, more were increasingly alarmed by the spread of politically charged commentary and sought ways to shut the critics up. That ultimately was done by various means.

One was talking with activists to hear their views and try to restrain them. On several occasions in late 1956, VCP leaders met with NVGP participants to listen to their grievances and caution them against becoming too provocative. In 1988–89, authorities talked numerous times with CFRF organizers. While they listened to CFRF leaders' concerns, they also urged them to keep forums small and to stop publishing the group's magazine.[8]

Meetings with and warnings from authorities did not stop *Nhân Văn* and *Giai Phẩm* participants in 1956 or CFRF leaders in 1988–89. Therefore authorities emphasized other measures. Several party-state publications produced articles countering the views of NVGP participants, claimed they sought to undermine the political system, and labeled them "anarchists," "revisionists," "opportunists," and "anti-party reactionaries."[9] Against the CFRF, national and Hồ Chí Minh City officials maneuvered to replace its principal leaders with people they could count on to tame the organization.[10]

Another action by authorities was to obstruct and ultimately stop the publication of *Nhân Văn*, *Giai Phẩm*, and CFRF's magazines. In 1956, when paper and ink were in short supply, authorities made it hard for *Nhân Văn*, *Giai Phẩm*, and other independent magazines to purchase those materials. And by the end of that year, Hà Nội authorities had ordered all of these publications to stop. By 1958, the national government had imposed censorship procedures, concentrated publishing in party-state enterprises, and eliminated all private publishing houses.[11] Thirty years later, when the state relaxed censorship and other restrictions on publications, CFRF was able to find printers to produce three issues of its magazine. But subsequent party-state directives to all printing houses prevented the CFRF from publishing a planned fourth issue.[12]

Other measures authorities took against NVGP participants were harassment and punishment short of arrest and imprisonment. Security police threatened and interrogated numerous *Giai Phẩm* and *Nhân Văn* contributors and their families, forced some to leave Hà Nội, and for years thereafter prevented many others from publishing, teaching, showing their artistic creations, or being employed in work using their professional talents.[13]

Some of the NVGP and CFRF participants were imprisoned. Of the roughly sixty contributors to *Nhân Văn* and *Giai Phẩm*, five were arrested and convicted of espionage. Their prison sentences ranged from five to fifteen years. The longest sentences were for the two who had resisted their interrogators most strenuously before being tried in court. An internal report from the judge showed that the verdicts had been decided prior to court proceedings and the trial was rigged against the defendants.[14] Of the dozen or so principal CFRF leaders, four were arrested for abusing their liberties; each was imprisoned for less than a year. Some years later, two of them were imprisoned again for a few months after they published overseas their accounts of CFRF's activities and other autobiographical material.[15]

Comparisons to the Present

The NVGP affair and CFRF activism each lasted only a few years, in which time authorities shut down the controversial publications, punished dissenters, and smothered opposition. By contrast, since 1995 public political criticism in Vietnam has persisted for two decades. And during that time the number of people who openly spoke out grew and their activities became far more diverse than had occurred earlier. Moreover, critics from the mid-1990s through 2015 included not only people who were opposed to particular policies or wanted modest reforms, but also dissidents who objected to the entire regime and sought democratization.

Helping to explain these different durations are the dissimilar conditions in which authorities acted. At the time of the NVGP affair, the VCP and people generally in northern Vietnam were still recovering from a decade of war against France and a tumultuous exodus of thousands of fellow citizens who had moved to the southern half of the country at the war's end. The VCP was also completing a massive redistribution of agricultural land and trying to rectify mistakes committed during that process. Many authorities, concerned that the party-state remained weak, wanted to focus on strengthening its institutions and abilities to govern. Another high priority was building a socialist system and bolstering Vietnam's relations with the Soviet Union, China, and other Communist Party-governed countries from which the VCP sought substantial support in order to consolidate its rule, create socialism, and fend off enemies, particularly the government in the southern half of Vietnam backed by the United States. In these conditions, tolerance for criticism, even though it did not challenge the VCP's rule, was brief. The measures taken to stifle it also enhanced the party's control over the production and circulation of ideas, which most authorities reckoned helped to stabilize their rule, advance the socialist project, and bring the VCP's stance in line with the crackdown on critics taking place by the late 1950s in China and the Soviet Union.

By the mid-1980s, the party-state was well established, not just in the north but throughout Vietnam, having vanquished the U.S. and Sài Gòn government's armies. It could control the media and monitor potential dissenters throughout the country. Its grip on the economy, however, had been slipping since the late 1970s, and it was moving away from a centralized, state-directed economic system toward what became known as "renovation" and a "market economy with socialist orientations." In this context and that of the "glasnost" and "perestroika" reforms endorsed by Mikhail Gorbachev in the Soviet Union, Vietnam's regime loosened constraints on publications and other avenues for public expression. By the late 1980s, however, emerging political challenges to communist governments in Eastern Europe and the Soviet Union itself made many Vietnamese authorities highly nervous, as did pointed criticisms and defiance by several Vietnamese writers and groups, including the CFRF. Still retaining the means to clamp down on perceived emerging political dissent, party-state leaders quickly used them.

By the mid-1990s, however, Vietnamese authorities' control over citizens' behavior had noticeably diminished. It declined further in subsequent years, allowing political views and activities to diversify.[16] A former Vietnamese journalist was amazed when surveying Vietnam in about 2009 that "the ruling party has been adopting an increasingly receptive and relaxing approach to the media in particular and civil society in general. . . . I have been many times struck by the way the [VCP] tolerates people who dare to open their mouth to speak against its policies or to expose corruption and other misdeeds of its senior members. . . . The current level of freedom is something nobody would think of about ten years ago."[17]

The market economy significantly reduced authorities' domination over people's lives, interests, and thinking and contributed to the emergence of an increasingly varied civil society.[18] And with the spread of new, multifaceted communication technologies, party-state agencies could no longer tightly constrain the content and sources of people's information. Many officials, while often anxious about this situation and debating how best to manage it, generally came to embrace this outcome as a necessity for the country's development. Also, most Vietnamese leaders became more mindful of foreign scrutiny of the way they treated societal groups and organizations, particularly their critics. No longer able to rely primarily on communist regimes elsewhere, Vietnam's leaders cultivated economic, diplomatic, and political relations with countries and associations around the world, especially those touting democratic institutions and processes. Consequently, numerous national authorities figured that the regime could not afford to be deemed absolutely repressive.

Under this combination of conditions, authorities in contemporary Vietnam, unlike their predecessors, were unable and unwilling to stop most regime critics. Authorities, however, did react to regime critics in ways similar to methods used during the NVGP affair and CFRF activism: interaction, denunciation, obstruction, intimidation, and confinement, which included imprisonment for some.

Interaction and Dialogue

Some observers of Vietnam have detected factions among party-state leaders who make contending claims and arguments about policies, resources, and other political issues.[19] How to deal with dissidents has been one of those issues. Analysts and dissidents themselves have said that "reformers" or "modernizers" within the regime's leadership are more open than others to considering a range of opinions and widening the political system. Although few details are available, some among the modernizers have urged interaction with regime critics.

Võ Văn Kiệt, Vietnam's prime minister from 1991 to 1997 and a senior adviser to the government for years afterward, favored "expanding dialogue" between authorities and democratization advocates. Authorities, he elaborated in an interview, should foster an open exchange of views with such activists. That approach, he added, is better than being heavy-handed. Moreover, he said, officials should treat critics with civility rather than imposing degrading labels on them. He also supported revamping National Assembly elections so as to significantly increase the number of delegates who are not members of the VCP.[20] Although Võ Văn Kiệt died in 2008, other national officials reportedly express similar views during their closed deliberations about responses to dissidents.[21]

On several occasions local officials met informally with dissidents to discuss political issues.[22] One instance was a lengthy conversation in 2008 between a colonel in the security police and Nguyễn Khắc Toàn, a dissident whose activism had landed him in prison for four years (2002–6). For two hours in a modest café in Hà Nội, Nguyễn Khắc Toàn and the colonel, who had often interrogated him in police headquarters, had a frank exchange of views about corruption, laws, legal institutions, and Vietnam's political system.[23] Whether either man's positions changed as a result is unknown. Nguyễn Khắc Toàn noticed, however, that the colonel referred to him and others like him as "political activists," which Toàn regarded as more respectful than the terms often used in official news sources: "political opportunists," "regime malcontents," and "transgressors of criminal law."[24]

In February 2013, some members of the National Assembly committee responsible for revising the nation's 1992 constitution met with a delegation advocating democratization.[25] The delegation, which included some prominent regime critics, represented the initial six dozen people who had signed a petition in January condemning the committee's draft constitution for not being based on democratic principles.[26] At the meeting, the delegation elaborated their position, gave the committee the petition and a proposal for a democratic constitution, and asked the committee to circulate widely both documents as part of the public discussion about the constitution that the committee itself was encouraging. The committee members were reportedly gracious and said they would consider the material. The committee never publicly circulated the delegation's documents but interaction between the National Assembly's committee and the delegation continued in written exchanges.

Denunciation, Obstruction, and Intimidation

The party-state has multiple agencies responsible for detecting and hindering, if not stopping, regime critics and others perceived to be threats to the country.[27] Detention, arrest and imprisonment are the most severe methods the government has used against them, but there are also less onerous measures.

One is to denounce and, in the eyes of regime critics, slander those who dissent. During the late 1990s and early 2000s, party-state mass media rarely commented about individual dissidents. Later, however, authorities and their media frequently mocked them. Prime Minister Nguyễn Tấn Dũng's personal website, for instance, featured accounts dismissing critics as "phony democrats" and "saboteurs masquerading as democrats."[28] Several party-state authorities and media accounts alleged that dissidents' real agenda is to put themselves in power and repatriate to Vietnam people who are viscerally anti-communist and had failed at governing half the country before 1975. At a minimum, according to numerous such reports, regime critics are supported by outsiders, especially overseas Vietnamese, who oppose the VCP.[29] A frequent allegation is that many who claim to advocate democracy are mainly interested in living off the contributions received from their relatives, friends, and external backers.[30] Another one is that dissidents, by berating and lying about the VCP and its government, are unpatriotic and ungrateful for the huge sacrifices their forebears made in order to overthrow colonial rule, defeat aggressors, and secure the nation's independence.[31]

The party-state used various methods to impede democratization advocates and their organizations. It tapped and cut phone lines to numerous dissidents' residences; blocked their mobile phones; hacked their e-mails; tracked their Internet usage; confiscated files, publications, letters, and computers from their homes; stymied their employment; and badgered their families. Over two-thirds of the sixty-eight regime critics in my study endured such adversities. Authorities often interfered with and sometimes managed to shut down dissident organizations and websites.[32] The Ministry of Public Security has units whose primary tasks are to monitor phone calls and Internet traffic and counter, if not sabotage, Internet material and sites deemed incorrect, malicious, or threatening. Hà Nội alone, announced one city official in 2012, had nine hundred staff members doing this kind of work. Their accomplishments included establishing nineteen websites and four hundred online accounts used to refute objectionable stories and commentaries, steer Internet discussions in ways favorable to the regime, and circulate pro-government materials.[33] Authorities also allegedly placed spies among dissidents and created organizations pretending to be pro-democracy but which were actually traps to ensnare regime critics.[34]

Security police typically shadowed regime critics wherever they went, keeping a record of whom they met, when, and where, and sometimes pestering the people they saw. Dissidents who had served prison sentences usually remained on parole and closely monitored for years afterward. Police and hired groups often disrupted the marriage ceremonies, parties, and even funerals of regime critics and their families. Numerous dissidents reported their homes being pelted with garbage and rocks, their motorcycle tires slashed, and being hit by speeding vehicles, which also targeted their family members.[35] The secretary of a pro-democracy publication *Tự Do Dân Chủ*

[Freedom and Democracy], Dương Thị Xuân, claimed, with photos as evidence, that security police in late 2008 destroyed her entire house.[36] Authorities said her house was illegal because the area, on the outskirts of Hà Nội, was zoned for agriculture. Neighbors reported, however, that the police disturbed no other homes in the vicinity.

One victim of much harassment was Huỳnh Ngọc Tuấn. After being arrested in 1992 for his anti-government activities and imprisoned for ten years, he resumed writing essays against the VCP regime and joined pro-democracy organizations, including Bloc 8406. Between 2011 and 2014, he and his children reported, authorities prevented him from being employed and periodically ransacked their home, confiscated their books and other belongings, interrupted their travels, and threw boulders, rotten fish, poisonous snakes, and excrement into their house. Police also beat him, on one occasion breaking his breastbone.[37]

Numerous signers of the Declaration on Freedom and Democracy were beaten by men thought to be plain-clothed police or tough guys hired by authorities.[38] Security police and their hired men waylaid and mugged dissidents, among them Trần Khải Thanh Thủy and her husband in October 2009. Afterwards, she said, the security police made the event look as if she and her husband had attacked them.[39] Nguyễn Bắc Truyển, a lawyer in Hồ Chí Minh City imprisoned during 2007–12 for spreading propaganda against the state, was assaulted three times in 2013–14 by men thought to be government security agents. One beating broke his nose. On another occasion, men riding a motorcycle deliberately ran into him and his wife, causing him to be hospitalized for head injuries.[40] Authorities also assaulted other regime critics.[41]

Confinement

Among the most severe forms of repression is confinement, which can range from detention and interrogation to arrest and imprisonment. Confinement, however, does not happen to all regime critics and the extent of their confinements varies. Also, confinement rarely stops people from continuing their dissent. Using these two variables—extent of confinement and persistence of dissent—I identified six clusters among the sixty-eight regime critics under study (table 5.1). An examination of these clusters suggests reasons why authorities' actions toward these dissidents varied.

Table 5.1. Summary of data regarding sixty-eight regime critics in Vietnam as of December 2015

	Number	Birth year (%)				Average age (years)	Residence (%)			DRV links		VCP links		Military veteran		Confrontational approach	
		<1946	1946–1954	1955–1975	>1975		HN	HCMC	Other	Info #	% with	Info #	% with	Info #	% yes	Info #	% with
All	68	28	15	47	10	57.5	32	29	39	56	43	46	50	37	57	41	58
Cluster																	
1.	4	100				86.0	50	25	25	3	100	4	100	3	100	2	0
2.	15	33	20	40	7	59.5	47	27	27	13	69	11	64	10	70	7	28
3.	34	21	6	59	15	55.0	32	35	32	29	31	21	39	16	56	22	64
4.	10	30	30	30	10	59.6	30	10	60	8	37	7	57	6	33	8	87
5.	2			100		53.5	50	50		1	0	2	0	0	0	1	0
6.	3		33	67		56.3			100	2	0	1	0	2	0	1	100

NOTATIONS

Cluster codes:

1. No detention or arrest despite frequent public criticism of the regime.

2. Arrest and/or detention, often frequently, but no conviction and imprisonment even though public dissent against the regime continued.

3. Convicted and imprisoned once but not again even though public dissent against the regime continued.

4. Convicted, imprisoned, released; resumed public dissent; convicted and imprisoned again. (Five of the ten were in prison again as of late 2015. Of the other five, one died in 2008, one was forced to leave Vietnam, and three resumed public political dissent in Vietnam.)

5. Still in prison after being convicted for the first time.

6. Stopped public dissent against the regime after being detained, tried, and convicted.

Average age: Average age of the regime critics as of 2015 (not including those who had passed away earlier).

Residence: HN = Hà Nội; HCMC = Hồ Chí Minh City; Other = elsewhere in Vietnam.

DRV links: Office holder or other significant participation by the person or his or her parents or grandparents in the Democratic Republic of Vietnam (DRV) government (1945–75).

VCP links: Vietnamese Communist Party membership, current or past, by the individual or his or her parents or grandparents.

Military veteran: Former member of the military supporting the VCP.

Confrontational approach: Past or present advocacy of a confrontational approach to replacing the party-state with a democratic political system.

Info #: Number of individuals for whom the relevant information is publicly available.

% with: Percentage of individuals for whom relevant information is publicly available who have DRV links, or have VCP links, or take a confrontational approach to regime change.

% yes: Percentage of individuals for whom information is publicly available who are military veterans.

Source: Based on publicly available information collected and tabulated by the author.

In the first cluster are four dissidents who, as far as I can determine, suffered no confinement—police neither detained, arrested, nor imprisoned them. The four are Trần Đại Sơn, Đặng Văn Việt, Trần Lâm, and Lữ Phương. Partial explanations for this exceptional treatment may be that all had served in the government or military during Vietnam's wars against France and the United States, were VCP members, and were senior citizens when they began to openly criticize the regime.

Trần Đại Sơn (1931?–2006), a party member for over fifty years and an army veteran of several wars, began in 2003 to publicly chastise the security police and other party-state institutions.[42] Đặng Văn Việt (1920–), an army veteran who later was a high-ranking official in a government bureau for irrigation, signed the Declaration on Freedom and Democracy and was a founding editorial board member of the Internet-based dissident publication *Tổ Quốc* [Homeland] in 2006.[43] Trần Lâm (1924–2014) had a long career in the Vietnamese government, including being a member of Vietnam's Supreme Court. Beginning about 2005, he sharply criticized authorities. He also defended several dissidents in court, was on the editorial board of Homeland when it started, and frequently wrote for that publication.[44] Lữ Phương (1938–) served in the underground movement fighting the government in southern Vietnam and the United States. In the early 1990s he began to publicly criticize the regime.[45]

Authorities confined sixty-four of the sixty-eight dissidents. The most common confinement was detainment at police stations where interrogations could last for hours, sometimes days. Many dissidents were detained several times.[46] According to their accounts, the police wanted them to detail their political views, involvement in unauthorized organizations and publications, and relations with other critics. Besides getting information, police also used the interrogations to frighten dissidents and threaten harsher measures if they continued to criticize the VCP and its government. Sometimes the police became physical, slapping, punching, and beating the people being questioned.

Among the sixty-four regime critics who were confined, often several times and some for several weeks, fifteen were released without being incarcerated and resumed public dissident activities. They compose cluster 2 in table 5.1.

Five people in this cluster left Vietnam. Bạch Ngọc Dương went to Cambodia in May 2007 after being hounded by police. Lê Trí Tuệ, one of the founders in October 2006 of the Independent Trade Union of Vietnam, reportedly fled to Cambodia in 2007 to escape constant harassment, more interrogations, and arrest.[47] Nguyễn Chính Kết left Vietnam in late 2006 to be the foreign representative of Bloc 8406, the pro-democracy network created by some signers of the Declaration on Freedom and Democracy.[48] Dương Thu Hương, a novelist, moved to France in 2006 in order to be at liberty to write. Bùi Kim Thành, the only dissident, so far as I know, whom authorities confined in a mental hospital (twice), was reportedly released on condition she leave Vietnam. She became active in anti-Vietnam regime organizations in the United States.[49]

Why the remaining ten people in the second cluster were not arrested, tried, and convicted may be due in part to all having significant connections to the regime. Five were or had been VCP members, and four of those were also military veterans. Three of the five—Bùi Minh Quốc, Trần Độ, and Vũ Cao Quận—had long careers serving their country and the party-state prior to becoming, in their senior years, critical of the political system. The other two—Nguyễn Quang A and Phạm Chí Dũng—were much younger but had been VCP members for years and had also worked for the government.[50] Two of the additional five people in the second cluster had long careers serving the party-state before becoming democratization advocates. Hoàng Tiến fought in wars against France and the United States; Nguyễn Thanh Giang was in the military briefly and was then a government scientist for thirty years. Giang's wife also had a career in the government and was a VCP member. Her father, also a party member, gave his life fighting French forces in 1950. The parents or other close family members of Dương Thị Xuân, Đỗ Nam Hải, and Nguyễn Phương Anh—the final three in this group of ten—were VCP members, government officials, or war veterans.[51]

Personal and familial connections to the regime and ties to relatives and friends still in the government and VCP may have provided these ten individuals and other dissidents like them with significant protection against extreme repression. Much in Vietnamese politics, scholarship suggests, involves personal relationships and networks that, while not guaranteeing benefits, can deliver advantages and safeguards.[52]

A second possible reason for not being convicted and jailed pertains to approaches taken to democratization. Available information makes fairly clear what approach six of the ten took (information for the other four is inadequate). Of those six, five took nonconfrontational approaches, which were more tolerable to authorities. Only Đỗ Nam Hải advocated confrontation.

His own explanation in 2010 about why he was not jailed bears on a third possible reason. Authorities, he said, weighed the advantages and disadvantages to the regime before arresting dissidents. Thus far, he speculated, officials thought arresting him would not be worth the trouble.[53] Ordinary police officers and security agents do not decide to arrest regime critics. Such decisions are made at high levels, particularly in the Ministry of Public Security and even sometimes by the prime minister. Those authorities consider many factors, including adverse consequences arrests might have on the government's domestic and international relations.[54] For instance, two likely reasons Nguyễn Quang A was not arrested are that he took a nonconfrontational approach to regime change and he was well known to government officials in Europe and the United States and well respected in Vietnam, even by many who disagreed with his political views.[55]

Forty-nine of the regime critics in my study were charged with crimes, sentenced, and imprisoned. They were among the approximately three hundred Vietnamese jailed since the mid-1990s for politically related violations of law.[56]

The forty-nine imprisoned regime critics include thirty-four who, after being released, resumed their public political criticisms yet were not arrested again (cluster 3, table 5.1). Two questions to ponder are why they were imprisoned rather than only detained, and why they weren't jailed again. Available information suggests possible answers.

Among the regime critics for whom I have information, those in cluster 3 were noticeably less likely to have personal connections to the regime than those in cluster 2 (see table 5.1): 31 percent compared to 69 percent had links to the Democratic Republic of Vietnam (DRV)—that is, connections to the revolution and war against France, the United States, and the Sài Gòn government pre-1975; 39 percent compared to 64 percent had VCP links; and 56 percent compared to 70 percent had done military service. These figures suggest that having personal connections to the party-state was no guarantee against arrest, but lacking them increased a dissident's chances of being imprisoned. Another higher risk factor is the confrontational approach for democratizing that 64 percent of the dissidents in cluster 3 favored during the period leading to their incarceration, much less than the 28 percent of those in cluster 2.

As for why critics in cluster 3 were not rearrested, the explanation for eight of the thirty-four is they left Vietnam. Hàng Tấn Phát, Huỳnh Việt Lang, Nguyễn Ngọc Quang, Trần Quốc Hiền, Trương Quốc Huy, and Vũ Hoàng Hải fled to escape further harassment, detention, and possible arrest; and Cù Huy Hà Vũ and Tạ Phong Tần were compelled by authorities to leave. The advanced ages of another seven—Chân Tín, Lê Hồng Hà, Nguyễn Mạnh Sơn, Nguyễn Xuân Nghĩa, Phạm Quế Dương, Trần Dũng Tiến, and Trần Khuê, all over sixty-four years old when released from prison—likely protected them from further imprisonment. In the 1990s and early 2000s, authorities arrested and imprisoned a number of dissidents who were in their late sixties and even in their seventies. But after 2005, possibly because authorities became more mindful of international scrutiny over how the party-state treated critics, only two of all forty-nine incarcerated dissidents were sixty-five years or older when arrested.[57] Recent release from prison may explain why an additional three people in this cluster—Lê Thanh Tùng, Nguyễn Tiến Trung, and Vi Đức Hồi—were not rearrested as of late 2015.

One of remaining sixteen people in cluster 3, Lê Chí Quang, resumed dissident activities after being released from prison in 2004 but, possibly due to illness, stopped around 2009. Nguyễn Văn Túc and Trần Đức Thạch are military veterans and from families who participated in revolutions against France and to reunite Vietnam, backgrounds that may have helped them not to be rearrested.[58] Nonconfrontational approaches to democratization may be a partial reason why an additional five—Hà Sĩ Phu, Lê Thăng Long, Phạm Bá Hải, Phạm Hồng Sơn, and Phạm Thanh Nghiên—were not rearrested. Another three—Lê Công Định, Lê Thị Công Nhân, and Nguyễn Vũ Bình—had shifted from espousing confrontation to supporting the civil society approach.[59]

Meanwhile, however, the five who still took a confrontational approach—Huỳnh Ngọc Tuấn, Lê Nguyên Sang, Nguyễn Bắc Truyển, Nguyễn Bình Thành, and Nguyễn Khắc Toàn—also were not incarcerated again. This plus the fact that very few regime critics have been imprisoned more than once even though they continued to advocate democratization raises the possibility that authorities may reason that if a first imprisonment doesn't stifle dissent, a second one is also unlikely to do so.

That has been the case for all ten dissidents who were reincarcerated (cluster 4, table 5.1). Their multiple prison terms did not stop their opposition. Of the eight whose approaches to democratization are known from their statements and actions, seven endorsed confrontation, additional evidence that authorities treat people taking this stance more harshly than other regime critics.

Five in cluster 4 were among the earliest and most determined regime critics. Hoàng Minh Chính, a philosophy scholar, was purged from the VCP and imprisoned during 1967–72 for criticizing, not publicly but within party circles, Vietnam's policies regarding China and the Soviet Union. In 1981, soon after he had accused VCP leaders of violating Vietnam's constitution, authorities imprisoned him for another seven years. And in November 1995, at the age of seventy-three, he was incarcerated another year for distributing writings against the party.[60] After being released from prison, he was not arrested again even though he became a founding member and leader of the Vietnamese Democratic Party in 2006.[61] By then he was eighty-four and sickly, conditions that may have stopped further repression; he died in 2008. Trần Anh Kim, a former military officer, was first imprisoned in 1995–97 for, he said, exposing the corruption by authorities in Thái Bình, his home province. In 2009, authorities accused him of trying to overthrow the government and sentenced him to five and a half years' imprisonment.[62]

Nguyễn Văn Tính was a teacher in northern Vietnam in the early 1960s when he wrote to Hồ Chí Minh and other leaders to oppose the war in the south. After trying to establish an opposition political party in 1967, he was imprisoned until 1974. Subsequently, he often spoke against the regime, was detained many times, and was convicted in 2009 for spreading propaganda against the state and jailed for three years.[63] Nguyễn Đan Quế, a physician in Hồ Chí Minh City, began in 1976 to criticize the government's healthcare and human rights policies and created a short-lived dissident newspaper. In 1978, authorities sentenced him to ten years' imprisonment for rebellious and reactionary activities. In 1991, he was sentenced to twenty years for attempting to overthrow the government; he was freed after seven years in prison. His third incarceration was July 2004 to September 2005 for abusing his democratic rights and jeopardizing the state and society.[64] Nguyễn Văn Lý, a Roman Catholic priest in Huế, was imprisoned in 1983–92 for disturbing the peace, and jailed again in 2001 for four years for parole violations and sabotaging national unity. In early 2007, some months after he coauthored the Declaration on Freedom and Democracy and helped to create Bloc 8406, a court sentenced him to eight years for spreading propaganda against the state. When he suffered several strokes, authorities released him in March 2010 but returned him to prison a few years later after his health improved.[65]

The remaining five people in cluster 4 are a lawyer, three laborers, and a writer. The lawyer is Nguyễn Văn Đài, who is featured in chapter 4. Đoàn Huy Chương, a factory worker involved in organizing independent labor unions, is discussed in chapter 1. Hồ Thị Bích Khương, once a contract laborer in South Korea and a market vendor in her home province Nghệ An in central Vietnam, began exposing corruption and other abuses in the mid-1980s. Police often beleaguered her and her family; in 2005 they detained her for six months. She subsequently participated in demonstrations in Hà Nội and in 2006 joined Bloc 8406. In April 2007, authorities arrested her and, months later, sentenced her to two years' imprisonment for spreading propaganda against the state, the same charge on which she was rearrested in December 2010 and given a five-year sentence.[66] Nguyễn Kim Nhàn, a worker in a province north of Hà Nội, began criticizing the VCP government publicly in the mid-1990s. After joining others to fly banners with anti-government slogans, he was convicted in 2009 for spreading propaganda against the state and imprisoned for eighteen months. Soon after being released in 2011, authorities arrested him again for the same offense and sentenced him to five and a half years' imprisonment.[67] Writer Trần Khải Thanh Thủy, an editorial board member of *Homeland*, was a founding member in 2006 of the Independent Trade Union of Vietnam, which the government deemed illegal.[68] In early 2007, she was imprisoned for disturbing the peace. After nine months in jail, authorities released her for health reasons. In 2010, authorities tried her and her husband for assaulting police officers and sentenced her to three and a half years' imprisonment. They released her in 2011 on condition she leave Vietnam; she went to the United States.[69]

In cluster 5 are two regime critics who were still in prison as of late 2015 for the first time. One was Trần Huỳnh Duy Thức, featured in chapter 4. The other was Nguyễn Ngọc Cường, who was arrested in 2011 for spreading propaganda against the state.[70]

In 2012, seventeen regime critics in my study were still serving their first prison terms; by 2015 all but the two just named had been released. Meanwhile, few dissidents were imprisoned for the first time. Explanations for the declining number of new imprisonments come from regime critics themselves.

One is that by 2013 the party-state had intensified harassment and physical attacks on critics but avoided arresting and prosecuting them. This, wrote one dissident, is a "more sophisticated strategy" for authorities that better "conceals their human rights violations" and thereby "softens international criticism."[71] Another regime critic offered a second explanation for why practically "no one has been arrested and convicted for political offenses recently," even though critics and their writings, speeches, blogs, and petitions had proliferated. The reason "is because . . . our actions don't pose a danger" to the regime. We dissidents, he proposed, must "bump our heads against the ceiling" of what authorities will countenance even though doing so will likely mean going to prison.[72] Put together, these explanations suggest that maybe high-level authorities thought the party-state could withstand a great deal of criticism and that such toleration enhanced Vietnam's international standing.

Cluster 6 has Đoàn Văn Diên, Lê Thị Lệ Hằng, and Trần Thị Lệ Hồng. They were arrested in 2007 and, after serving their sentences, stopped their political dissent, at least in public, because of their penalties and other reasons.[73] That this cluster has but three individuals indicates that imprisoning critics is only a marginally effective repressive measure; far more democratization advocates continued their open opposition to the regime despite having been jailed. This suggests that regime critics have considerable determination and commitment and that authorities are somewhat tolerant of dissent and unable to stifle it.

Prison Sentences and Conditions

Before the year 2000, nearly half of the thirteen offenses for which regime critics were incarcerated were rather heavy-duty: espionage, trying to overthrow the government, joining reactionary organizations, rebellion, and revealing state secrets (see table 5.2, top half). Since 2000, those charges constituted less than one-fifth of the offenses for which dissidents were imprisoned. The rest were lighter, such as abusing one's freedom and democratic rights, disturbing the peace, and spreading propaganda against the state. The last of these, which appeared only once prior to 2000, constituted over 60 percent of all offenses for which dissidents were incarcerated from then on.

Prison terms, too, tended to become shorter (see table 5.2, bottom half). Prior to 2000, almost 60 percent of incarcerated dissidents were imprisoned

Table 5.2. Offenses and imprisonments for forty-nine regime critics

	Year arrested						
	<1990	1990–1994	1995–1999	2000–2004	2005–2009	2010–2015	Total*
Offense code							
1.		1		1	23	8	33
2.			1	3			4
3.			1	4	1	1	7
4.		1			6		7
5.					1		1
6.	2				1		3
7.	1						1
8.			1				1
9.	1				1	1	3
10.	2	2		1		1	6
Total	6	4	3	9	33	11	66

	Year arrested						
–	<1990	1990–1994	1995–1999	2000–2004	2005–2009	2010–2015	Total*
Years incarcerated**							
<1				1	2		3
1 < 2			3	3	2	1	9
2 < 3			1	1	6		8
3 < 4		1			7	1	9
4 < 5				4	6		10
5 < 6	1				5	3	9
6 < 7					2		2
7 < 8	2	1				2	5
8 or more	2	1			2	1	6
Total	5	3	4	9	32	8	61

NOTATIONS

Offense codes: 1. spreading propaganda against the state; 2. espionage; 3. abusing freedoms and/or democratic rights; 4. trying to overthrow the government and/or inciting others to oppose the government; 5. working with foreign elements against the state; 6. joining reactionary organizations; 7. rebellion; 8. revealing state secrets; 9. disturbing the peace or security; 10. other or unknown.

* The number of offenses and incarcerations exceeds forty-nine, the number of regime critics in my study who were imprisoned, because some dissidents were convicted of more than one offense and imprisoned more than once.

** For the seven dissidents still in prison (five in cluster 4 and the two in cluster 5), this tabulation uses sentences. In the past, over half of those convicted were incarcerated for a shorter time than their original sentences stipulated.

Source: Based on publicly available information collected and tabulated by the author.

Table 5.3. Incarcerations of forty-nine regime critics compared to original sentences for forty-eight of them

| | In prison for full sentence | | Imprisonment shorter than original sentence | | | | Total | |
| | | | By less than 1 year | | By 1 year or more | | | |
	#	%	#	%	#	%	#	%
Cluster 3	15	47	3	9	14	43	32**	99*
Cluster 4	6	46	3	23	4	31	13***	100
Cluster 6	1	33	1	33	1	33	3	99*
Total	22	46	7	14	19	40	48	100

NOTATIONS

Cluster code:

3. Convicted and imprisoned once but not again even though public criticism against the regime continued.

4. Convicted, imprisoned, released; resumed public dissent; convicted and imprisoned again.

6. Stopped public dissent against the regime after being detained, tried, and convicted.

* Less than 100% due to rounding.

** Less than the thirty-four dissidents in cluster 3 due to missing information for two individuals.

*** There were more than thirteen incarcerations for the ten dissidents in cluster 4 but information is incomplete for some of the prison terms.

Source: Based on publicly available information collected and tabulated by the author.

for five years or longer (two of them, Nguyên Đan Quế and Huỳnh Ngọc Tuấn, served ten years each). Since then, less than one-third of incarcerations were that long. Nearly half of the prison terms since the beginning of 2000 were less than four years, and that includes dissidents still serving sentences that could end up being shortened. In the forty-eight incarcerations for which both sentence and prison term are available, less than half of the imprisoned dissidents served their full sentence. Forty percent had reductions of a year or more (see table 5.3).

Some sentences were reduced by appellant courts but more often dissidents were freed early for good behavior, poor health, and domestic and international pressures. The latter, according to informed sources, largely explains why the party-state in 2014 released several critics early, among them three dissidents: Cù Huy Hà Vũ (served three years four months of a seven-year sentence), Nguyễn Tiến Trung (four years nine months of a seven-year sentence), and Vi Đức Hồi (three years, six months of an eight-year sentence).[74] The three regime critics' families, all with personal connections to VCP officials, persistently pressed for their release. In 2012–14, other Vietnamese signed petitions and demonstrated on their behalf, particularly when Cù Huy Hà Vũ went on hunger strikes to protest prison officers' mistreatment of him and other inmates. Ambassadors, U.S. Congress members, and other foreign officials often requested Vietnamese authorities to release these and other critics. Meanwhile, party-state leaders wanted Vietnam to be included in the Trans-Pacific Partnership then being negotiated. That, plus aspiring to enhance its image after becoming a member of the Human Rights Commission of the United Nations, also likely influenced the Vietnamese authorities' decisions to free the prisoners.

Prison terms are specified in Vietnam's criminal code. For instance, the code says the prison sentence for spreading propaganda against the state is three to twenty years; for abusing one's freedom and democratic rights, the range is between a simple warning and seven years' imprisonment; for attempting to overthrow the government or inciting others to do so, the sentence can vary from five years in prison to death.[75]

Consequently, people convicted for the same offense and even tried at the same time have received different sentences. The approaches regime critics took for democratization do not appear to be related to sentences.[76] An accused who had relatives in influential positions within the government, military, police, or VCP might have been treated less harshly than others. Being known internationally, especially among human rights organizations and United Nations agencies, also may help to explain lighter sentences. Another factor is the assessment of judges, or the higher authorities instructing them, of how menacing the offense or the offender is.[77] Sentences may also vary because of the accused's demeanor.[78] A defendant who appeared contrite was likely to get a shorter sentence than another one who, in the eyes of interrogators, prosecutors, and other officials, was belligerent. An example is the sentence of Trần Huỳnh Duy Thức to sixteen years' imprisonment while the three men tried with him by the same court for the same offense—trying to overthrow the government—received five- and seven-year sentences. Speculations about why Thức's sentence was much heavier include that he was less known outside Vietnam than were the other three, and that he, unlike the other three, was argumentative in court and said police had beaten him.[79] On the other hand, Hồ Thị Bích Khương was sentenced to two years in prison, less than the minimum for propagandizing against the state, even though during her trial, she wrote in her memoir, she interrupted and insulted the judges.[80]

Conditions in prisons were dismal. The only positive thing about them is that they were more tolerable than the gulags in the Soviet Union and the notorious prisons of the Republic of Vietnam (RVN) in the southern half of the country before reunification.[81] Prisoners lived in cramped cells, often with poor sanitation and ventilation.[82] During initial months in jail, regime critics typically were interrogated numerous times. Some reported being locked in solitary confinement for days or beaten by prison guards and other inmates. Imprisoned dissidents normally lived with other prisoners convicted of a wide range of crimes. Meals were spare and sometimes so awful that inmates refused to eat. Prisoners worked most of the day: gardening, raising pigs and other livestock, making handicrafts, cleaning and repairing prison facilities, and doing chores. Apparently much of the food fed to them came from what they produced. If they fell sick, they usually received medical attention, although not necessarily promptly. Recreation time and resources were sparse. Frequently prisoners were allowed to read newspapers and magazines provided by authorities, watch some television programs, and listen to selected radio broadcasts. Visits from relatives and friends were restricted and closely monitored. Occasionally, authorities permitted foreign diplomats and representatives from international organizations to visit imprisoned dissidents.

Being a regime critic in Vietnam is risky. Even though the sixty-eight dissidents considered in this chapter were neither violent nor favored armed struggle, authorities' reactions were often heavy-handed. Officials messed up many regime critics' lives—took away their jobs, intimidated their relatives and friends, interfered with their daily lives, interrogated them, sometimes beat them, and frequently detained or imprisoned them.

Nevertheless, data in this and chapter 4 do not support a conclusion that the party-state tolerated little or no dissent or opposition. Instead, the data show that the regime has been somewhat tolerant even of people who oppose the present political system and seek democratization. And as earlier chapters reveal, toleration has been even greater toward public critics <u>not</u> aiming to overhaul the political system.

In the mid-1950s and late 1980s, the VCP government rather quickly and decisively silenced public political criticism with repression ranging from denunciation to imprisonment. From the mid-1990s to 2015, authorities used a similar array of oppressive measures but with much less effect, largely because the regime's control over society had significantly abated as the market economy spread, diverse communication technologies became widely accessible, and authorities became sensitive to domestic and international perceptions of how they dealt with critics.

This chapter shows that repression against regime critics was not uniform. A few dissidents were not detained despite years of publicly opposing the political system. Several regime critics were detained but never imprisoned even though they persistently and openly advocated democratization. Others were imprisoned, but after getting out of jail and resuming their public dissent, they were not imprisoned again. Only a few served additional prison terms.

Analysis of the data suggests some reasons for the variation. Elderly regime critics were less vulnerable to imprisonment, especially after 2005, than younger ones. Personal or familial connections to the regime by having been in the VCP, the military, or the government reduced the likelihood of being imprisoned or, if imprisoned, the risk of being rearrested after being released and resuming public dissent. Dissidents who pursued one of the nonconfrontational approaches to democratization also were less apt to be arrested or imprisoned more than once.

This chapter also shows that during the 1995–2015 period, crimes for which dissidents were convicted became less onerous and the length of their imprisonment became shorter. Available data also suggest that over half of the regime critics who were incarcerated were released from prison before serving their full sentences. And between 2012 and 2015, the number of dissidents imprisoned decreased substantially.

Chapter 6

Reprise and Prospects

Workers striking for a living wage; villagers demonstrating against the theft of their fields; students, fishers, former government officials, and other Vietnamese protesting against Chinese aggression and imploring national authorities to support them; and hundreds of writers, businesspeople, scientists, academics, and other citizens openly contending that Vietnam must democratize and hundreds more Vietnamese signing petitions saying the same—these activities became a familiar part of Vietnam's public political life in 1995–2015. A couple of decades earlier, one could plausibly claim that Vietnamese citizens voiced little criticism in public about living conditions, land use, government policies and officials, or the political system. Since the mid-1990s, such an allegation would be false. Besides the activities and complaints just summarized, and detailed in previous chapters, citizens also criticized and organized against environmental degradation, substandard public education, demolition of neighborhoods and markets, and numerous other problems, more evidence that Vietnamese have been speaking out on political issues.

Public political criticism emerged and expanded because people were aggrieved, aggravated, and anxious to be heard. And, as a consequence of an expanding market economy and new communication technologies, they had the opportunities and means to organize and convey their demands. Here the Internet and mobile phones and their rapid spread and accessibility to most Vietnamese citizens were immensely important for speaking out, not just episodically or to quickly mobilize crowds, but to make arguments and justify demands over the course of months and years. Women and men, young and old, rural dwellers and urbanites—all could fairly readily and cheaply text, phone, blog, and post on websites their words, photos, and videos to voice grievances, make claims, announce demonstrations, describe protest marches, circulate petitions and open letters, send complaints to authorities, and do other things to convey their concerns far and wide. To a considerable degree, party-state authorities either let citizens speak or could not stop them. Concerted, extremely aggressive campaigns to halt all public political criticism would greatly risk an economic and political crisis that almost certainly would have created even more discontent and greater challenges to VCP rule.

Besides, party-state authorities often took rather seriously the idea that the government was "of the people, for the people, and by the people," a ubiquitous official motto that was more than a slogan. To maintain political, social, and economic order, authorities needed to listen to and heed, at least to an extent, people's concerns. Hence, they tolerated, even accommodated some of citizens' demands and demonstrations. Authorities usually sided with striking workers who insisted that employers were cheating and abusing them. Officials frequently found that villagers' claims were valid and increased compensation paid for fields that were appropriated. Authorities revised labor and land laws to meet some of the concerns of workers and villagers. Officials countenanced several demonstrations and other forms of protest against China and Vietnam-China relations. They tolerated a number of individuals who openly advocated democratization.

The points at which authorities' reactions became repressive varied with the issue and type of political activity. For labor, that point came when workers tried to form their own unions. Regarding land, authorities used police to evict people after disputes had persisted for several years and to disperse large demonstrations. Toward protests against China and Vietnam-China relations, authorities resorted to intimidation and force when demonstrations became lengthy, happened several weekends in a row, threatened to grow nationwide, or occurred in defiance of orders explicitly prohibiting them. Against those championing democratization, authorities used intimidation, threats, and periodic detention. They imprisoned many dissidents but not all. Regime critics who were senior citizens, had served in the military, had worked for the government, had personal connections to regime officials, or advocated nonconfrontational approaches to democratization were less likely to be jailed.

The political activities of workers, villagers, and self-described protectors of Vietnam against China evolved independently of each other. The political criticisms and activities of each of these three groups scarcely overlapped, and no noticeable coordination or mutual support appeared between striking workers and protesting villagers and very little between either of them and critics of China and Vietnam-China relations. Somewhat more evident was occasional collaboration between democratization advocates and villagers speaking out on land issues or workers attempting to form their own unions. Although reasons for these modest overlaps were not deeply probed in this study, available evidence suggests that party-state authorities stifled such interactions. It is also possible that workers and villagers had little time, energy, and other resources for anything beyond their own political concerns about their living conditions, families, and sources of income.

Considerably more interaction and overlap occurred between democratization advocates and anti-China activists. Probably few citizens who criticized China and Vietnam-China relations also favored democratization; most regime critics, however, also opposed China's actions against Vietnam and the party-state's reactions. Disappointment and frustration with how authorities dealt with China's incursions into their country influenced some Vietnamese to conclude that regime change was needed in order to preserve the nation. For others who already favored democratization, China's actions at Vietnam's expense constituted further evidence for why regime change was imperative.

Demonstrations, protests, petitions, and other public political activities regarding labor, land, nation, and democratization continued as this book was being completed. Those pertaining to labor, land, and nation will probably ebb and flow until solutions can put the controversies to rest. Public fervor for regime change and democratization could disappear if authorities mobilized the party-state's repressive mechanisms to smother it. I suspect that will not occur. Attempting it would risk not only considerable backlash from within Vietnamese society but widespread consternation and recrimination from numerous other nations and from international agencies. Since the late 1980s, the party-state has expended immense efforts to cultivate favorable, friendly relations with countries around the world. An all-out effort to destroy the democratization movement would jeopardize many of those ties. A better approach, party-state leaders are likely to wager, is to deal with regime critics and their activities in much the same way as has been done in recent years—toleration to some degree, harassment and intimidation to a considerable degree, and imprisonment from time to time. Consequently, the number of dissidents and other critics put in prisons is likely to rise and fall from year to year, as it has in the past two decades.

Meanwhile, issues not considered in this volume will also continue to be publicly debated and criticized. Religious groups, for instance, will probably persist in disputing party-state interference in their own internal affairs and constraints on where and how they worship. Environmental problems will still rouse Vietnamese citizens to decry corporations and government agencies that pollute water, foul air, and destroy favored landscapes and structures. Police brutality, another subject numerous citizens have condemned and organized against, will likely remain a target of public criticism.

To these and other matters on which Vietnamese citizens speak out, party-state authorities will react with a combination of responsiveness, toleration, and repression. They are apt to be most tolerant of and responsive to activities that are rather small and localized. They will likely take vigorous measures to prevent people in disparate locations who have similar political criticisms to organize nationwide or even province-wide. Just as officials during recent years repressed nascent independent labor unions and in 2014 nipped in the bud a would-be association among self-described victims of injustice, they will probably stymie other such organizing efforts. Similarly anathema to party-state officials will be collaboration among groups formed around separate issues. For instance, authorities probably will thwart attempts by villagers opposing land appropriations to coordinate their actions with workers striking for higher wages and will not allow numerous democratization advocates to aid those villagers and workers. Party-state leaders will remain highly vigilant to avoid waves of political discontent about distinct issues from merging to become a torrential storm threatening the regime.

Recent scholarship on Vietnam's political system offers a mixed, even contradictory picture of dynamics inside the party-state. Some studies reveal struggle and arguments within the VCP, between the VCP and various government ministries, between ministries and the National Assembly, within the National Assembly, and between national and local tiers of government. The struggles are often over policy options and ideas, with conservatives, moderates, and reformers taking different positions, presenting competing interpretations, and predicting alternative scenarios. Contestation can also be over turf, personal connections, and access to resources for the benefit of individual officials and their allies.[1] One study concludes that the party-state is scarcely more than a patchwork of networks composed of interpersonal relationships in which policy differences are much less important than patronage and personal benefits.[2] One prominent analyst suggests that the national level of the party-state has become less and less able to govern because authorities cannot agree on how to tackle corruption and undertake critically needed reforms in public health, education, and banking. Real governing occurs at the provincial and subprovincial levels, particularly those run by officials who have learned to innovate, attract investments, and solve problems.[3] Yet other studies highlight the party-state's ability to foster remarkable economic growth, greatly reduce poverty, and substantially improve living standards for a huge proportion of Vietnam's population. Analyses also portray the abilities of party-state institutions to deal reasonably effectively with the contending interests that emerged as the political economy diversified and to improve methods for making authorities accountable to their peers at each level of government and to their superiors and subordinates at different levels.[4]

Meanwhile, analyses of state-society relations show fairly uniformly that Vietnam's political system has long included considerable discussion and engagement between rulers and ruled. Most of these studies use "state-society relations" as a shorthand expression for complex phenomena and recognize that neither "state" nor "society" is a homogeneous entity and that the two are intermingled. Agencies and authorities of the state are part of society; citizens—individually and in groups and organizations—are not wholly autonomous from the state. What this scholarship shows is that if governance in Vietnam ever was solely or primarily national party-state authorities imposing their will on citizens in a top-down manner, it no longer is and has not been for decades. In earlier periods, the importance of societal pressures and influences on authorities' actions and policies was difficult to discern. Since the mid-1990s, such interactions between society and the party-state have become more evident and public. They do not characterize the entire political system but they are a significant feature.

To summarize this feature, some scholarship describes state-society relations in Vietnam as "dialogical," meaning there is two-way communication and influence between citizens and authorities.[5] Such dialogue does not mean citizens are as powerful as authorities; it simply means their actions and preferences are important aspects of interactions between them and party-state entities. Citizens' communication can be direct, verbal, or organized; it can also be indirect, nonverbal, or unorganized, conveyed through things people do or do not do that heed or ignore what authorities expect or demand.[6]

In an earlier period, when VCP rule encouraged citizens to publicly display support and compliance but deterred and repressed public criticism and resistance, citizens communicated their discontent through quiet, private, and subtle behavior that did not comply with official expectations and requirements. Over time, such behavior cumulatively contributed to undermining the centralized economy and to releasing pent-up energy and creativity across the nation.[7]

This book shows that after the mid-1990s, the dialogical aspect of state-society relations became very visible and included citizens influencing authorities' actions and policies regarding labor, land, foreign relations, and democratization. Recent analyses of other topics also show that engagement between authorities and the people has become much more public and that changes in policies, practices, and other aspects of governance come not only from party-state agencies but also from citizens and civic organizations.[8] A study of Vietnam's National Assembly found that many representatives, especially those nominated at local levels rather than at the national level, are often responsive to constituents' concerns and criticisms.[9] Other research showed that political dynamics in Vietnam include debates and pressures between the tiers of the party-state and between officials at each level and the businesspeople, craftspeople, workers, peasants, and other citizens in each jurisdiction.[10] Contentious political discourse in contemporary Vietnam now includes such fundamental governance issues as the content of the country's constitution, the role of the VCP, and the meaning of nationalism.[11]

That dialogue between citizens and authorities is more public does not, of course, mean citizens run the country or that authorities are beholden only to societal interests and pressures. We can recognize that dialogical engagement involves authorities listening and responding positively to people's concerns while at the same time acknowledge that authorities often act without input from citizens and frequently dismiss, even repress citizens' criticisms and protests, as evidence in this book also demonstrates.

Furthermore, the dialogical aspect of Vietnam's political system does not mean the country is on the brink of having multiparty elections, freedom of the press and speech, and other institutions common in procedural democracies. Indeed, it does not even mean Vietnam is firmly on a path to such democratization.[12] After all, social science literature is fairly clear that democratization involves a combination of numerous factors. One of them often is the extent to which groups, associations, organizations, and other societal activities can thrive and become sources of information, ideas, and inspiration different from those that regime authorities and institutions provide. Such activities have greatly multiplied in Vietnam, and some of them influence authorities' actions and policies and champion political causes. These are promising developments for possible democratization in Vietnam. Another favorable factor concerns ideology. Democratization is often associated with the sharp decline in the credibility of the ideologies and doctrines of an existing regime. The two principal ideologies that Vietnam's party-state avows are communism and nationalism. To many Vietnamese citizens, however, communism appears to be a facade because party leaders and members rarely practice what they preach. Even sizable portions of VCP members reportedly do not really believe in communism.[13] Meanwhile, the claim of party-state authorities to be the chief defenders of the nation is undermined by their apparent inability to stop China's encroachments into Vietnam.

Several other factors, however, appear not to be favorable for democratization in the near future. Party-state leaders, despite their internal debates and rivalries, appear highly united by their determination to maintain the present political system. Also, there is little significant pressure on them from outside the country to do otherwise. Internally, too, pressures to democratize are modest. The democratization movement is a significant development in Vietnam but remains small. And thus far it lacks substantial support among workers and middle-class people, two sectors of society that have been highly important for democratization in many other countries. If democratization became attractive to a sizable proportion of villagers and urban workers, in the context, for instance, of a major collapse of the nation's economy, then internal pressure for regime change could increase rapidly. In protests against land appropriations and corruption, villagers often criticized authorities for being undemocratic. But unknown or thus far untapped is the extent to which villagers' expectations and ideas about democracy overlap and reinforce those of democratization advocates. Meanwhile, the party-state regime continues to enjoy considerable legitimacy in Vietnamese society.[14] Much of that is due to the major improvements in living conditions—better incomes, greater freedom, more opportunities for personal and family advancement—that most Vietnamese have experienced within their own lifetimes.

Some of that legitimacy comes from the very fact that party-state authorities dialogue with citizens about their interests, concerns, and criticisms.[15] That has contributed to enhancing people's lives and their regard for the political system. True, Vietnamese often have negative views of and experiences with party-state authorities. But many also see officials and government agencies listening to and accepting the arguments, criticisms, and proposals of individuals, groups, and communities. Maybe the political system can continue in the same direction it has been going in recent decades, evolving more elaborate and public dialogical interactions between party-state agencies and societal groups and interests without changing the regime.[16]

Appendix

Cited Party-State Newspapers

For readers unfamiliar with newspapers cited in endnotes that are produced by Vietnam's party-state entities, this list, arranged alphabetically by Vietnamese title, provides the publisher for each one.

An Ninh Thủ Đô [Security in the Capital], Public Security Police [Công An] office in Hà Nội.

Báo Xây Dựng [Construction News], Ministry of Construction [Bộ Xây Dựng].

Công An Nghệ An [Nghệ An Public Security], Public Security Police [Công An] office in Nghệ An province.

Công An Nhân Dân [People's Public Security], Ministry of Public Security Police [Bộ Công An]

Dân Sinh [People's Livelihood], Ministry of Labor, Invalids and Social Affairs [Bộ Lao Động-Thương Binh và Xã Hội].

Đại Đoàn Kết [Great Unity], Homeland Front [Mặt Trận Tổ Quốc].

Hà Nội Mới [New Hà Nội], Hà Nội Committee of the Vietnamese Communist Party [Thành Ủy Cộng Sản Việt Nam, Thành phố Hà Nội].

Lao Động [Labor], Vietnam General Confederation of Labor [Tổng Liên Đoàn Lao Động Việt Nam].

Người Cao Tuổi [Elderly People], Vietnam's Association of Elderly People [Hội Người Cao Tuổi Việt Nam].

Người Lao Động [Worker], Vietnam General Confederation of Labor's branch in Hồ Chí Minh City [Liên Đoàn Lao Động Thành phố Hồ Chí Minh].

Nhân Dân [People], Central office of the Vietnamese Communist Party [Trung ương của Đảng Cộng Sản Việt Nam].

Nông Dân Việt Nam [Vietnamese Peasant], Vietnam Peasants' Association [Hội Nông Dân Việt Nam].

Pháp Luật [Law], Ministry of Justice [Bộ Tư Pháp].

Pháp Luật TP Hồ Chí Minh [Hồ Chí Minh City Law], People's Committee, Hồ Chí Minh City [Ủy ban Nhân dân, Thành phố Hồ Chí Minh].

Quân Đội Nhân Dân [People's Army], Ministry of National Defense [Bộ Quốc Phòng].

Sài Gòn Giải Phóng [Sài Gòn Liberation], Hồ Chí Minh City Committee of the Vietnamese Communist Party [Đảng bộ, Đảng Cộng Sản Việt Nam, Thành phố Hồ Chí Minh].

Sài Gòn Tiếp Thị [Sài Gòn Market], Hồ Chí Minh City Center to Expedite Commerce and Investment [Trung tâm Xúc tiến Thương mại và Đầu tư Thành phố Hồ Chí Minh].

Thanh Hóa [Thanh Hóa province newspaper], Thanh Hóa province Committee of the Vietnamese Communist Party [Đảng bộ, Đảng Cộng Sản Việt Nam, tỉnh Thanh Hóa].

Thanh Niên [Young People], Youth Union of Vietnam [Hội Liên Hiệp Thanh Niên Việt Nam].

Tiền Phong [Vanguard], Hồ Chí Minh Communist Youth League, central office [Cơ quan Trung ương, Đoàn Thanh Niên Cộng Sản Hồ Chí Minh].

Tuần Báo Văn Nghệ [Arts and Literature Weekly], Hồ Chí Minh City Associations for Literature and Arts [Liên Hiệp các Hội Văn Học-Nghệ Thuật Thành phố Hồ Chí Minh].

Tuổi Trẻ [Youth], Hồ Chí Minh Communist Youth League, Hồ Chí Minh City [Đoàn Thanh Niên Cộng Sản Hồ Chí Minh, Thành phố Hồ Chí Minh].

NOTES

Introduction

1. Analyses of the emergence and diversity of societal groups include Thiem H. Bui, "The Development of Civil Society and Dynamics of Governance in Vietnam's One Party Rule," *Global Change, Peace & Security* 25, no. 1 (2013): 77–93; Joseph Hannah, "Local Non-government Organizations in Vietnam: Development, Civil Society and State-Society Relations" (PhD diss., University of Washington, 2007); Ben J. Tria Kerkvliet, Russell H. K. Heng, and David W. H. Koh, eds., *Getting Organized in Vietnam* (Singapore: Institute of Southeast Asian Studies, 2003); Mark Sidel, "The Emergence of a Non-profit and Philanthropy Sector in the Socialist Republic of Vietnam," in *Emerging Civil Society in the Asia Pacific Community*, ed. Tadashi Yamamoto (Singapore: Institute of Southeast Asian Studies, 1995), 293–304; Philip Taylor, ed., *Modernity and Re-enchantment: Religion in Post-revolutionary Vietnam* (Singapore: Institute of Southeast Asian Studies, 2007); William Taylor et al., *Civil Society in Vietnam: A Comparative Study of Civil Society Organizations in Hanoi and Ho Chi Minh City* (Hà Nội: Asia Foundation, 2012); Carlyle A. Thayer, "Vietnam and the Challenge of Political Civil Society," *Contemporary Southeast Asia* 31 (April 2009): 1–27; Andrew Wells-Dang, *Civil Society Networks in China and Vietnam* (New York: Palgrave Macmillan, 2012); Jörg Wischermann,

"Civil Society Action and Governance in Vietnam," *Journal of Current Southeast Asian Affairs* 2 (2010): 3–40.

2. In addition to my own observations in Vietnam since my first visit in 1989, this paragraph draws on several studies, including Michael L. Gray, "Control and Dissent in Vietnam's Online World" (Tia Sang Vietnam Research Report, February 2015), accessed March 12, 2015, http://www.tiasangvietnam.org/wpcontent /uploads/2015/02/TSVN.Backgrounder.Social.Media_.Jan15.pdf; Bill Hayton, *Vietnam: Rising Dragon* (New Haven, CT: Yale University Press, 2010), 135–58; David G. Marr, ed., *The Mass Media in Vietnam* (Canberra: Department of Political and Social Change, Australian National University, 1998); Catherine McKinley and Anya Schiffrin, "Leninist Lapdogs to Bothersome Bloggers in Vietnam," in *State Power 2.0: Authoritarian Entrenchment and Political Engagement Worldwide*, ed. Muzammil H. Hussain and Philip Howard (Burlington, VT: Ashgate, 2013), 125–37; Björn Surborg, "On-line with the People in Line: Internet Development and Flexible Control of the Net in Vietnam," *Geoforum* 39 (2008): 344–57, doi:10.1016/j.geoforum.2007.07.008.

3. These four by no means exhaust the range of political criticism in contemporary Vietnam. For instance, my research initially included religious groups and environmentalists' petitions, demonstrations, and other political actions, but material on those and the other topics became so voluminous that I had to scale back.

4. Such assessments appear in several Freedom House reports between 2009 and 2015. For example, "Freedom in the World—Vietnam (2010)," Freedom House, May 29, 2011, http://freedomhouse.org/template.cfm?page+363&year=2010; and "Vietnam: Country Report, 2015," Freedom House, accessed December 18, 2015, https://freedomhouse.org /report/freedom-world/2015/vietnam.

5. Zachary Abuza, *Renovating Politics in Contemporary Vietnam* (Boulder, CO: Lynne Rienner, 2001), 38. Even in 2001, the statement was hyperbolic.

6. Human Rights Watch, *World Report 2013* (New York: Human Rights Watch, 2013), Vietnam chapter; Human Rights Watch, "Vietnam: Country Summary," January 2015, Human Rights Watch, accessed June 30, 2015, https://www.hrw.org/sites /default/files/related_material/vietnam_9.pdf; U.S. Department of State, *2010 Country Reports on Human Rights Practices: Vietnam* (Washington, DC: U.S. Department of State, 2011). More measured than the U.S. Department of State's report for 2010 are its *Country Reports on Human Rights Practices for 2011: Vietnam* (Washington, DC: U.S. Department of State, 2012) and *Vietnam 2014 Human Rights Report* (Washington, DC: U.S. Department of State, 2015).

7. John Kleinen, *Vietnam: One-Party State and the Mimicry of Civil Society* (Bangkok: Research Institute on Contemporary Southeast Asia, 2015), 10.

8. Stein Tønnesson, "The 'Vietnam Peace': How Priorities in Vietnam's External and Internal Policies Changed after 1987" (paper presented at the International Studies Association convention, New York City, February 18, 2009), 7.

9. Bill Hayton, "The Limits to Political Activity in Vietnam," July 14, 2010, East Asia Forum, accessed July 15, 2010, http://www.eastasiaforum.org/2010/07/14/the-limits -to-political-activity-in-vietnam/.

10. David Koh, "Political Reform and Democratization in Vietnam," in *East Asian Democracy and Political Changes in China: A New Goose Flying?*, ed. Zhengxu Wang and Colin Duerkop (Singapore: Konrad Adenauer Stiftung, 2008), 82–83.

11. Juan J. Linz, *Totalitarian and Authoritarian Regimes* (Boulder, CO: Lynne Rienner, 2000), 61, 63.

12. Linz, *Totalitarian and Authoritarian*, 159; Juan J. Linz, "An Authoritarian Regime: Spain," in *Mass Politics: Studies in Political Sociology*, ed. Erik Allardt and Stein Rokkan (New York: Free Press, 1970), 264.

13. For some of that debate, see Adam Fforde, "Vietnam in 2004: Popular Authority Seeking Power?," *Asian Survey* 45, no. 1 (2005): 146–52; Fforde, "Vietnam in 2012: The End of the Party," *Asian Survey* 53, no. 1 (2013): 101–108; Martin Gainsborough, *Vietnam: Rethinking the State* (New York: Zed Books, 2010); Tuong Vu, "Persistence amid Decay: The Communist Party of Vietnam at 83," in *Politics in Contemporary Vietnam: Party, State, and Authority Relations*, ed. Jonathan D. London (New York: Palgrave Macmillan, 2014), 21–41; Tuong Vu, *Vietnam's Communist Revolution: The Power and Limits of Ideology* (New York: Cambridge University Press, 2017).

14. Linz, *Totalitarian and Authoritarian*, 65; Carl J. Friedrich and Zbigniew K. Brzezinski, *Totalitarian Dictatorship and Autocracy* (Cambridge, MA: Harvard University Press, 1956), 9–10.

15. Although the political systems in Vietnam and China have major similarities, they also have significant differences. See Edmund Malesky, Regina Abrami, and Yu Zheng, "Institutions and Inequality in Single-Party Regimes: A Comparative Analysis of Vietnam and China," *Comparative Politics* 43 (July 2011): 401–419; Regina Abrami, Edmund Malesky, and Yu Zheng, "Vietnam through Chinese Eyes: Divergent Accountability in Single-Party Regimes," in *Why Communism Did Not Collapse: Understanding Authoritarian Regime Resilience in Asia and Europe*, ed. Martin K. Dimitrov (New York: Cambridge University Press, 2014), 237–75; Anita Chan, Benedict J. Tria Kerkvliet, and Jonathan Unger, eds., *Transforming Asian Socialism: China and Vietnam Compared* (Boulder, CO: Rowman & Littlefield, 1999).

16. "Leninism" refers to features of each country's Communist Party. Jonathan London, "Viet Nam and the Making of Market-Leninism," *Pacific Review* 22 (July 2009): 375–99; London, "Market-Leninism" (Working Paper No. 124, Southeast Asia Research Centre, City University of Hong Kong, 2012).

17. Carlyle A. Thayer, "Political Legitimacy in Vietnam under Challenge," in *Political Legitimacy in Asia*, ed. John Kane, Hui-Chieu Loy, and Haig Patapan (New York: Palgrave Macmillan, 2011), 56–58; Steve Tsang, "Consultative Leninism: China's New Political Framework," *Journal of Contemporary China* 18 (November 2009): 865; Xi Chen, *Social Protest and Contentious Authoritarianism in China* (New York: Cambridge University Press, 2012); Baogang He and Mark E. Warren, "Authoritarian Deliberation: The Deliberative Turn in Chinese Political Development," *Perspectives on Politics* 9 (June 2011): 269–73; Rebecca MacKinnon, "China's 'Networked Authoritarianism,'" *Journal of Democracy* 22 (April 2011): 33–35; Andrew C. Mertha, *China's Water Warriors: Citizen Action and Policy Change* (Ithaca, NY: Cornell University Press, 2008), 5, 151–57; Andrew J. Nathan, "Authoritarian Resilience," *Journal of Democracy* 14

(January 2003): 6–7; Robert Weller, "Responsive Authoritarianism," in *Political Change in China: Comparisons with Taiwan*, ed. Bruce Gilley and Larry Diamond (Boulder, CO: Lynne Rienner, 2008), 117–18.

18. Edmund Malesky and Jonathan London, "The Political Economy of Development in China and Vietnam," *Annual Review of Political Science* 17 (2014): 413.

19. I have borrowed "responsive-repressive" from Harold Crouch's study of Malaysian politics where the national government exercises authoritarian powers to "preserve political stability and the continued domination of the Malay elite" but is also sensitive to countervailing social forces, popular pressures, and opposition. Thus it often tackles "challenges with a combination of repressive and responsive measures." Harold Crouch, *Government and Society in Malaysia* (Ithaca, NY: Cornell University Press, 1996), 244.

20. Brantly Womack, "Modernization and the Sino-Vietnamese Model," *International Journal of China Studies* 2 (August/September 2011): 170.

21. Le Hong Hiep, "The One-Party State and Prospects for Democratization in Vietnam," *ISEAS Perspective*, no. 63 (2013): 8. Also see Benedict J. Tria Kerkvliet, "Governance, Development, and the Responsive-Repressive State in Vietnam," *Forum for Development Studies* 37 (March 2010): 33–60.

22. Teresa Wright, "Stable Governance and Regime Type," in *State-Society Relations and Governance in China*, ed. Sujian Guo (Lanham, MD: Lexington Books, 2014), 177. Wright's larger point is that analysts "need to view regime type not as a dichotomy between authoritarianism and democracy" (174).

23. Isaac Manfred Elfstrom, "Resistance, Repression, and Responsiveness: Workers and the State in China" (PhD diss., Cornell University, 2017), 193.

24. In Vietnamese, "ward" is *phường* and "subdistrict" is *xã*. Often *xã* is translated as "commune," which can mislead readers into thinking it is a unit of communal living or communal residency, which it is not. It is the basic administrative unit in rural areas, which is how Vietnamese dictionaries define the word. Many subdistricts have two or more villages.

25. For some studies of complexities within the party-state since the early 1990s, see David W. P. Elliott, *Changing Worlds: Vietnam's Transition from Cold War to Globalization* (New York: Oxford University Press, 2012); Gainsborough, *Vietnam*; Thomas Jandl, *Vietnam in the Global Economy: The Dynamics of Integration, Decentralization, and Contested Politics* (Lanham, MD: Lexington Books, 2013); Edmund Malesky and Paul Schuler, "Nodding or Needling: Analyzing Delegate Responsiveness in an Authoritarian Parliament," *American Political Science Review* 106 (August 2010): 1–21; Thaveeporn Vasavakul, "Authoritarianism Reconfigured: Evolving Accountability Relations within Vietnam's One-Party Rule," in *Politics in Contemporary Vietnam*, ed. Jonathan London (New York: Palgrave Macmillan, 2014), 42–63; Alexander L. Vuving, "Vietnam: A Tale of Four Players," in *Southeast Asian Affairs 2010*, ed. Daljit Singh (Singapore: Institute of Southeast Asian Studies, 2010), 367–91; Vuving, "Vietnam in 2012: A Rent-Seeking State on the Verge of a Crisis," in *Southeast Asian Affairs 2013*, ed. Daljit Singh (Singapore: Institute of Southeast Asian Studies, 2013), 325–47.

26. See, for example, Alan R. Ball, *Modern Politics and Government*, 5th ed. (London: Macmillan, 1993), 20–21; Benedict J. Tria Kerkvliet, *The Power of Everyday Politics: How Vietnamese Peasants Transformed National Policy* (Ithaca, NY: Cornell Univer-

sity Press, 2005), 21–22; Adrian Leftwich, "Politics: People, Resources, and Power," in *What Is Politics?*, ed. Adrian Leftwich (Oxford: Basil Blackwell, 1984), 63–70; Hugh T. Miller, "Everyday Politics in Public Administration," *American Review of Public Administration* 23, no. 2 (1993): 99–100; Gerry Stoker, "Introduction," in *Theory and Methods in Political Science*, ed. David Marsh and Gerry Stoker (London: Macmillan, 1995), 5–7.

1. Labor

1. Thanh Hải, "Chỉ có thể 'nói' bằng đình công!" [Can "Speak" Only by Striking!], May 12, 2005, *Lao Động* [Labor], accessed May 5, 2006, http://www.laodong.com.vn /pls/bld/folder$.view_item_detail(129565); Thanh Hải, "Chỉ mới nhượng bộ 3/8 'yêu sách' của CN" [Conceding only 3/8 of Workers' "Demands"], May 13, 2005, *Lao Động*, accessed May 5, 2006, http://www.laodong.com.vn/pls/bld/folder$.view_item _detail(129710); Thanh Hải, "100% yêu sách của công nhân được đáp ứng" [100% of Workers' Demands Are Met], *Lao Động*, May 14, 2005, 1–2. To strike was the last resort for those wanting or needing a job at the factory. For many others their last resort was to quit, which reportedly hundreds of Keyhing Toy factory workers did over several years.

2. The main method for collecting news reports was to regularly monitor from 2004 three newspapers that circulated widely in Vietnam and reported extensively on laborers' conditions, complaints, and strikes as well as actions of the party-state and its Vietnam General Confederation of Labor [Tổng Liên Đoàn Lao Động Việt Nam], hereafter referred to as the VGCL, and the confederation's unions. Two VGCL newspapers, *Lao Động* and *Người Lao Động* [Worker], are the sources for most of the accounts. *Thanh Niên* [Young People] is the third newspaper regularly checked since 2004. I also have articles, but less systematically gathered, that these three newspapers published in 1992, 1993, 1995, 1996, and 2000. For some of those articles I thank Michael Karadjis. The supplementary method for finding reports was to search online for information about particular enterprises, organizations, individuals, strikes, and other events. That method frequently led to additional news sources.

3. I am reasonably confident that Vietnamese journalists related rather well what workers told them. I base this on having read a large number of news accounts stretching over several years, using a diversity of sources, talking to Vietnamese researchers interested in labor issues, and reading studies by scholars who have interviewed workers. This is not to say the reporting is evenhanded for all sides of the strikes and related events. Some reports are; many, however, focus on workers and their problems, complaints, ambitions, and demands. Given my interest in wanting to understand precisely those views, that focus is helpful.

4. The figures for the proportion of strikes at foreign-invested enterprises come from the VGCL, as reported in "Quan hệ lao động nhiều bất ổn" [Much Instability in Labor Relations], September 6, 2007, *Lao Động*, accessed September 10, 2007, http://www .laodong.com.vn/Home/congdoan/2007/9/53933.laodong; Bảo Duy, "Để đình công đúng luật" [To Strike According to Law], September 13, 2016, Công Đoàn Việt Nam

[Vietnam Trade Union], accessed April 26, 2017, http://www.congdoanvn.org.vn/tin-tuc/quan-he-lao-dong-505/de-dinh-cong-dung-luat-125532.tld; Do Quynh Chi and Di van den Broek, "Wildcat Strikes: A Catalyst for Union Reform in Vietnam?," *Journal of Industrial Relations* 55, no. 5 (2013): 286. The workforce figures are based on data in *Niên Giám Thống Kê Statistical Yearbook of Vietnam 2009* (Hà Nội: Nxb Thống Kê, 2010), 61; and *Niên Giám Thống Kê Statistical Yearbook of Vietnam 2015* (Hà Nội: Nxb Thống Kê, 2016), 135, 138.

5. "Tranh chấp LĐ và đình công gia tăng" [Labor Conflicts and Strikes Increase], May 24, 2005, *Lao Động*, accessed May 5, 2006, http://www.laodong.com.vn/pls/bld/folder$.view_item_detail(130531); Trần Ngọc Angie, *Ties That Bind: Cultural Identity, Class, and Law in Vietnam's Labor Resistance* (Ithaca, NY: Southeast Asia Program, Cornell University, 2013), 145, 200–201. Far fewer strikes occurred in enterprises from such other places as Europe, Hong Kong, Japan, and Singapore.

6. Trần Ngọc Angie, *Ties That Bind*, 183–85.

7. Vĩnh Tùng, "Làm gì để hạn chế tranh chấp, đình công?" [How Can Conflicts and Strikes Be Limited?], *Người Lao Động*, November 3, 2000, 3. I have not found figures for the number of all disputes since 2000.

8. Quốc Bình and Thế Yên, "Thấy gì qua cuộc lãn công ở Cty LD Tỷ Xuân?" [What's to Be Seen from the Slowdown at Ty Xuan Company?], October 23, 2006, *Lao Động*, accessed October 25, 2006, http://www.laodong.com.vn/Home/congdoan/tranhchapld/2006/10/8081.laodong.

9. Lê Tuyết and Hoàng Hoan, "Ai bảo lương, thưởng tết tăng?" [Who Says Wages and New Year Bonuses Rise?], January 28, 2013, *Lao Động*, accessed April 12, 2017, http://laodong.com.vn/xa-hoi/ai-bao-luong-thuong-tet-tang-100900.bld.

10. "Hạn chế cả quyền làm mẹ của người lao động" [Limiting a Worker's Motherhood Rights], October 31, 2006, *Lao Động*, accessed November 2, 2006, http://www.laodong.com.vn/Home/congdoan/tranhchapld/2006/10/9129.laodong.

11. For a revealing analysis of news coverage about workers' protests, see Angie Ngọc Trần, "The Third Sleeve: Emerging Labor Newspapers and the Response of Labor Unions and the State to Workers' Resistance in Vietnam," *Labor Studies Journal* 32 (September 2007): 257–79. Of course, many newspapers and magazines pay little attention to workers or are more partial to employers and businesses.

12. Cao Hùng, "Xin nghỉ việc, không được trả lương?" [Quitting—Because Not Being Paid?], July 4, 2005, *Lao Động*, accessed May 4, 2006, http://www.laodong.com.vn/pls/bld/folder$.view_item_detail(133579).

13. "Doanh nghiệp sách Thành Nghĩa—TPHCM" [Thành Nghĩa Books, Hồ Chí Minh City], July 31, 2007, *Lao Động*, accessed August 1, 2007, http://www.laodong.com.vn/Home/congdoan/tranhchapld/2007/7/48269.laodong.

14. Dương Bội Ngọc, "Vụ lãn công của 300 công nhân Cty TNHH Wonderful" [Slowdown by 300 Workers at Wonderful Company], December 31, 2007, *Lao Động*, accessed February 6, 2008, http://www.laodong.com.vn/Home/congdoan/tranhchapld/2007/12/71188.laodong.

15. Dương Minh Đức, "Một ngày 3 vụ đình công về lương—thưởng" [Three Strikes in One Day over Wages and Bonuses], January 9, 2008, *Lao Động*, accessed January 25, 2008, http://www.laodong.com.vn/Home/congdoan/tranhchapld/2008/1/72247.

laodong; Dương Minh Đức, "Lương, thưởng chưa tương xứng với công lao động" [Wages and Bonuses Not Yet Acceptable to Workers], January 14, 2008, *Lao Động*, accessed January 25, 2008, http://www.laodong.com.vn/Home/congdoan/tranh chapld /2008/1/72907.laodong.

16. Vĩnh Tùng, "Không nên xem lợi nhuận là tất cả" [Profits Should Not Be the Top Priority], July 11, 2007, *Người Lao Động*, accessed July 11, 2007, http://www.nld .com.vn/tintuc/cong-doan/194987.asp; Trung Tâm Hỗ Trợ Phát Triển Quan Hệ Lao Động (CIRD) [Center for Labor Relations Development], Bộ Lao Động-Thương Binh và Xã Hội [Ministry of Labor, Invalids and Social Affairs, MoLISA], "Các yêu sách đình công" [Strike Demands], December 5, 2015, Quan hệ Lao động [Labor Relations], accessed April 12, 2017, http://quanhelaodong.gov.vn/cac-yeu-sach-dinh-cong/.

17. Khánh Linh, "Lay lắt chờ lương" [Waiting a Long Time for Wages], *Người Lao Động*, September 24, 2012, 6.

18. Examples are analyzed by Tu Phuong Nguyen, "Workers' Strikes in Vietnam from a Regulatory Perspective," *Asian Studies Review* (2017): 8–9, doi:10.1080/10357823. 2017.1298568.

19. For several details and an overview of the issue, see "Vỡ Quỹ bảo hiểm, những báo động đáng sợ?" [Social Insurance Fund Broken, Frightening Warnings?], May 10, 2014, *Công An Nghệ An* [Nghệ An Public Security], accessed April 17, 2017, http:// congannghean.vn/kinh-te-xa-hoi/201405/vo-quy-bao-hiem-nhung-bao-dong-dang-so -482445/.

20. Suhong Chae, "Spinning Work and Weaving Life: The Politics of Production in a Capitalistic Multinational Textile Factory in Vietnam" (PhD diss., City University of New York, 2003), 77–86; December and January issues of *Lao Động*, *Người Lao Động*, and *Thanh Niên* for most years between 2004 and 2015.

21. A decree (Nghị Định 03/2006/NĐ-CP) that took effect in February 2006 changed the 625,950 *đồng* per month minimum wage to 870,000 *đồng* per month for workers in foreign-invested establishments located in Hà Nội and Hồ Chí Minh City. The increases were less in other "zones." Further details are in Trần Ngọc Angie, *Ties That Bind*, 138–40; "Vietnam Minimum Wages 2008–2017," Trading Economics, accessed May 4, 2017, http://www.tradingeconomics.com/vietnam/minimum-wages. The value of the Vietnamese currency in relation to the U.S. dollar was approximately 11,000 *đồng*/US$ in 1995; 14,200 *đồng*/US$ in 2000; 15,800 *đồng*/US$ in 2005; 19,100 *đồng*/US$ in 2010; and 21,900 *đồng*/US$ in 2015.

22. Minh Anh, "Đời sống hàng triệu công nhân chật vật" [Millions of Workers Struggling to Live], March 9, 2011, Gia đình Net [Family Internet], accessed March 10, 2011, http://giadinh.net.vn/20110309082552333p0c1002/doi-song-hang-trieu-cong-nhan -chat-vat-chinh-sach-bi-khiem-khuyet.htm; Trần Ngọc Angie, *Ties That Bind*, 197; "Vietnam's Minimum Wage Leaves Its Workers Impoverished," April 22, 2013, *Thanh Niên*, accessed April 23, 2013, http://www.thanhniennews.com/index/pages/20130414 -vietnam-minimum-wage-leaves-working-group-in-poverty.aspx.

23. Interview with prominent Vietnamese economist Lê Đăng Doanh, May 26, 2008, Radio Free Asia (RFA), accessed May 27, 2008, http://www.rfa.org/vietnamese /in_depth/Interview_with_economist_LeDangDoanh_about_wave_of_labor_strikes _in_Vietnam_NNguyen-05262008103135.html; Kaxton Siu and Anita Chan, "Strike

Wave in Vietnam, 2006–2011," *Journal of Contemporary Asia* (2014), esp. 10–14, doi 10.1080/00472336.2014.903290.

24. "Hai công nhân bị trói chân tại nơi làm việc" [Two Workers' Legs Tied to Their Workplace], April 12, 2007, Vietnam.net, accessed April 19, 2007, http://www .vietnamnet.vn/xahoi/laodong/2007/04/683865/.

25. "Bữa ăn ngày càng tệ" [Meals Worsen by the Day], July 2, 2007, *Người Lao Động*, accessed July 5, 2007, http://www.nld.com.vn/tintuc/cong-doan/194162.asp; Ngô Sơn, "Thiếu chất, giảm lượng, nguy cơ ngộ độc cao" [Malnutrition, Insufficient Intake, High Risk of Poisoning], July 12, 2008, *Lao Động*, accessed July 15, 2008, http:// www.laodong.com.vn/Home/congdoan/2008/7/97213.laodong; Kaxton Siu, "The Working and Living Conditions of Garment Workers in China and Vietnam," in *Chinese Workers in Comparative Perspective*, ed. Anita Chan (Ithaca, NY: Cornell University Press, 2015), 127–28.

26. "Vì sao hơn 5.000 cuộc đình công không do công đoàn lãnh đạo?" [Why More Than 5,000 Strikes Lack Union Leadership?], July 26, 2013, *Lao Động*, accessed April 26, 2017, http://laodong.com.vn/cong-doan/vi-sao-hon-5000-cuoc-dinh-cong-khong -do-cong-doan-lanh-dao-129494.bld.

27. There is a similar analysis by Tu Phuong Nguyen, "Labour Law and (In)justice in Workers' Letters in Vietnam," *Asian Journal of Law and Society* (2017): 1–19, doi: 10.1017/als.2017.29.

28. Lê Trí Tuệ, quoted in a RFA report by Đỗ Hiếu, "Tình trạng đối xử bất công đối với công nhân tại Việt Nam" [Unjust Treatment of Workers in Vietnam], May 1, 2007, Mạng Ý Kiến [Opinion Net], accessed May 3, 2007, http://ykien.net/blog/?p=1225.

29. "Làm công khổ lắm!" [Work Is So Hard!], August 29, 2007, *Người Lao Động*, accessed August 30, 2007, http://www.nld.com.vn/tintuc/cong-doan/200603.asp.

30. Yến Trinh and Chí Quốc, "Nhọc nhằn đời công nhân" [A Worker's Weary Life], October 22, 2007, *Tuổi Trẻ* [Youth], accessed April 4, 2008, http://www.tuoitre.vn /Tianyon2/Index.aspx?ArticleID+225522&ChannelID=89; "Nỗi buồn cơm áo" [The Sorrow of Making a Living], February 28, 2006, *Lao Động*, accessed May 4, 2006, http:// www.laodong.com.vn/pls/bld/folder$.view_item _detail(150350).

31. For a description of typical living quarters, see Siu, "The Working and Living Conditions of Garment Workers," 126–27.

32. "Công nhân lao động đang sống và làm việc như thế nào" [How Laborers Live and Work], April 24, 2014, Trung tâm Hỗ trợ thanh niên công nhân [Center for Assisting Young Laborers], accessed April 14, 2017, http://congnhanbinhphuoc.org.vn/vi /news/Thong-tin-ve-Cong-nhan-Doanh-nghiep/Cong-nhan-lao-dong-dang-song-va -lam-viec-nhu-the-nao-275/.

33. Tuấn Sơn and Mai Hương, "Đời sống công nhân ở TPHCM" [Workers' Lives in Hồ Chí Minh City], August 23, 2007, *Sài Gòn Giải Phóng* [Sài Gòn Liberation], accessed August 27, 2007, http://www.sggp.org.vn/xahoi/2007/8/117054/#.

34. See, for example, Thu Trà, Thu Hương, and Ngô Sơn, "'Thắt dạ dày' vì chuyện áo cơm" ["Tightening Your Belt" for the Hard Times], March 7, 2008, *Lao Động*, accessed March 12, 2008, http://www.laodong.com.vn/Home/phongsu/2008/3/79370 .laodong; Cao Hùng and Giảng Hải, "Lao động nghèo loay hoay giữa đô thị" [Poor Laborers Struggling in the City], March 8, 2008, *Lao Động*, accessed March 12, 2008,

http://www.laodong.com.vn/Home/phongsu/2008/3/79572.laodong; Trần Ngọc Angie, *Ties That Bind*, 186–90.

35. The writers of the letter were Huỳnh Ngọc Cảnh, a laborer in the AMATA industrial zone in Đồng Nai province; Nguyễn Tấn Hoành, from the Điện Bàn industrial zone, Quảng Nam; Nguyễn Tấn Dung, working in the Biên Hòa II industrial zone, Đồng Nai; Dương Thái Phong, Huyền Tiên, Trương Long, Vũ Hà, Trần Tá, Võ Hải, and Nguyễn Thị Tuyết, all from the Tân Bình and Vĩnh Lộc industrial areas of Hồ Chí Minh City; and Hoàng Anh Tuấn, employed in the Gia Định shoe factory, Sài Gòn. Found at Dan Chu Net, accessed April 25, 2006, http://www.danchu.net /ArticlesChinhLuan/0.0.0.Collection.2006.I/HuynhNgocCanh.601.htm. Also see interview with one of the letter writers, Nguyễn Tấn Hoành, March 24, 2006, RFA, accessed April 21, 2006, http://www.doi-thoai.com/baimoi0306_336.html.

36. Nguyễn Thiện Nhân, "Đình công căng thẳng tại Công ty Shin Sung Vina (Long An) kéo dài 8 ngày chưa kết thúc!" [After Eight Days Still No End to the Tense Strike at Shin Sung Vina Company in Long An], April 8, 2015, Giải Pháp Dân Chủ cho Việt Nam [Democratic Solution for Vietnam], accessed April 17, 2017, https:// giaiphapdanchu.wordpress.com/2015/04/08/dinh-cong-cang-thang-tai-cong-ty-shin -sung-vina-long-an-keo-dai-8-ngay-chua-ket-thuc/; "Đình công bước sang ngày thứ 4" [Strike Enters a Fourth Day], March 30, 2015, Kênh, accessed April 17, 2017, http:// kenh13.info/dinh-cong-buoc-sang-ngay-thu-4-gay-tac-nghen-quoc-lo-1a.html; "Tại sao công nhân Pou Yuen đình công phản đối luật bảo hiểm xã hội mới?" [Why Are Pou Yuen Workers Striking to Oppose the New Social Insurance Law?], March 31, 2015, Dân Luận [People Discuss], accessed April 17, 2017, https://www.danluan.org/tin-tuc/20150331 /tai-sao-cong-nhan-pouyuen-dinh-cong-phan-doi-luat-bao-hiem-xa-hoi-moi.

37. Kỳ Anh, "Vụ 90.000 công nhân đình công" [The Strike by 90,000 Laborers], March 30, 2015, CafeBiz, accessed April 17, 2017, http://cafebiz.vn/cau-chuyen-kinh -doanh/vu-90000-cong-nhan-dinh-cong-tap-doan-giay-dep-pou-yuen-la-ai -20150330174314048.chn.

38. "Tiếp tục đình công lớn ở Tp HCM" [Huge Strike Continues in Hồ Chí Minh City], March 30, 2015, British Broadcasting Corporation (BBC), accessed April 26, 2017, http://www.bbc.com/vietnamese/vietnam/2015/03/150330_workers_strike_insurance _update.

39. "Tại sao công nhân Pou Yuen đình công."

40. In at least one instance, a security guard, following his superior's order, drove a large truck into a workers' picket line in front of the company's driveway, causing many injuries and killing a pregnant employee. One of the several news reports about this is N. Anh and T. Dũng, "Bảo vệ lao xe tải vào công nhân đình công bị khởi tố" [Security Guard Who Drove Truck into Striking Workers Is Being Prosecuted], June 24, 2011, VnExpress, accessed June 27, 2011, http://vnexpress.net/gl/phap-luat/2011/06/bao-ve-lao -xe-tai-vao-cong-nhan-dinh-cong-bi-khoi-to/.

41. "Công nhân hãng giày Nike đình công" [Nike Shoemakers Go on Strike], November 29, 2007, BBC, accessed April 4, 2008, http://www.bbc.co.uk/vietnamese /vietnam/story/2007/11/071129_nike_factory_strike.shtml.

42. Chi Do Quynh, "Coordination among Strikes and Prospects for Pattern Bargaining in Vietnam," *Global Labour Column*, no. 234 (May 2016): 1.

43. "Vietnam: Labour Strikes Increased by 30%," August 16, 1999, Reuters, accessed August 20, 1999, http://elisa.anu.edu.au:8080/current/0000026.bsk/AA6RC00C.htm.

44. Calculated from figures in Linh Nguyên, "Quyền lợi người lao động trong hội nhập kinh tế" [Workers' Rights in a Mixed Economy], May 15, 2007, *Lao Động*, accessed May 21, 2007, http://www.laodong.com.vn/Home/congdoan/2007/5/36279.laodong.

45. Nguyên Thủy, "'Liên khúc' đình công" ["Potpourri" of Strikes], March 3, 2006, *Thanh Niên*, accessed April 13, 2006, http://www3.thanhnien.com.vn/Xahoi/2006/3/3/140573.tno.

46. The main sources for this discussion are "Hơn 400 người đập phá trong cuộc biểu tình bị bắt" [More Than 400 Demonstrators Arrested for Vandalism], May 14, 2014, VnExpress, accessed May 16, 2014, http://vnexpress.net/tin-tuc/phap-luat/hon-400-nguoi-dap-pha-trong-cuoc-bieu-tinh-bi-bat-2990338.html; Nguyệt Triều and Xuân Thủy, "Nhiều kẻ kích động công nhân trong cuộc biểu tình phản đối Trung Quốc" [Many Labor Agitators in the Demonstration against China], May 14, 2014, VnExpress, accessed May 16, 2014, http://vnexpress.net/tin-tuc/thoi-su/nhieu-ke-kich-dong-cong-nhan-trong-cuoc-bieu-tinh-phan-doi-trung-quoc-2990053.html; Huy Đức, "Mồi lửa và đống củi" [Flames and Firewood], May 19, 2014, Viet Studies, accessed May 22, 2014, http://www.viet-studies.info/kinhte/HuyDuc_MoiLua@DongCui.htm; Huong Le Thu, "The Anti-Chinese Riots in Vietnam: Responses from the Ground," *ISEAS Perspective*, no. 32 (May 27, 2014): 1–8.

47. Vũ Thủy, "20 năm qua: Chưa có cuộc đình công nào đúng luật" [In the Past 20 Years, No Strike Has Followed the Law], August 13, 2015, *Tuổi Trẻ* [Youth], accessed April 12, 2017, http://tuoitre.vn/tin/chinh-tri-xa-hoi/20150813/20-nam-qua-chua-co-cuoc-dinh-cong-nao-dung-luat/948135.html. Over the years, VGCL and MoLISA officials issued similar statements; an example is in Quang Chính, "Kiến nghị Đảng ra nghị quyết về giai cấp công nhân" [Petitioning the Party to Issue a Resolution about the Working Class], *Lao Động*, August 25, 2006, 2.

48. Huyền Ngân, "Vì sao các cuộc đình công đều trái luật?" [Why Are Strikes Contrary to the Law?], February 3, 2006, VnEconomy, accessed October 20, 2006, www.congdoanvn.org.vn; Thanh Van, "Strikes Double in 2011," January 10, 2012, Vietnam.net, accessed March 14, 2012, http://english.vietnamnet.vn/en/society/17535/strikes-double-in-2011.html; Trung Tâm Hỗ Trợ Phát Triển Quan Hệ Lao Động (CIRD) [Center for Labor Relations Development], Bộ Lao Động-Thương Binh và Xã Hội [MoLISA], "Thống kê đình công theo các doanh nghiệp có hay không có công đoàn" [Strike Statistics by Enterprises With or Without a Union], October 5, 2015, Quan hệ Lao động, accessed April 12, 2017, http://quanhelaodong.gov.vn/thong-ke-dinh-cong-theo-cac-dn-co-hay-khong-co-cong-doan/.

49. For elaboration, see Simon Clarke, Chang-Hee Lee, and Do Quynh Chi, "From Rights to Interests: The Challenge of Industrial Relations in Vietnam," *Journal of Industrial Relations* 49, no. 4 (2007): 545–68; Do Quynh Chi and Di van den Broek, "Wildcat Strikes."

50. For examples of such organizations in Hồ Chí Minh City, see Joseph Hannah, "Local Non-government Organizations in Vietnam: Development, Civil Society and State-Society Relations" (PhD diss., University of Washington, 2007), 184–90.

51. Examples are the open letter of March 27, 2006 from Thích Quảng Độ, a well-known leader of the Unified Buddhist Church of Vietnam [Giáo Hội Phật Giáo Việt Nam Thống Nhất] living in Hồ Chí Minh City, *Thông Luận* [Thorough Discussion], April 2006, 18–19; and statements by regime critics in Vietnam: Đỗ Nam Hải, Nguyễn Chính Kết, Trần Anh Kim, and Nguyễn Phong, "Kháng thư số 01 của Liên minh Dân chủ Nhân quyền Việt Nam" [Protest Letter Number 1 of the Democracy and Human Rights Alliance of Vietnam], November 24, 2006, *Tự Do Ngôn Luận* [Free Speech], accessed July 10, 2009, http://www.tdngonluan.com/tailieu/tl_lmdcnq_khangthu_01 .htm; Huỳnh Việt Lang (also known as Huỳnh Nguyên Đạo), "Anh Chị Em Cần Lao Dấn Bước" [Brothers and Sisters Need to Take the Plunge], February 14, 2006, Đảng Dân Chủ Nhân Dân [People's Democratic Party], accessed February 23, 2007, http://www.freewebs.com/dangdanchunhandan/.

52. A study of humor among factory workers provides some unusual evidence of such shared conditions and desires: Nghiem Lien Huong, "Jokes in a Garment Workshop in Hà Nội: How Does Humour Foster the Perception of Community in Social Movements," *International Review of Social History* 52, supplement issue (2007): 209–23.

53. This is well elaborated in the article by Siu and Chen, "Strike Wave," 8–10.

54. This is a theme in Trần Ngọc Angie, *Ties That Bind*, esp. chaps. 5 and 6.

55. "Nêu một vụ việc đình công xảy ra vào năm 2013 và bình luận về tính hợp pháp của cuộc đình công đó" [A Commentary to Consider Whether a Strike in 2013 Is Lawful], January 31, 2015, Trường Đại Học Luật Hà Nội [Hà Nội College of Law], accessed April 26, 2017, http://www.dhluathn.com/2015/02/neu-mot-vu-viec-inh-cong -xay-ra-vao-nam.html.

56. Dương Bội Ngọc, "Hậu quả từ vi phạm nghiêm trọng Luật Lao động" [Consequences of Serious Violations of the Labor Law], December 21, 2006, *Lao Động*, accessed January 3, 2007, http://www.laodong.com.vn/Home/congdoan/tranhchapld /2006/12/16021.laodong.

57. Ngọc Nga, "Cực lắm đời công nhân!" [Workers' Desperate Lives!], October 20, 2007, *Tuổi Trẻ*, accessed April 4, 2008, http://www.tuoitre.com.vn/Tianyon2/Index.aspx ?ArticleID=225252 &ChannelID=118.

58. Dương Minh Đức, "Công nhân đình công đòi nâng lương và thưởng tết" [Striking Workers Demand Higher Wage and New Year Bonus], February 3, 2007, *Lao Động*, accessed February 15, 2007, http://www.laodong.com.vn/Home/congdoan /tranhchapld /2007/2/22437.laodong.

59. My count of strikes for which I have information and Chi Do Quynh, "Coordination among Strikes," 1.

60. D. M. Đức and Q. Minh, "Người lao động đình công đòi tăng lương tối thiểu tại các doanh nghiệp FDI ở TP.Hồ Chí Minh" [Striking Laborers Demand Higher Minimum Wages at Foreign-Invested Enterprises in Hồ Chí Minh City], January 4, 2006, *Lao Động*, accessed May 4, 2006, http://www.laodong.com.vn/pls/bld/folder$ .view_ item_detail(146952).

61. Trần Ngọc Angie, *Ties That Bind*, 207–10, 240–48.

62. Dương Minh Đức, "Gần 18.000 công nhân đình công, đòi nâng lương tối thiểu" [Nearly 18,000 Workers Strike for Higher Minimum Wage], December 29, 2005, *Lao Động*, accessed May 4, 2006, http://www.laodong.com.vn/pls/bld/folder$

.view_item_detail(146579); Dương Minh Đức, "Hơn 5.000 công nhân đình công đòi nâng lương tối thiểu" [More Than 5,000 Laborers Strike for Higher Minimum Wage], December 30, 2005, *Lao Động*, accessed May 4, 2006, http://www.laodong.com .vn/pls/bld/folder$.view_item_detail(146723). For additional details about the strike, see Angie Ngọc Trần, "Alternatives to the 'Race to the Bottom' in Vietnam: Minimum Wage Strikes and Their Aftermath," *Labor Studies Journal* 32 (December 2007): 435–38.

63. Lê Thanh Hà, "Đình công và quan hệ lao động ở Việt Nam" [Strikes and Labor Relations in Vietnam], *Nghiên cứu Kinh tế* [Economics Research], no. 362 (July 2008): 58; Chi Do Quynh, "Coordination among Strikes," 1.

64. For more on this last point, see the analysis by Dương Minh Đức, "Lương, thưởng chưa tương xứng."

65. Vĩnh Tùng, "Làm gì để hạn chế tranh chấp" summarizes the involvement of local officials in resolving strikes during 1995–2000. For more recent evidence, see Simon Clarke, "The Changing Character of Strikes in Vietnam," *Post-Communist Economies* 18 (September 2006): 350–54; Mark Anner and Xiangmin Liu, "Harmonious Unions and Rebellious Workers: A Study of Wildcat Strikes in Vietnam," *ILR Review* 69 (January 2016): 3–28.

66. Ban Bí Thư, Ban Chấp hành Trung Ương, Đảng Cộng Sản, Việt Nam [Secretariat, Central Executive Committee, VCP], Chỉ thị [Instruction] 22-CT/TW, Hà Nội, June 5, 2008.

67. For examples, see Bảo Chân, "Thực hiện Bộ luật Lao động tại Khánh Hòa" [Implementing the Labor Code in Khánh Hòa], February 9, 2007, *Lao Động*, accessed February 15, 2007, http://www.laodong.com.vn/Home/congdoan/tranhchapld /2007/2 /23357.laodong; MoLISA findings cited in Thanh Van, "Strikes Double in 2011"; Trần Ngọc Angie, *Ties That Bind*, 117.

68. Phần Đấu, "Đình công 6 lần/năm tại 1 doanh nghiệp" [Six Strikes in One Year at an Enterprise], April 7, 2008, *Lao Động*, accessed April 8, 2008, http://www.laodong .com.vn/Home/congdoan/2008/4/83477.laodong.

69. Hà Dịu, "Huê Phong: Gần 4.000 công nhân đã quay lại làm việc" [Huê Phong: Nearly 4,000 Laborers Returned to Work], May 5, 2008, Vietnam.net, accessed May 7, 2008, http://www.vietnamnet.vn/xahoi/2008/05/781502/.

70. Quoted in Mai Hương and Quý Lâm, "Vì sao công nhân đình công triền miên?" [Why Do Workers Strike Incessantly?], April 15, 2008, *Sài Gòn Giải Phóng*, accessed May 8, 2008, http://www.sggp.org.vn/vi-sao-cong-nhan-dinh-cong-trien-mien-285633 .html. The same account indicates that the company's director, although claiming to be Vietnamese, was actually from China. For more about the Huê Phong company and labor protests there, see Trần Ngọc Angie, *Ties That Bind*, 239–40, 307–10.

71. Đỗ Sơn, "Bắc Giang: Hơn 100 công nhân bị sa thải vô cớ" [In Bắc Giang Province, over 100 Workers Fired Without Cause], January 6, 2006, ViệtBáo [Việt News], accessed May 7, 2008, http://vietbao.vn/Xa-hoi/Bac-Giang-Hon-100-cong -nhan-may-bi-sa-thai-vo-co/70035915/157/; Đỗ Văn and Chí Tùng, "Kết thúc thắng lợi sau 12 ngày đình công" [Victory after a 12-Day Strike], May 25, 2005, *Lao Động*, accessed May 7, 2008, http://www1.laodong.com.vn/pls/bld/display$.htnoidung (36,130595).

72. Lê Tuyết, "Vụ 900 CN ngừng việc đòi quyền đi vệ sinh" [900 Workers Stop Work, Want the Right to Go to the Toilet], March 14, 2014, *Lao Động*, accessed April 14, 2017, http://laodong.com.vn/cong-doan/vu-900-cn-ngung-viec-doi-quyen-di-ve-sinh -cty-khang-dinh-lam-dung-luat-186144.bld.

73. Viet Labor, "About Viet Labor," April 13, 2015, Lao Động Việt [Viet Labor], accessed April 14, 2017, https://laodongviet2.files.wordpress.com/2015/04/about-vl-eng -free-viet-labor-federation-ldv-20150414.pdf. The two groups in 2006 were Công Đoàn Độc Lập Việt Nam [Independent Trade Union of Vietnam, ITUV] and Hiệp Hội Đoàn Kết Công-Nông [United Workers-Farmers Association]. In 2014, the Phong trào Lao động Việt Nam [Vietnam Labor Movement] and ITUV joined with another organization established in Poland in late 2006, Ủy ban Bảo vệ Người Lao động Việt Nam [Committee to Protect Vietnamese Workers], to form Liên đoàn Lao động Việt Tự do [Free Viet Labor Federation, also called Viet Labor]. Hiệp Hội Đoàn Kết Công-Nông, Bản Tuyên Bố [Announcement], October 30, 2006, *Tự Do Ngôn Luận*, accessed February 23, 2007, http://www.tdngonluan.com/tailieu.htm; Trần Ngọc Thành, "TPP & 'Công đoàn độc lập Việt Nam'" [TPP (Trans-Pacific Partnership) and "Independent Trade Unions in Vietnam"], June 14, 2015, *Tự Do Ngôn Luận*, July 1, 2015, 26–29.

74. Phạm Linh, Hiệp Hội Đoàn Kết Công-Nông [United Workers-Farmers Association], "Ủng Hộ cuộc Khiếu Kiện của Dân Oan" [Support the Plea for Justice by Victims of Injustice], July 15, 2007, *Điện Thư* [Electronic Letter], no. 65 (July 2007): 4–5; "Viet Nam: Farmers' Union Crushed," May 2007, Amnesty International, accessed May 2, 2007, http://web.amnesty.org/appeals/index/vnm-010507-wwa-eng; Nguyễn Văn Huy, "Hai vụ án thô bạo đáng lưu ý" [Two Cases of Brutality Deserving Attention], *Thông Luận*, February 2009, 13–14.

75. Party-state newspapers, Vietnamese bloggers, and international news outlets wrote about Đoàn Huy Chương (Nguyễn Tấn Hoành), his companions, their activities, and trials. Two items are "Xét xử vụ án phá rối an ninh" [Judgement in the Case Regarding Disturbance of Public Security], October 27, 2010, *Lao Động*, accessed April 6, 2017, http://laodong.com.vn/phap-luat/xet-xu-vu-an-pha-roi-an-ninh-44246 .bld; and Khoa Diễm, "Ba nhà dân chủ ở Trà Vinh sẽ ra tòa không có luật sư" [Three Democracy Advocates in Trà Vinh Will Appear in Court Without Lawyers], January 24, 2011, RFA, accessed May 24, 2011, http://www.rfa.org/vietnamese/Human Rights/three-labor-activists-going-to-trial-without-lawyers-kdiem-01242011203947 .html.

76. One incident was reported by Dương Bội Ngọc, "Quan hệ lao động ngày càng rạn nứt" [Labor Relations Becoming More Fractured], April 4, 2007, *Lao Động*, accessed April 17, 2007, http://www.laodong.com.vn /Home/congdoan/tranhchapld /2007/4/30521.laodong.

77. The only account I have seen of a few laborers possibly being arrested for striking is in Siu and Chan, "Strike Wave in Vietnam," 16.

78. This has been stated by numerous reports, newspaper articles, and party-state officials. See, for example, "Giải pháp hạn chế đình công" [Addressing Strike Restrictions], May 18, 2006, *Pháp Luật* [Law], accessed October 20, 2006, www.congdoanvn .org.vn; Vũ Thủy, "20 năm qua."

79. Tellingly, officials rarely said, at least in public, that the strikes were "illegal" [*không hợp pháp, không hợp lệ,* or *bất hợp pháp*]. Instead they usually described the strikes as "spontaneous" [*tự phát*].

80. For examples, see Mạnh Quân, "Không thể coi cuộc đình công chưa đúng trình tự, thủ tục là bất hợp pháp" [Strikes That Don't Conform to Procedures Should Not Be Seen as Illegal], March 30, 2006, *Thanh Niên*, accessed April 13, 2006, http://www3.thanhnien.com.vn/Xahoi/2006/3/30/143752.tno; "Đình công và quan hệ lao động ở Việt Nam" [Strikes and Labor Relations in Vietnam], April 19, 2011, MoLISA, accessed April 26, 2017, http://www.molisa.gov.vn/vi/Pages/chitiettin.aspx?IDNews =20884; Tiến Dũng, "Chủ tịch Quốc hội Nguyễn Sinh Hùng" [National Assembly President Nguyễn Sinh Hùng], March 27, 2012, VnExpress, accessed April 9, 2013, http://vnexpress.net/gl/xa-hoi/2012/03/luong-cong-chuc-khong-the-thap-nhu-luong-toi -thieu/; Bảo Duy, "Để đình công đúng luật."

81. Also see Trần Ngọc Angie, *Ties That Bind*, 138, 197, 262.

82. Quốc Hội [National Assembly], "Bộ Luật Lao Động" [Labor Code], June 18, 2012, articles 91 and 92. Inflation was 7 percent in 2013, 4 percent in 2014, and 1 percent in 2015 (World Bank website, accessed May 4, 2017); minimum wages for urban industrial areas rose from 2.35 million *đồng* per month in 2013 to 3.10 million *đồng* per month in 2015 (Trading Economics, accessed May 4, 2017, http://www.tradingeconomics.com/vietnam /minimum-wages).

83. Report from the MoLISA cited by Hà Nam, "Năm 2015, cả nước xảy ra 245 cuộc đình công" [The Nation Had 245 Strikes in 2015], January 1, 2016, Voice of Vietnam, accessed April 12, 2017, http://vov.vn/tin-24h/nam-2015-ca-nuoc-xay-ra-245-cuoc -dinh-cong-464800.vov.

84. Tran Van Minh, "Vietnam Meets Demands to End Strike," April 1, 2015, *St. Louis Post-Dispatch*, accessed April 3, 2015, http://www.stltoday.com/news/vietnam-meets -demands-to-end-strike-in-nike-adidas-factory/article_ee8c49e0-8888-5549-91e4 -0df140036177.html#.

85. Chính phủ [Government (of Vietnam)], "Báo Cáo: Về quy định tại Điều 60 Luật Bảo hiểm xã hội năm 2014 về bảo hiểm xã hội một lần" [Report Regarding Lump Sum in Article 60 of the 2014 Social Insurance Law], số 226/BC-CP [Number 226/BC-CP], May 19, 2015, 3–4. In 2007–14, the report said, 80 percent of workers chose to receive their social insurance benefits as lump sum payments; only 20 percent opted for a monthly pension after reaching retirement age (2).

86. Quốc Hội, "Nghị Quyết: Về việc thực hiện chính sách hưởng Bảo Hiểm Xã Hội một lần đối với người lao động" [Resolution Regarding Implementing a Policy for Lump Sum Social Insurance Benefits to Laborers], số 93/2015/QH13 [No. 93/2015/ QH13], June 22, 2015.

87. Hồng Thanh and Vũ Hoàng Long, "Quốc hội nghe trình sáu dự án luật" [National Assembly Hears Six Reports on Draft Legislation], June 1, 2006, *Nhân Dân* [People], accessed October 24, 2006, http://www.nhandan.com.vn/tinbai/?top=37&sub=50&Article =63688.

88. Jonathan Stromseth, "Reform and Response in Vietnam: State-Society Relations and the Changing Political Economy" (PhD diss., Columbia University, 1998), 207–26.

89. For samples of these discussions, see Văn Tiến, "Công nhân quá sức chịu đựng mới đình công" [Workers Put Up with More Than They Can Endure before Striking], May 4, 2006, Vietnam.net, accessed March 22, 2007, http://www.vietnamnet.vn/xahoi/laodong/2006/05/567168/; "Nơi chưa có công đoàn thì ai lãnh đạo đình công?" [Who Leads Strikes Where No Union Exists?], August 11, 2006, *Lao Động*, accessed October 20, 2006, http://www. congdoanvn.org.vn/printdocument.asp?MessageID =674; Đ. Bình and N. Linh, "Người lao động được cử ban đại diện để tổ chức đình công" [Workers' Representatives May Organize Strikes], September 27, 2006, *Tuổi Trẻ*, accessed September 28, 2006, http://www.tuoitre.com.vn/Tianyon/Index.aspx?ArticleID=164055&ChannelID=3.

90. Quốc Hội, "Luật sửa đổi, bổ sung một số điều của Bộ Luật lao động" [Revised Law and Amendments for the Labor Code], November 19, 2006, chapter 14, article 172a.

91. For some news coverage of the discussions, see "Không đình công khi có tranh chấp lao động về quyền?" [No Strike When a Labor Conflict Is about Rights?], *Đại Đoàn Kết* [Great Unity], August 11, 2006, 1, 6; "Hội nghị Quốc Hội" [National Assembly Conference], *Pháp Luật*, August 11, 2006, 3; "Chỉ được đình công khi chủ không chấp hành cách giải quyết của cơ quan Nhà nước" [Strikes Permitted Only When Employer Does Not Abide by State Offices' Solutions], September 27, 2006, *Tiền Phong* [Vanguard], accessed September 28, 2006, http://www.tien phongonline.com.vn/Tianyon/Index.aspx?ArticleID=61546&ChannelID=2.

92. Quốc Hội, "Luật sửa đổi," chapter 14, article 173.

93. Quốc Hội, "Bộ Luật Lao Động" [Labor Code], June 18, 2012, chapter 14, articles 209 and 210. For some explanations about these changes, see Trần Ngọc Angie, *Ties That Bind*, 115–19; Do Quynh Chi, "Employee Participation in Vietnam" (Dialogue Working Paper No. 42, International Labour Organization, Geneva, 2012), 23–25.

2. Land

1. Of the twenty-three cases depicted in documents and verbal accounts given to us in two visits to the park during September and October 2012, thirteen (57 percent) were about families evicted from or forced to sell their farms or the low compensation they received for their farms. Usually mixed in were accusations of corruption. Complaints in the other ten cases had to do with pension payments, family reputations, imprisonments, military veteran entitlements, and physically abusive local authorities. Mai Xuân Thưởng park is named for a young Vietnamese opposed to colonial rule killed by French officials in 1887. Nearby is a smaller park with a statue of Lý Tự Trọng—another young man who opposed French rule and was executed in 1931—where some of the people we met also camped. Periodically, police required long-staying park users to leave.

2. Luật Đất Đai Năm 2003 (Đã được sửa đổi, bổ sung năm 2009–2010) [Land Law of 2003, with modifications made in 2009–2010], article 38, clause 1. Similar provisions were included, with more elaboration, in the country's revised land law of 2013, article 61.

3. Data for the amount of land taken from landholders are sparse and somewhat inconsistent. My figures draw on World Bank, *Compulsory Land Acquisition and Voluntary Land Conversion in Vietnam* (Hà Nội: World Bank, 2011), 16; Lê Hiểu, "Về vấn đề chuyển đổi mục đích sử dụng đất nông nghiệp trong quá trình công nghiệp hóa, đô thị hóa" [Regarding the Changing Use of Agricultural Land during Industrialization and Urbanization], *Tạp chí Quản lý Nhà nước* [Journal of State Management], no. 174 (July 2010): 34; Đặng Kim Sơn and Nguyễn Đỗ Anh Tuấn, *Chính sách Đất đai cho phát triển tại Việt Nam: Cơ hội hay Thách thức?* [Land Policy for Development in Vietnam: Opportunity or Challenge?] (Hà Nội: Trung Tâm Tư Vấn Chính Sách Nông Nghiệp, 2011), 63. The number for farming people affected is based on the figure in Lê Hiểu, "Về vấn đề," 35, that every hectare no longer farmed displaces thirteen workers [*người lao động*]. Some sources say the figure is eleven or twelve workers displaced; others say more.

4. "Tố cáo khiếu nại" [Denunciation Complaint], May 2, 2012, BBC, accessed July 19, 2012, www.bbc.co.uk/vietnamese/vietnam/2012/05/120502_land_dispute_conference .shtml; Nguyễn Tấn Phát, "Những bất cập hiện nay của chính sách đất đai và thách thức đối với phát triển tam nông ở Việt Nam" [Land Policy Shortcomings and Challenges for Three-Pronged Agricultural Development in Vietnam], *Nghiên Cứu Kinh Tế* [Economic Research], no. 366 (November 2008): 65–66; Việt Lê Quân, "Câu hỏi sau vụ chống cưỡng chế ở Hải Phòng" [Questions after the Resistance to Coercion in Hải Phòng], January 10, 2012, Vietnam.net, accessed January 13, 2012, http://tuanvietnam .vietnamnet.vn/2012-01-09-cau-hoi-sau-vu-chong-cuong-che-o-hai-phong. For the years 2012–15, I collected, with the gracious help of Andrew Wells-Dang, figures for complaints and petitions submitted to particular government agencies in some years or fractions of years but we could find no government-wide number for any year or for the four-year period.

5. I could not find figures for the number of demonstrations for any year or period. These data probably exist in the Ministry of Public Security [Bộ Công An] but are not available to outside researchers.

6. I excluded land protests in midland and mountainous areas of the country and those that were primarily extensions of disputes among members of extended families.

7. "Đơn Khiếu Nại: V/v Bị thu hồi đất tại Khu Công Nghiệp Hố Nai" [Written Complaint: Suffering Land Retrieval at the Hố Nai Industrial Zone], March 15, 2005, Tiếng Dân Kêu [Lament of the People], accessed December 1, 2006, http://www.tieng-dankeu.net/.

8. Tạ Nguyên, "Đồng Nai: huyện Trảng Bom giải 'bài toán' đối với hộ bị thu hồi đất" [Đồng Nai province: Trảng Bom District Untangling "Dilemmas" for Households Losing their Land], July 10, 2009, Bộ Tài Nguyên và Môi Trường [MoNRE], accessed April 30, 2013, http://www.monre.gov.vn/v35/default.aspx?tabid=428&cateID =4&id=68576&code=6QZCN68576.

9. Thành Nguyên, "Bố trí tái định cư" [Preparing Resettlement Sites], July 29, 2011, *Người Cao Tuổi* [Elderly People], accessed April 30, 2013, http://nguoicaotuoi.org.vn/story .aspx?id=6360&lang=vn&zone=7&zoneparent=0.

10. Đoan Trang, "Nguyện vọng xin lại đất canh tác của bà con là chính đáng" [People Have Legitimate Hopes of Retrieving Their Fields], *Người Lao Động* [Worker],

October 18, 2000, 7; "Mất hàng trăm, nghìn hecta đất nhưng không thấy ai bị bỏ tù" [Hundreds, Thousands of Hectares Lost but No One Jailed], August 11, 2005, *Tuổi Trẻ* [Youth], accessed April 30, 2013, http://tuoitre.vn/Chinh-tri-Xa-hoi/93067/Mat-hang -tram-nghin-hecta-dat-nhung-khong-thay-ai-bi-bo-tu.html.

11. "Dân Hố Nai về Sài Gòn biểu tình đòi tài sản bị nhà nước cướp đoạt" [Demonstrating in Sài Gòn, People of Hố Nai Demand Property that the State Seized], August 3, 2009, Người Việt [Vietnamese People], accessed August 10, 2009, http://www .nguoi-viet.com/absolutenm/anmviewer.asp?a=99086&z=2.

12. Tạ Nguyên, "Đồng Nai"; Thành Nguyên, "Viết tiếp bài Bố trí tái định cư" [Continuing the Article: Preparing Resettlement Sites], March 2, 2012, *Người Cao Tuổi*, accessed April 30, 2012, http://nguoicaotuoi.org.vn/story.aspx?id=7365&lang=vn&zone =7&zoneparent=0.

13. "Quyết Định của Chủ tịch Ủy ban Nhân dân Thành phố Hồ Chí Minh" [Decision of the Chairman of the People's Committee, Hồ Chí Minh City], June 27, 2002, Lê Hiền Đức, accessed May 17, 2013, http://lehienduc2013.blogspot.com/2013/05/tiep -theo-vu-quan-9-cuop-at-trai-phap.html; "Quận 9, khu công nghệ cao" [District 9, High-Tech Industrial Zone], March 12, 2008, Mạng Ý Kiến [Opinion Net], accessed March 19, 2008, http://ykien0711.blogvis.com/2008/03/12/qu%e1%ba%adn-9-khu -cong-ngh%e1%bb%87-cao-anh-minh-k%e1%bb%83-chuy%e1%bb%87n -v%e1%bb%a3-anh-b%e1%bb%8b-b%e1%ba%aft/; Điếu Cày and Chông Tre, "Khi những công dân chống tham nhũng bị tham nhũng đàn áp" [When the Corrupt Repress Citizens Resisting Corruption], March 12, 2008, *Thông Luận* [Thorough Discussion], accessed March 19, 2008, www.thongluan.org/vn/modules.php?name=News&file =article&sid=2614.

14. Trà Mi, "Công an bắt giữ nhiều người khiếu kiện đất đai ở quận 9" [Police Detain Many Appealing for Justice Regarding District 9 Land], March 14, 2008, RFA, accessed March 19, 2008, www.rfa.org/vietnamese/in_depth/2008/03/14/ People_ Complain_About_Land_Seizures_put_in_jail_part1_TMi/; Điếu Cày and Chông Tre, "Khi những công dân." "Appeal for justice" is a brief translation of *khiếu kiện*. A fuller translation, for which I'm grateful to Nguyễn Điền, could be "appeal for justice or redress," or "sue for justice and/or redress."

15. "Họ là những người dũng cảm chống tham nhũng" [They're the Valiant People Fighting Corruption], March 6, 2008, Tiếng nói Dân chủ [Voice of Democracy], accessed March 11, 2008, www.ptdcvn.org/modules.php?name=News&file=article&sid =2223#.

16. This paragraph is based on reports by demonstrators themselves, sympathetic bloggers, a government document, and various news accounts. Among the sources are Viện Kiểm Sát Nhân Dân Quận 9 [People's Control Office, District 9], "Cáo Trạng" [Indictment], December 24, 2007, Hoa be, accessed October 5, 2011, http://hoabe .multiply.com/journal/item/31/31?&show_interstitial=1&u=%2Fjournal%2Fitem; "Chị Nguyễn Thị Mỹ Vân, một trong 3 người phụ nữ bị cáo" [Nguyễn Thị Mỹ Vân, One of Three Female Defendants], January 19, 2008, Hoa be, accessed October 5, 2011, http:// hoabe.multiply.com/journal/item/245/245; "Công an đã tiến hành bắt hàng loạt người dân liên quan đến vụ ngày 22-11-2007" [Security Police Carried Out Duties when Detaining Masses of People Connected to the November 22, 2007 Event], March 2, 2008,

Tiếng nói Dân chủ, accessed March 11, 2008, www.ptdcvn.org/modules.php?name =News&file=article&sid=2207#; "Đi tìm hiểu hoàn cảnh nhà anh Minh chị Trang" [Studying the Circumstances of Minh and Trang's Family], February 26, 2008, Tiếng nói Dân chủ, accessed March 11, 2008, www.ptdcvn.org/modules.php?name=News&file =article&sid=2188#.

17. "Quận 9, TP.Hồ Chí Minh: Những vụ cưỡng chế dân để lấy đất lạ lùng" [District 9, Hồ Chí Minh City: Instances of Unprecedented Coercion to Seize Land], June 3 and 5, 2009, *Đại Đoàn Kết* [Great Unity], June 15, 2009, http://baodaidoanket.net/ddk /mdNews.ddk?id=17067 and http://baodaidoanket.net/ddk/mdNews.ddk?id=17130; Trà Mi, "Công an bắt giữ nhiều người"; Điếu Cày and Chông Tre, "Khi những công dân"; Võ Đắc Danh, "Trên đồng bưng Sáu Xã" [On Six Villages' Hiding Grounds], June 2008, 2013, Đào Hiếu, accessed June 26, 2013, http://daohieu.wordpress.com /category/th%E1%BB%9Di-s%E1%BB%B1-tren-d%E1%BB%93ng-b%C6%B0ng-sau -xa. Accounts in party-state sources confirming aspects of residents' charges about authorities violating laws and regulations include "Cty 'gia đình' thâu tóm ... khu công nghệ?" ["Family" Company Seizing ... Industrial Zone?], April 2, 2008, *Lao Động* [Labor], accessed October 22, 2011, http://laodong.com.vn/Home/Cty-gia-dinh-thau -tom-khu-cong-nghe/201110/82834.laodong; "Chính quyền làm sai" [Authorities' Wrongdoings], April 21, 2008, *Lao Động*, accessed April 21, 2008, http://www.laodong .com.vn/Home/phapluat/2008/4/85536.laodong; Nhóm PV Pháp Luật [Law Journalist Group], "Thu hồi đất của dân không đúng luật" [Unlawful Confiscation of People's Land], June 17, 2009, MoNRE, accessed July 25, 2013, www.monre.gov.vn/v35/default .aspx?tabid=428&cateID=4&id=67079&code=CZ0YR67079; "Ông phó chủ tịch khỏa lấp sai phạm bằng cách nào?" [How Did a Vice-Chairman Cover Up Wrongs?], October 8, 2009, *Đại Đoàn Kết*, accessed July 25, 2013, http://www.daidoanket.vn/index.aspx? Menu=1390&chitiet=3099&Style=1.

18. "Công an đã tiến hành"; Bùi Trúc Linh, "Viết cho những người dân Q. 9 (TpHCM) đang bị bắt vì chống tham nhũng" [Writing for the District 9 (Hồ Chí Minh City) People Arrested for Fighting Corruption], March 9, 2008, Tiếng nói Dân chủ, accessed March 11, 2008, www.ptdcvn.org/modules.php?name=News&file=article&sid =2234#.

19. Võ Đắc Danh, "Trên đồng bưng Sáu Xã"; Bùi Trúc Linh, "Viết cho những người dân Q. 9." Among additional accounts regarding compensation are "Dân khiếu kiện 'gây rối trật tự'" [Appeal for Justice People "Cause Disorder"], March 16, 2008, BBC, accessed March 19, 2008, www.bbc.co.uk/vietnamese/vietnam/story/2008 /03/080314_khieukien_quan9.shtml; Thép Bút, "Đã sai lại càn quấy" [Breaching and Rebelling], 2009, Đào Hiếu, accessed March 7, 2013, http://daohieu.wordpress.com /category/th%E1%BB%9Di-s%E1%BB%B1-c%C6%B0%E1%BB%9Bp-d%E1%BA %A5t/.

20. Võ Đắc Danh, "Trên đồng bưng Sáu Xã"; Thép Bút, "Đã sai lại"; Nguyễn Xuân Ngữ, "Đơn kêu oan của một cựu chiến binh vì bị cưỡng chế thu hồi đất sai pháp luật" [A Veteran Files Protest against Illegal Forced Repossession of Land], March 10, 2013, TTNGBT, accessed May 21, 2013, http://ttngbt.wordpress.com/2013/04/22/don-keu -oan-cua-mot-cuu-chien-binh-vi-bi-cuong-che-thu-hoi-dat-sai-phap-luat/.

21. "Giải thích của chính quyền quận 9 về các khiếu kiện của dân oan" [District 9 Authorities' Explanation of Pleas from Victims of Injustice], March 15, 2008, RFA, accessed March 19, 2008, www.rfa.org/vietnamese/in_depth/2008/03/15/People_Complain_ About_Land_Seizures_put_in_jail_part2_TMi/; Ủy Ban Nhân Dân Thành Phố Hồ Chí Minh [People's Committee, Hồ Chí Minh City], "Về xử lý đơn tố cáo của ông Nguyễn Xuân Ngữ, Quận 9" [Settling Nguyễn Xuân Ngữ's Denunciation, District 9], January 19, 2011 (on file with author).

22. For an interview with the lawyer, Lê Trần Luật, see "Luật sư kiện công an ngăn cản biện hộ cho dân oan" [Attorney Sues Security Police for Hindering Defense of Victims of Injustice], June 30, 2008, RFA, accessed August 1, 2008, www.rfa.org/vietnamese/in_depth/lawyer_sues_police_for_blocking_disposition_a_first_case_MLAm-06302008172852.html.

23. "Đơn Tố Cáo" [Denunciation], April 4, 2013, Lê Hiền Đức, accessed May 3, 2013, http://lehienduc2013.blogspot.com/2013/04/cong-dan-quan-9-to-cao-le-thanh-hai.html.

24. "Văn phòng luật sư tư vấn sai pháp luật" [Law Office Gave Wrong Advice about Law], *Báo Xây Dựng* [Construction News], July 12, 2009, Luật Việt [Vietnamese Law], accessed March 11, 2012, http://www.luatviet.org/Home/tin-tuc-phap-luat/tin-trong-nuoc/2009/8235/Van-phong-luat-su-tu-van-sai-phap-luat.aspx; Duy Tuấn, "Phó chủ tịch Hà Nội 'đề nghị xử lý' một luật sư" [Hà Nội Vice Chairman "Suggests Taking Measures" Regarding a Lawyer], January 4, 2010, Vietnam.net, accessed January 18, 2010, http://www.vietnamnet.vn/bandocviet/theodauthu/201001/Pho-Chu-tich-Ha-Noi-de-nghi-xu-ly-mot-luat-su-887607/; Duy Tuấn and Thu Hương, "Tiền đền bù 1m2 đất chỉ mua được 2 kg thit bò" [Compensation for One Square Meter of Land Can Buy Only 2 Kilos of Beef], January 6, 2010, Vietnam.net, accessed January 18, 2010, www.vietnamnet.vn/bandocviet/theodauthu/201001/Tien-den-bu-1m2-dat-chi-mua-duoc-2kg-thit-bo-888016/. HUD's Vietnamese name is Tổng Công Ty Đầu Tư Phát Triển Nhà và Đô Thị.

25. "Hà Nội: 5/1/2010: Cưỡng chế GPMB" [Hà Nội, January 5, 2010: Forced Land Clearing], December 26, 2009, *Báo Xây Dựng*, accessed March 11, 2012, http://kientruc.vn/tin_trong_nuoc/ha-noi-5-1-2010-cuong-che-gpmb-thu-hoi-dat-xay-dung-khu-do-thi-moi-tay-nam-ho-linh-dam/14658.html; Duy Tuấn and Thu Hương, "Tiền đền bù."

26. Nguyễn Trọng Ty, Luật sư [Attorney], Kính gửi: Ban Biên Tập *Báo An Ninh Thủ Đô* [Letter to Editorial Board, Capital Security News], July 7, 2009 (on file with author); Duy Tuấn and Thu Hương, "Thuyết phục, 'ép' dân không được thì cưỡng chế" [If Persuading and "Squeezing" People Fails, Use Coercion], January 7, 2010, Vietnam.net, accessed January 18, 2010, http://www.vietnamnet.vn/bandocviet/theodauthu/201001/Thuyet-phuc-ep-dan-khong-duoc-thi-cuong-che-888224/; "Khiếu kiện tại dự án khu đô thị tây nam Linh Đàm" [Appeals for Justice at the Southwest Linh Đàm Urban Project], June 29, 2009, *Hà Nội Mới* [New Hà Nội], accessed March 11, 2012, http://timnhadat.com/forum/Default.aspx?g=posts&m=3770.

27. Duy Tuấn and Thu Hương, "Thuyết phục"; Nguyễn Trọng Ty, Kính gửi; Duy Tuấn, "Phó chủ tịch Hà Nội"; T. Chính, "Văn phòng luật sư tư vấn sai luật" [Law Office Gave Wrong Advice about Statute], June 26, 2009, *An Ninh Thủ Đô* [Security in

the Capital], accessed April 11, 2012, www.anninhthudo.vn/An-ninh-doi-song/Van
-phong-Luat-su-tu-van-sai-luat/351179.antd.

28. Duy Tuấn and Thu Hương, "Thuyết phục."

29. Duy Tuấn and Thu Hương, "Tiền đền bù"; Duy Tuấn and Thu Hương,
"Thuyết phục"; Duy Tuấn, "Cám cảnh làng rau ngày cận tết" [The Grim Scene in
Vegetable Village on the Eve of Tet], January 27, 2010, Diễn đàn Lịch sử Việt Nam
[Vietnam History Forum], accessed April 9, 2012, http://lichsuvn.info/forum/showthread
.php?t=10465.

30. Duy Tuấn and Thu Hương, "Tiền đền bù."

31. Duy Tuấn and Thu Hương, "Thuyết phục."

32. "Hà Nội: 5/1/2010"; Duy Tuấn and Thu Hương, "Thuyết phục"; Duy Tuấn,
"Không có tên trong quyết định vẫn bị thu hồi đất" [Even Those Not Listed in the Resolution Had Their Land Taken], January 28, 2010, ViệtBáo [Viet News], accessed
March 11, 2012, http://vietbao.vn/Xa-hoi/Khong-co-ten-trong-quyet-dinh-van-bi-thu
-hoi-dat/20891915/126/.

33. Two years later, in Hải Phòng province in northern Vietnam, families fighting to
retain land being taken from them actually did make a landmine that wounded several
policemen.

34. See articles from RFA reprinted in *Tự Do Ngôn Luận* [Free Speech], March 15,
2011, 12–14. In December 2008, a villager in Thái Bình province objecting to land being taken from his family reportedly doused himself and a subdistrict chairman with
gasoline. Before he could strike a match, other people intervened (document given to
me by a protester in Mai Xuân Thưởng park, written by the man's attorney, Đặng
Ngọc Phúc, "Bào chữa bảo vệ quyền, lợi ích hợp pháp cuả anh Trần Văn Sự" [Protect-
ing the Legal Rights and Interests of Trần Văn Sự], May 15, 2009, 2.

35. This paragraph is based on comments villagers made to journalists and my conversations in Hà Nội during September and October 2012 with some demonstrating
villagers, a lawyer, a civil society advocate, and a researcher.

36. This and several other aspects of the stance of villagers resonates with the findings by Nguyen Van Suu, "The Politics of Land: Inequality in Land Access and Local
Conflicts in the Red River Delta since Decollectivization," in *Social Inequality in Vietnam and the Challenges to Reform*, ed. Philip Taylor (Singapore: Institute of Southeast
Asian Studies, 2004), 285–87.

37. Bằng A villagers saying this are quoted in Duy Tuấn and Thu Hương, "Tiền
đền bù." The written complaint from Phú Sơn households in 2005 cited earlier ("Đơn
Khiếu Nại") indicated that turning over their land "for the benefit and welfare of the
public" would be different from surrendering their land to benefit the "profit and self-
interest" of individuals.

38. "*Tôi ghét nhà nước, tôi ghét đảng, tôi ghét đất nước, tôi ghét hết.*" Another exception is the passage quoted earlier from an April 2013 letter by some District 9 residents.

39. Sources for this paragraph are primarily Trung Dinh Dang, "Post-1975 Land
Reform in Southern Vietnam: How Local Actions and Responses Affected National
Land Policy," *Journal of Vietnamese Studies* 5 (Fall 2010): 92–96; Benedict J. Tria Kerkvliet, "Rural Society and State Relations," in *Vietnam's Rural Transformation*, ed. Benedict J. Tria Kerkvliet and Doug J. Porter (Boulder, CO: Westview Press, 1995), 74–80.

40. *Đại Đoàn Kết*, April 10–16, 1993, 6; *Nông Dân Việt Nam* [Vietnamese Peasant], August 1993, 11; Ban Chấp Hành Trung Ương [Central Executive Committee (of the VCP)], "Báo Cáo tình hình tranh chấp ruộng đất ở nông thôn hiện nay" [Report: Situation in the Countryside Regarding Conflicts over Agricultural Land], September 27, 1990 (on file with author).

41. This and the following discussion of rightful resistance draw on Kevin J. O'Brien and Lianjiang Li, *Rightful Resistance in Rural China* (Cambridge: Cambridge University Press, 2006), esp. 1–24, 42–49, 54–63, 67–69.

42. Two other studies notice similarities and difference between land protests in contemporary Vietnam and rightful resistance: Danielle Labbé, *Land Politics and Livelihoods on the Margins of Hanoi, 1920–2010* (Vancouver: University of British Columbia Press, 2014), 147–52; and Nguyen Thi Thanh Binh, "Multiple Reactions to Land Confiscations in a Hanoi Peri-urban Village," *Southeast Asian Studies* 6 (April 2017): 99, 103–104, 112. Also resonating with some of the Vietnamese protesters' claims to justice and fairness are Erik Harms's findings in "Social Demolition: Creative Destruction and the Production of Value in Vietnamese Land Clearances," in *State, Society and the Market in Contemporary Vietnam*, ed. Hue-Tam Ho Tai and Mark Sidel (London: Routledge, 2013), 60–68.

43. This summary draws on dozens of sources. To get an overview of people's demands and the centrality of land, see the words from a sampling of their banners and posters: "Nội dung những biểu ngữ khiếu kiện" [Content of Appeal for Justice Banners], July 2007, Tiếng Dân Kêu, accessed July 20, 2007, http://www.tiengdankeu.net/.

44. "Nông dân vẫn tập trung khiếu kiện" [Peasants Keep Appealing for Justice], July 18, 2007, BBC, accessed July 19, 2007, http://www.bbc.co.uk/vietnamese/vietnam/ story/2007/07/070718_viet_protests.shtml.

45. Examples are cited in written accusations by demonstrator Lư Thị Thu Duyên, "Đơn Tố Cáo" [Denunciation], July 26, 2007, Đối Thoại [Dialogue], accessed August 2, 2007, www.doi-thoai.com/baimoiđđ_350.html; and a statement signed by fifty-seven protesters from seven provinces, Đơn Thỉnh Nguyện [Petition], July 7, 2007, Mạng Ý Kiến, accessed July 12, 2007, http://ykien.net/blog/?p=1865.

46. "Dân chúng Tiền Giang kéo về biểu tình trước văn phòng II Quốc Hội" [Tiền Giang People Flock to Demonstration at National Assembly Office II], June 28, 2007, RFA, accessed July 2, 2007, http://www.rfa.org/vietnamese/in_depth/2007/06/28/ Land_claimants_from_TienGiang_have_demonstrated_in_HCMcity/; "Phỏng vấn chị Cao Quế Hoa, đại diện đoàn biểu tình của người dân Tiền Giang" [Interview with Cao Quế Hoa, Spokesperson for a Group of Demonstrators from Tiền Giang], July 3, 2007, RFA, accessed December 23, 2010, http://www.rfa.org/vietnamese/vietnam/Anti GovernmentDemonstrationContinueInHCMCT_Khanh-20070703.html; "Tuần lễ thứ 3" [Week 3 (of the protests)], July 9–12, 2007, Tiếng Dân Kêu, accessed July 22, 2007, http://www.tiengdankeu.net/; Lư Thị Thu Duyên, "Tường thuật v/v công an Sài Gòn & Gò Vấp bắt giữ người trái phép" [Recounting Illegal Arrests by Sài Gòn and Gò Vấp Police], September 20, 2007, Mạng Ý Kiến, accessed October 3, 2007, http://ykien.net /blog/?p=2649.

47. "TP HCM biểu tình" [Hồ Chí Minh City Demonstrations], June–July, 2007, Tiếng Dân Kêu, accessed July 22, 2007, http://www.tiengdankeu.net/; "Dân chúng

Tiền Giang kéo về"; "Tuần lễ thứ 4" [Week 4 (of the protests)], July 13–20, Tiếng Dân Kêu, accessed July 22, 2007, http://www.tiengdankeu.net/; "Từ nơi biểu tình ở Sài Gòn" [From the Demonstration Site in Sài Gòn], July 6, 2007, ViệtBáo, accessed November 21, 2007, http://www.vietbao.com/?ppid=45&pid=114&nid=110666.

48. Cao Quế Hoa, Lê Thị Nguyệt, and Nhóm phóng viên người đưa tin sự thật từ thành phố Sài Gòn [Reporters Bringing Truthful News from Sài Gòn], "Đồng bào tỉnh Tiền Giang biểu tình tại Sài Gòn" [Tiền Giang Compatriots Demonstrate in Sài Gòn], July 1, 2007, Tổ quốc Danh dự Trách nhiệm [Duty and Honor to the Homeland], accessed December 18, 2010, www.toquocdanhdutrachnhiem.com/danoantiengiang2 .html; "Một bà cụ dân oan chia sẻ về đoạn trường khiếu kiện" [Elderly Woman, a Victim of Injustice, Shares the Pains of Appealing for Justice], July 10, 2007, Tiếng Dân Kêu, accessed July 22, 2007, http://www.tiengdankeu.net/; "Đại diện giáo hội Phật giáo Việt Nam Thống nhất thăm dân oan" [Representatives of the United Buddhist Church of Vietnam Visit Victims of Injustice], July 13, 2007, Tiếng Dân Kêu, accessed July 22, 2007, www.tiengdankeu.net/; "Thỉnh nguyện thư của một số Tín hữu Công giáo Việt Nam" [Petition of Several Vietnamese Catholics], July 11, 2007, Bản tin từ Huế [News from Huế], accessed June 8, 2013, http://bantintuhue.blogspot.com/2007/07/thnh-nguyn -th-ca-mt-s-tn-hu-cng-gio-vit_22.html.

49. "Phỏng vấn nhà văn Nguyễn Xuân Nghĩa, thành viên mới của Ban điều hành Khối 8406" [Interview with Writer Nguyễn Xuân Nghĩa, New Member of Bloc 8406's Coordinating Committee], August 3, 2007, RFA, accessed August 7, 2007, http://www .rfa.org/vietnamese/in_depth/2007/08/03/WriterNguyenXuanNghiaNewlyAppointe-dExecutiveMemberBloc8406_GMinh/. Among the ad hoc groups were Ủy ban yểm trợ người khiếu kiện [Committee to Assist Those Appealing for Justice] and Nhóm phóng viên người đưa tin sự thật từ thành phố Sài Gòn [Reporters Bringing Truthful News from Sài Gòn]. Regarding Bloc 8406, see chapter 4.

50. Cao Quế Hoa, Lê Thị Nguyệt, and Nhóm phóng viên người đưa tin sự thật từ thành phố Sài Gòn, "Đồng bào"; "Dân chúng Tiền Giang kéo về"; "Sẵn sàng đối thoại với người khiếu kiện" [Ready to Dialogue with People Appealing for Justice], July 12, 2007, BBC, accessed July 12, 2007, http://www.bbc.co.uk/vietnamese/vietnam/story /2007/07/070712_peasant_protest_update.shtml. Cao Quế Hoa and Lê Thị Nguyệt were protesters from Tiền Giang province who occasionally wrote and frequently gave interviews about the events.

51. Lư Thị Thu Duyên, "Đơn Tố Cáo."

52. Đỗ Thông Minh, "Ngọn lửa đấu tranh (I)" [Flame of Struggle, part 1], July 20, 2007, Đàn Chim Việt [Việt Flock], accessed August 24, 2007, www.danchimviet.com /php/modules.php?name=News&file=article&sid=3635; Ngọc Anh, "Tiếp cứu dân oan lên án bạo quyền" [Continue to Rescue Victims of Injustice Condemning Tyranny], June 28, 2007, Mạng Ý Kiến, accessed June 29, 2007, http://ykien.net/blog; "Dân chúng Tiền Giang kéo về."

53. Quang Minh, "Bản tin nhanh từ thủ đô Hà Nội" [Quick News Bulletin from Hà Nội], July 2, 2007, Đối Thoại, accessed July 6, 2007, www.doi-thoai.com/baimoi0707 _034.html; "Hàng trăm nông dân Tánh Linh—Bình Thuận bị áp bức bất công từ quê ra Hà Nội khiếu kiện" [Hundreds of Oppressed, Mistreated Peasants from Tính Linh district, Bình Thuận Province, Go to Hà Nội Appealing for Justice], July 9, 2007, Tiếng

Dân Kêu, accessed July 20, 2007, www.tiengdankeu.net/; Đỗ Thông Minh, "Ngọn lửa đấu tranh."

54. "Dân chúng Tiền Giang kéo về." Also see "Biểu tình của đồng bào Tiền Giang sang ngày thứ 7" [Day 7 of Tiền Giang Compatriots' Demonstrations], June 28, 2007, Mạng Ý Kiến, accessed June 29, 2007, http://ykien.net/blog; Đỗ Thông Minh, "Ngọn lửa đấu tranh."

55. "Tuần lễ thứ 3"; "Tuần lễ thứ 4"; Trần Văn Hải, "Tâm thư 1 người trực tiếp nhìn cảnh CSVN càn quét đồng bào dân oan tại văn phòng Quốc Hội 2" [Heartfelt Letter by a Witness of Vietnamese Communists Mopping Up Victims of Injustice at National Assembly Office 2], July 21, 2007, ViệtBáo, accessed November 21, 2007, www.vietbao .com/?ppid=45&pid=114&nid=111420; "500 người lên TP HCM khiếu kiện về địa phương" [500 People Appealing for Justice in Hồ Chí Minh City], July 20, 2007, Vietnam .net, accessed August 23, 2007, http://www.vietnamnet.vn/xahoi/doisong/2007/07/720475/. Some Vietnamese authorities claimed that the protesters were dispersed peacefully: "Giải quyết khiếu kiện: Phải tôn trọng và lắng nghe dân" [To Resolve Appeals for Justice: Respect and Listen Intently to the People], July 23, 2007, Vietnam.net, accessed August 23, 2007, http://www.vietnamnet.vn/chinhtri/2007/07/721201/.

56. For examples, see Việt Hà, "Hàng trăm nông dân biểu tình tại Hà Nội" [Hundreds of Peasants Demonstrate in Hà Nội], April 10, 2012, RFA, accessed September 16, 2012, http://webwarper.net/ww/www.rfa.org/vietnamese/in_depth/hundred-farmers -protest-in-hanoi-04102012055619.html; "Nhìn lại nhân quyền Việt Nam năm 2014" [Another Look at Human Rights in Vietnam during 2014], January 2015, Dân Làm Báo [Citizen Journalist], accessed August 31, 2015, http://danlambaovn.blogspot.com /2015/01/nhin-lai-nhan-quyen-viet-nam-2014.html.

57. UDIC's actual name is Công ty Đầu tư và Phát triển Đô thị Việt Hưng. The Vietnamese name for Ecopark is Khu Đô Thị Thương Mại Du Lịch Văn Giang. The three Văn Giang subdistricts (*xã*) are Cửu Cao, Phụng Công, and Xuân Quan (sometimes written as Xuân Quang). Among the sources for this and the next two paragraphs are Phạm Viết Đào, "8,2 tỷ USD cho chiếc Bánh Vẽ" [8.2 Billion U.S. Dollars for a Fraudulent Project], April 2012, Dân Làm Báo, accessed June 26, 2013, http:// danlambaovn.blogspot.com.au/2012/04/82-ty-usd-cho-chiec-banh-ve-khu-o-thi .html#more; Nguyễn Nại Dương, "Bão nổi lên rồi từ vùng quê Hưng Yên thân yêu" [Rising Storm from Beloved Hưng Yên], *Tự Do Ngôn Luận*, September 15, 2006, 28–30; "Thông cáo báo chí của nông dân Văn Giang" [Press Release from Văn Giang Peasants], August 10, 2012, Ba Sàm [Gossip], accessed August 15, 2012, http://anhbasam .wordpress.com/2012/08/11/thong-cao-bao-chi-cua-nong-dan-van-giang/; a document from four attorneys helping the Văn Giang villagers: Trần Vũ Hải, Nguyễn Anh Vân, Lưu Vũ Anh, and Hà Huy Sơn, "Kiến nghị số 05 liên quan đến dự án Ecopark-Hưng Yên gửi Thủ Tướng Chính Phủ" [Petition Number 5 to the Prime Minister Regarding the Ecopark-Hưng Yên Project], January 16, 2013, Ba Sàm, accessed January 24, 2013, http://anhbasam.wordpress.com/2013/01/21/1565-kien-nghi-so-05-lien-quan-den-du -an-ecopark-hung-yen/; my conversations with two Văn Giang villagers, Hà Nội, October 2012.

58. Examples of reports and photos of Văn Giang villagers protests: "Nông dân về Hà Nội khiếu kiện" [To Plea for Justice Peasants Flock to Hà Nội], February 21, 2012,

BBC, accessed February 21, 2012, www.bbc.co.uk/vietnamese/vietnam/2012/02/120221
_ecopark_protest.shtml; "Bão nông dân đồng loạt nổi lên khắp nơi" [Peasant Storm
Rising All Over], September 12, 2012, Cầu Nhật Tân, accessed September 13, 2012,
http://caunhattan.wordpress.com/2012/09/12/van-giang-bao-lai-noi-len/; "Hàng trăm
người biểu tình ở Hà Nội" [Hundreds Demonstrate in Hà Nội], April 27, 2011, RFA,
accessed November 12, 2011, http://www.rfa.org/vietnamese/vietnamnews/protest-in-
hanoi-04272011122519.html. In October–November 2012, I witnessed several Văn Giang
villagers' demonstrations in Hà Nội.

59. For a summary of the August 2012 meeting, see Phóng Viên Tự Do [Freelance
Correspondents], "Tường thuật buổi đối thoại giữa Bộ Tài Nguyên và Môi Trường
với người dân Văn Giang" [Recounting the Dialogue between Văn Giang Residents
and MoNRE], August 21, 2012, Ba Sàm, accessed March 7, 2013, http://anhbasam
.wordpress.com/2012/08/21/1217-tuong-thuat-vu-doi-thoai-giua-bo-tai-nguyen-va-moi
-truong-voi-nguoi-dan-van-giang/. YouTube has several clips from the meeting; for examples, see http://www.youtube.com/watch?v=KIOxhwNIrEw&feature=plcp; http://
www.youtube.com/watch?v=GD_irlKH_1A&feature=plcp.

60. Nguyễn Quang A, "Chính phủ có cố ý làm trái luật đất đai?" [Did the Government Deliberately Violate the Land Law?], November 9, 2012, Ba Sàm, accessed November 15, 2012, http://anhbasam.wordpress.com/2012/11/09/1366-chinh-phu-co-co-y
-lam-trai-luat-dat-dai/; Đặng Hùng Võ, "Giáo sư Đặng Hùng Võ nói lại về vụ Văn
Giang" [Professor Đặng Hùng Võ Talks Again about Văn Giang Issue], December 10,
2012, Vietnam.net, accessed June 26, 2013, http://vietnamnet.vn/vn/chinh-tri/tuanvietnam
/100018/giao-su-dang-hung-vo-noi-lai-ve-vu-van-giang.html; Đặng Hùng Võ, "Thư
phúc đáp thư mời đối thoại 'phúc thẩm' của nông dân Văn Giang" [Reply to Văn
Giang Peasants' Invitation to a "Review" Dialogue], December 18, 2012, Ba Sàm, accessed December 23, 2012, https://anhbasam.wordpress.com/2012/12/20/1485-gs-dang
-hung-vo-gui-thu-khuoc-tu-cuoc-doi-thoai-phuc-tham-voi-nguoi-dan-van-giang/.

61. "Hưng Yên: Dân cắm cờ xuống đất, phản đối chính quyền" [Hưng Yên: People
Stick Flags in Fields, Oppose Authorities], January 8, 2009, RFA, accessed January 9,
2009, http://www.rfa.org/vietnamese/in_depth/thousands-of-farmers-in-HungYen-
province-protest-regarding-land-dispute-TGiao-01082009102235.html; "Vụ Văn Giang:
Chính quyền cưỡng chế" [Văn Giang Case: Authorities Use Force], April 24, 2012, BBC,
accessed April 29, 2012, http://xuandienhannom.blogspot.com.au/2012/04/bbc-ua-tin
-trang-nhat-ve-vu-cuong-che.html; "Văn Giang: Chính quyền tỉnh lên tiếng" [Văn
Giang: Provincial Authorities Speak Up], April 26, 2012, BBC, accessed June 4, 2012,
http://www.bbc.co.uk/vietnamese/vietnam/2012/04/120426_van_giang_views.shtml.
A portion of the April 2012 clash appeared on YouTube: http://www.youtube.com/watc
h?v=FVkt7ZgnBLE&feature=player_embedded#.

62. X. Long, "Tuyên án 8 người gây rối tại dự án Ecopark-Văn Giang" [Eight
Sentenced for Causing Disorder in Ecopark Project, Văn Giang], July 12, 2016, *Tuổi
Trẻ*, accessed September 16, 2016, http://tuoitre.vn/tin/phap-luat/20160712/xet-xu-8
-nguoi-gay-roi-tai-du-an-ecopark-van-giang/1135672.html.

63. "Hàng nghìn nông dân biểu tình" [Thousands of Peasants Demonstrate],
January 7, 2009, BBC, accessed January 14, 2009, http://www.bbc.co.uk/vietnamese/
vietnam/story/2009/01/090107_hung_yen_dispute.shtml; "Lại xảy ra xô xát vì đất đai ở

Hưng Yên" [Recurrent Violence over Land in Hưng Yên], February 5, 2009, RFA, accessed February 13, 2009, http://www.rfa.org/vietnamese/in_depth/brief-violence-occurred-in-HungYen-regarding-land-dispute-TGiao-02052009150524.html; "Vụ thu hồi đất ở Văn Giang" [Retrieving Land in Văn Giang], May 8, 2012, Tin Mới [News], accessed June 3, 2013, http://www.tinmoi.vn/vu-thu-hoi-dat-o-van-giang-hung-yen-bai-2-duoc-mat-01883258.html; Trần Vũ Hải, Lưu Vũ Anh, and Hà Huy Sơn, "Kiến nghị số 01 liên quan đến dự án Ecopark-Văn Giang" [Petition Number 1 Regarding Ecopark-Văn Giang Project], May 22, 2012, Ba Sàm, accessed September 16, 2012, http://webwarper.net/ww/anhbasam.wordpress.com/2012/05/23/1025-ban-kien-nghi-gui-thu-tuong/. This last document is one of several petitions attorneys for Văn Giang villagers sent to the prime minister.

64. Conversations with four Văn Giang villagers, Hà Nội, October-November 2012; "Hàng nghìn nông dân"; "Lại xảy ra xô xát."

65. Conversations with two Văn Giang villagers, Hà Nội, October 2012; Nguyễn Tường Thụy, "Chính quyền tỉnh Hưng Yên phải chịu trách nhiệm vụ hành hung nông dân Văn Giang" [Hưng Yên Provincial Authorities Must Be Responsible for Văn Giang Peasants Violence], *Tự Do Ngôn Luận*, July 15, 2012, 31–32; Công dân xã Xuân Quan [Citizens of Xuân Quan Subdistrict], "Đơn Tố Cáo Khẩn Cấp," Kính gửi Ông Bộ Trưởng Bộ Công An [Urgent Denunciation, Letter to Minister for Public Security], July 12, 2012, *Tự Do Ngôn Luận*, July 15, 2012, 32; Trần Vũ Hải, "Kiến nghị số 03 liên quan đến dự án Ecopark" [Petition Number 3 Regarding Ecopark Project], July 24, 2012, Ba Sàm, accessed September 16, 2012, http://webwarper.net/ww/anhbasam.wordpress.com/2012/07/25/1160/; Trần Vũ Hải, "Kiến Nghị số 04 Liên quan đến dự án Ecopark" [Petition Number 4 Regarding Ecopark Project], September 13, 2012, Ba Sàm, accessed September 15, 2012, http://webwarper.net/ww/anhbasam.wordpress.com/2012/09/14/1254-kien-nghi-so-04-lien-quan-den-du-an-ecopark-hung-yen/.

66. Early in the first century C.E., two sisters, Trưng Trắc and Trưng Nhị, led a rebellion against Chinese rule in a territory that became part of Vietnam.

67. Trần Vũ Hải, Nguyễn Anh Vân, Lưu Vũ Anh, and Hà Huy Sơn, "Kiến nghị số 05". Also see Trần Khải Thanh Thủy, "Chuyện ba làng từ tỉ phú xuống bần hàn" [Story of Three Villages, from Wealth to Misery], January 18–21, 2009, Người Việt, accessed January 22, 2009, www.nguoi-viet.com/absolutenm/anmviewer.asp?a=89687&z=2; www.nguoi-viet.com/absolutenm/anmviewer.asp?a=89724&z=157; Liên Đới [Jointly], accessed July 21, 2009, www.liendoi.net/news.php?readmore=2826.

68. Conversations with four Văn Giang villagers, Hà Nội, October–November 2012.

69. Danielle Labbé, "Media Dissent and Peri-urban Land Struggles in Vietnam: The Case of the Văn Giang Incident," *Critical Asian Studies* 47 (December 2015): 495–513.

70. Conversations with Lê Hiền Đức, two other people who helped Văn Giang protesters, and two Văn Giang villagers, Hà Nội, October–November 2012; also accounts of and by the villagers' lawyers and articles such as Trần Khải Thanh Thủy, "Chuyện ba làng" and "Đại biểu Quốc hội không về Văn Giang" [National Assembly Delegates Do Not Go to Văn Giang], November 18, 2012, BBC, accessed November 20, 2012, www.bbc.co.uk/vietnamese/vietnam/2012/11/121118_vangiang_land_disputes.shtml.

71. Trần Vũ Hải, Nguyễn Anh Vân, Lưu Vũ Anh, and Hà Huy Sơn, "Kiến nghị số 05."

72. "Tuyên Bố của dân Văn Giang, Dương Nội về hai vụ án liên quan đến nông dân Đoàn Văn Vươn tại Hải Phòng" [Announcement by Văn Giang and Dương Nội Residents about Two Cases Related to Đoàn Văn Vươn in Hải Phòng], March 25, 2013, Dân Làm Báo, accessed June 28, 2013, http://danlambaovn.blogspot.com/2013/03/tuyen-bo-cua-nong-dan-van-giang-duong.html#.Uc4xCtiOm4E; "Phiên tòa xét xử anh Đoàn Văn Vươn tại Hải Phòng" [Trial and Sentence of Đoàn Văn Vươn in Hải Phòng], April 2, 2013, Xuân Diện Hán Nôm, accessed April 2, 2013, http://xuandienhannom.blogspot.com/2013/04/tin-khan-cap.html.

73. "Biểu tình lớn ở Hà Nội phản đối TQ" [Large Anti-China Demonstration in Hà Nội], July 8, 2012, BBC, accessed July 24, 2012, www.bbc.co.uk/vietnamese/vietnam/2012/07/120708_second_antichina_protest.shtml.

74. "Thông báo thành lập Ban Vận Động Hiệp Hội Dân Oan Việt Nam" [Announcing a Committee to Establish an Association for Victims of Injustice in Vietnam], December 31, 2013, Ba Sàm, accessed March 7, 2014, http://basam.info/2013/12/31/2183-thong-bao-thanh-lap-ban-van-dong-hiep-hoi-dan-oan-viet-nam/; "Thông báo số 11 của những người định thành lập Hiệp Hội Dân Oan Việt Nam" [Announcement 11 of People Establishing the Association for Victims of Injustice in Vietnam], April 12, 2014, Dân Luận [People Discuss], accessed April 23, 2014, https://danluan.org/tin-tuc/20140412/nguyen-xuan-ngu-thong-bao-so-11-cua-nhung-nguoi-dinh-thanh-lap-hiep-hoi-dan-oan.

75. Chung Hoàng, "Phó chủ tịch Hưng Yên báo cáo Thủ tướng vụ Văn Giang" [Hưng Yên's Vice Chairman Reports to the Prime Minister about Văn Giang Case], May 2, 2012, Vietnam.net, accessed June 6, 2012, http://vietnamnet.vn/vn/chinh-tri/70570/pho-chu-tich-hung-yen-bao-cao-thu-tuong-vu-van-giang.html.

76. Conversations with two Văn Giang villagers, Hà Nội, October 2012; Trần Khải Thanh Thủy, "Chuyện ba làng"; Trần Vũ Hải, "Kiến nghị số 03"; Lê Hiền Đức correspondence to author, January 8, 2014; "'Dân oan' Văn Giang Kêu Gọi Trợ Giúp" [Văn Giang "Victims of Injustice" Call for Help], July 12, 2015, Lê Hiền Đức, accessed August 21, 2015, http://lehienduc2013.blogspot.com/2015/07/nhan-dan-van-giang-to-cao-chinh-quyen.html. This last document, issued by Văn Giang residents still demanding that their farms be returned to them despite Ecopark nearing completion, chronicles many events in their struggle from 2004 to 2015.

77. Chính Trực, "Nguyễn Xuân Diện: Người lớn nhưng 'cái đầu' không lớn" [Nguyễn Xuân Diện: He's Big but Not His Head], May 3, 2013, Nguyễn Tấn Dũng, accessed June 15, 2013, http://nguyentandung.org/nguyen-xuan-dien-nguoi-lon-nhung-cai-dau-khong-lon.html; Trần Khải Thanh Thủy, "Chuyện ba làng."

78. "Bào chữa cho nông dân chống cưỡng đoạt đất, một luật sư bị tạt acid" [Acid Thrown on Lawyer Defending Peasants Fighting Land Hijack], February 2009, Báo Sóng Thần [Tidal Wave News], accessed June 11, 2013, http://songthan.free.fr/archiver/0,,137,00.html; "Việc bắt người ở huyện Văn Giang (Hưng Yên)" [Arrest in Văn Giang District, Hưng Yên], June 13, 2008, *Công An Nhân Dân* [People's Security], accessed June 11, 2013, www.cand.com.vn/News/PrintView.aspx?ID=93101; "Nghi vấn từ một vụ tạt acid luật sư" [Doubts about Acid Being Thrown at Lawyer], February 3,

2009, *Pháp Luật* [Law] accessed June 11, 2013, www.luatviet.org/Home/tin-tuc-phap
-luat/tin-trong-nuoc/2009/7615/Nghi-van-tu-mot-vu-tat-axit-luat-su.aspx; "Hành xử kiểu
'lệ làng,' cán bộ thôn lĩnh án tù" [Practicing "Village Law," a Village Cadre Sentenced
to Jail], December 30, 2008, Vietnam +, accessed June 11, 2013, www.vietnamplus.vn
/Home/Hanh-xu-kieu-le-lang-can-bo-thon-linh-an-tu/200812/4319.vnplus.

79. Annette Miae Kim, *Learning to Be Capitalists* (New York: Oxford University
Press, 2008), 102–3, makes a similar observation, but credits news coverage of land controversies more than villagers' actions themselves.

80. Evidence about land protests support this statement. Also indicative are surveys
showing that respondents were more satisfied with the national government and the
National Assembly than they were with local and provincial authorities. CECODES,
Chỉ số Hiệu quả Quản trị và Hành chính Công cấp tỉnh ở Việt Nam (PAPI) [Vietnam
Provincial Government and Public Administration Performance Index] (Hà Nội: CE-
CODES, 2012), 113–14.

81. For examples of reports about the teams' work, see "Hoạt động của Đoàn Công tác
Chính phủ tại TPHCM" [Government Team Activities in Hồ Chí Minh City], *Người
Lao Động*, September 27, 2000, 4; "Phải xử lý tiêu cực, trả lại quyền lợi cho người dân"
[Solve Negativity, Reassure People of Their Rights], August 17, 2005, *Thanh Niên*
[Young People], accessed November 29, 2006, www3.thanhnien.com.vn/Nhadat/2005
/8/18/119329.tno; "Tiền Giang: Điều chỉnh tăng mức đền bù đất cho dân" [Tiền Giang:
Adjusting Level of Compensation for Land], August 22, 2007, Vietnam.net, accessed
August 23, 2007, http://www.vietnamnet.vn/xahoi/2007/08/732596/.

82. "500 người lên TP HCM"; "Tố cáo khiếu nại"; "Hoàn thiện cơ chế phối hợp
giải quyết khiếu nại, tố cáo" [Improve Mechanism to Coordinate the Resolution of Complaints and Denunciations], May 2, 2012, *Quân Đội Nhân Dân* [People's Army], accessed July 24, 2012, http://qdnd.vn/qdndsite/vi-VN/61/43/10/50/50/186900/Default
.aspx.

83. This is suggested in Kim, *Learning to Be Capitalists*, 106–7; Annette Kim, "Talk-
ing Back: The Role of Narrative in Vietnam's Recent Land Compensation Changes,"
Urban Studies 48, no. 3 (2010): 494, 496, 499; Nguyen Van Suu, "Contending Views and
Conflicts over Land in Vietnam's Red River Delta," *Journal of Southeast Asian Studies* 38
(June 2007): 313.

84. World Bank in Vietnam, Embassy of Denmark, and Embassy of Sweden, *Recognizing and Reducing Corruption Risks in Land Management in Vietnam* (Hà Nội:
National Political Publishing House, 2011), 48.

85. Andrew Wells-Dang, Pham Quang Tu, and Adam Burke, "Conversion of Land
Use in Vietnam through a Political Economy Lens," *Journal of Social Sciences and
Humanities* 2, no. 2 (2016): 139–40.

86. Lawyers helping Văn Giang protesters urged the prime minister to establish a
special commission to resolve the problem: Trần Vũ Hải, Lưu Vũ Anh, and Hà Huy
Sơn, "Kiến nghị số 01"; Trần Vũ Hải, Nguyễn Anh Vân, Lưu Vũ Anh, and Hà Huy Sơn,
"Kiến nghị số 05." Similar proposals came from other quarters of society.

87. See, for instance, comments by the deputy prime minister and the MoNRE:
Thái Thiện, "Sẽ lập đoàn công tác giải quyết các khiếu kiện phức tạp" [Body to Be Established to Resolve Complicated Appeals for Justice], August 15, 2007, Vietnam.net,

accessed August 23, 2007, http://www.vietnamnet.vn/xahoi/2007/07/718485/; Nguyễn Hưng - Tiến Dũng, "'528 vụ khiếu kiện tồn đọng là mầm mống mất ổn định'" ["528 Long-standing Appeal for Justice Cases Are Germs for Instability"], May 2, 2012, VnExpress, accessed May 17, 2012, http://vnexpress.net/gl/xa-hoi/2012/05/528-vu-khieu-kien -ton-dong-la-mam-mong-mat-on-dinh/.

88. For a newspaper account about the legal complexities and contradictions confronting local authorities, see "Thực hiện luật đất đai ở TP.HCM" [Implementing the Land Law in Hồ Chí Minh City], August 31, 2007, *Thanh Niên*, accessed September 10, 2007, http://www3.thanhnien.com.vn/Nhadat/2007/8/31/207017.tno. For an overview of land confiscation and compensation legalities, see World Bank, *Compulsory Land Acquisition*.

89. This statement and the next paragraph draw on several news accounts between 2000 and 2015; conversations during September–October 2012 and October 2016 in Hà Nội with a journalist and six researchers who investigate land issues; Đặng Kim Sơn and Nguyễn Đỗ Anh Tuấn, *Chính sách Đất đai*, 132–34, 138; Đặng Ngọc Dinh, chủ biên, *Giải quyết Xung đột và Phòng chống Tham nhũng* [Resolving Conflicts and Fending Off Corruption] (Hà Nội: Nxb Tri Thức, 2011), 73–108, 261–62; World Bank in Vietnam, Embassy of Denmark, and Embassy of Sweden, *Recognizing and Reducing Corruption Risks*.

3. Nation

1. On several occasions in September and October 2012 and October 2016, I observed the No-U group practice, watched them play other teams, and talked with No-U members. Some other teams wore jerseys with the team's name followed by "FC," initials commonly used for football (soccer) teams in Vietnam and other countries.

2. For a scholarly study of new Chinese in Vietnam since the 1990s, see Nguyen Van Chinh, "Recent Chinese Migration to Vietnam," *Asian Pacific Migration Journal* 22, no. 1 (2013): 7–30.

3. Bill Hayton's well-researched book *The South China Sea: The Struggle for Power in Asia* (New Haven, CT: Yale University Press, 2014) analyses these and other issues in the sea whose very name is contested.

4. "Bắn đạn bi, tàu Hải cảnh Trung Quốc áp sát nhiều giờ tàu cá Việt Nam" [Shooting Bullets, Chinese Coast Guard Close in on Vietnamese Fishing Boat], March 19, 2016, *Người Lao Động* [Worker], accessed April 7, 2016, http://nld.com.vn /thoi-su-trong-nuoc/ban-dan-bi-tau-hai-canh-trung-quoc-ap-sat-nhieu-gio-tau-ca-viet -nam-20160319132909344.htm.

5. I base this observation on over one hundred reports, mostly from Vietnamese newspapers, of encounters between Vietnamese fishing boats and Chinese vessels in 2005–15.

6. Việt Hà, "Ngư Việt Nam phải chịu đựng đến bao giờ" [How Long Do Vietnamese Fishers Have to Put Up with It?], May 6, 2010, RFA, accessed July 13, 2010, http://www.rfa.org/vietnamese/in_depth/Stories-of-a-fisherman-returned-from-

Hoang-Sa-05062010071515.html; "Gặp những người thân tàn ma dại trở về từ Hoàng Sa" [Meet the People in Bad Shape Who Returned from Paracel Islands], July 28, 2010, Vietnam.net, accessed August 2, 2010, http://www.vietnamnet.vn/psks/201007/Gap-nhung-nguoi-than-tan-ma-dai-tro-ve-tu-Hoang-Sa-925247/.

7. Trí Tín and Thiên Lý, "Bất chấp tàu Trung Quốc đe dọa, người dân quyết bám biển" [Despite Intimidation by Chinese Boats, People Are Determined to Remain on the Sea], May 30, 2011, VnExpress, accessed June 4, 2011, http://vnexpress.net/gl/xa-hoi /2011/05/bat-chap-tau-trung-quoc-de-doa-nguoi-dan-quyet-bam-bien/.

8. Nguyễn Chính Tâm, "Sức hậu thuẫn của toàn dân tộc" [The Power of Support from the Entire Nation], June 12, 2011, Tuần Việt Nam [Vietnam Week], accessed June 19, 2011, http://tuanvietnam.vietnamnet.vn/2011-06-10-suc-hau-thuan-cua-toan -dan-toc.

9. "Tàu đánh cá của ngư dân xã Hòa Lộc (Hậu Lộc) bị tàu lạ tấn công" [Unidentified Vessel Attacks Boat of Fishers from Hòa Lộc subdistrict (Hậu Lộc district)], *Thanh Hóa* [Thanh Hóa province newspaper], January 12, 2005, 4; Cao Ngọ and Ngọc Minh, "Những người thoát chết nói gì?" [What Do People Who Escaped Death Say?], *Thanh Niên* [Young People], January 15, 2005, 3; "8 ngư dân bị bắt giữ tại Hải Nam vẫn khỏe mạnh" [The Eight Fishers Held in Hainan Are in Good Health], January 22, 2005, ViệtBáo [Việt News], accessed May 6, 2016, http://vietbao.vn/Chinh-Tri/8-ngu -dan-bi-bat-giu-tai-Hai-Nam-van-khoe-manh/20368393/75/; Phạm Thanh Nghiên, "Uất ức—biển ta ơi" [Wrath of Our Sea], March 1, 2008, Đàn chim Việt [Việt Flock], accessed March 17, 2016, http://www.danchimviet.info/archives/30765/u%E1%BA%A5t-%E1%BB%A9c-bi%E1%BB%83n-ta-%C6%A1i/2008/03. Spellings of names for some of the nine Vietnamese who were killed vary in these and other sources.

10. Lê Quỳnh and Ngô Nguyên, "Tàu ngư dân Việt Nam bị nước ngoài bắt, đòi tiền chuộc, 'tàu lạ' thì được tha" [Foreign Country Abducts Vietnamese Fishers, Demands Ransoms; Unmarked Boat Got Away], March 31, 2010, *Sài Gòn Tiếp Thị* [Sài Gòn Market], accessed October 10, 2010, http://sgtt.vn/Thoi-su/120187/Tau-ngu -dan-Viet-Nam-bi-nuoc-ngoai-bat-doi-tien-chuoc-"tau-la"-thi-duoc-tha.html. Sometimes Filipinos, Indonesians, and Malaysians captured Vietnamese fishers; usually those instances were settled without the fishers paying money, losing their boats, or suffering other sizable losses. See, for example, observations by a Vietnamese border patrol officer in "Không để ngư trường của chúng ta bị thu hẹp" [Don't Let Our Fishing Zones Be Restricted], June 28, 2009, *Tiền Phong* [Vanguard], accessed July 7, 2009, http://www.tienphong.vn/Tianyon/Index.aspx?ArticleID=16475 7&ChannelID=2.

11. "Nhiều tàu cá của ngư dân Huế bị tàu Trung Quốc phá hoại" [Chinese Vessels Destroy Many Boats of Huế Fishers], April 15, 2016, VnExpress, accessed May 28, 2016, http://vnexpress.net/tin-tuc/thoi-su/nhieu-tau-ca-cua-ngu-dan-hue-bi-tau-trung-quoc -pha-hoai-3388006.html; Pamela Boykoff, "Vietnam Fishermen on the Front Lines of South China Sea Fray," May 22, 2016, CNN News, accessed May 28, 2016, http://www .cnn.com/2016/05/22/asia/vietnam-fisherman-south-china-sea/.

12. Simon Denyer, "How China's Fishermen Are Fighting a Covert War in the South China Sea," April 12, 2016, *Washington Post*, accessed May 28, 2016, https://www .washingtonpost.com/world/asia_pacific/fishing-fleet-puts-china-on-collision-course

-with-neighbors-in-south-china-sea/2016/04/12/8a6a9e3c-fff3-11e5-8bb1-f124a43f84dc
_story.html.

13. "Trong lúc đánh bắt ở ngư trường Trường Sa, một ngư dân Quảng Ngãi đã bị
tàu lạ bắn chết" [Unidentified Boat Shot Dead a Quảng Ngãi Man Fishing in Spratly
Island Waters], November 29, 2015, *Người Lao Động*, accessed April 26, 2016, http://nld
.com.vn/thoi-su-trong-nuoc/mot-ngu-dan-bi-ban-chet-o-truong-sa-20151129161431587
.htm; Paulus Lê Sơn, "Vì sao ngư dân Việt Nam tiếp tục bị bắn giết trên vùng biển
thuộc chủ quyền Việt Nam?" [Why Are Vietnamese Fishers Continually Being Killed
in Territorial Sea Belonging to Vietnam?], December 1, 2015, Tin Mừng Cho Người
Nghèo [Good News for the Poor], accessed April 7, 2016, http://www.tinmungchon-
guoingheo.com/blog/2015/12/01/vi-sao-ngu-dan-viet-nam-tiep-tuc-bi-ban-giet-tren-vung-
bien-thuoc-chu-quyen-viet-nam/.

14. Trí Tín and Thiên Lý, "Bất chấp tàu Trung Quốc"; Mac Lam and Gia Minh,
"Chinese Boats Cause Thousands of Dollars in Damage to Vietnamese Fishermen's
Nets," November 18, 2015, RFA, accessed May 30, 2016, http://www.rfa.org/english/
news/vietnam/chinese-boats-cause-thousands-of-dollars-in-damage-to-vietnamese-
fishermens-nets-11182015161046.html; Nguyễn Thanh Giang, "Hữu nghị nhưng phải
cảnh giác" [Friendship But Must Be Vigilant], April 26, 2014, *Tổ Quốc* [Homeland],
May 1, 2014, 20.

15. Lưu Nguyễn, "Những việc làm đi ngược tình hữu nghị" [Actions Contrary to
Friendship], July 1, 2009, *Pháp Luật TP Hồ Chí Minh* [Hồ Chí Minh City Law], accessed
July 2, 2009, http://www.phapluattp.vn/news/chinh-tri/view.aspx?news_id=259971;
"Trung Quốc 'thả ngư dân Việt Nam'" [China "Releases Vietnamese Fishers"],
August 11, 2009, BBC, accessed August 12, 2009, http://www.bbc.co.uk/vietnamese/
vietnam/2009/08/090811_china_fishermen_update.shtml; Gia Minh, "Tâm sự ngư dân"
[Inner Feelings of a Fisher], August 16, 2009, RFA, accessed August 24, 2009, http://
www.rfa.org/vietnamese/in_depth/Detained-fisherman-tells-the-story-gminh-08162
009121835.html.

16. For example, Trí Nguyễn, "Kiên quyết không để ngư dân nộp phạt cho Trung
Quốc" [Resolutely, Do Not Let Fishers Pay Fines to China], June 29, 2009, VnExpress,
accessed July 2, 2009, http://www.vnexpress.net/GL/Xa-hoi/2009/06/3BA10AA2/; Lê
Quỳnh and Ngô Nguyên, "Tàu ngư dân."

17. Nguyễn Hưng, "'Phải đưa ngư dân bị Trung Quốc bắt về nước'" ["Fishers
Taken by China Must Be Brought Home"], July 1, 2009, VnExpress, accessed July 2,
2009, http://www.vnexpress.net/GL/Xa-hoi/2009/07/3BA10B57/; Trí Tín and Thiên
Lý, "Bất chấp tàu Trung Quốc"; Mac Lam and Gia Minh, "Chinese Boats."

18. Quoted in Nguyễn Thanh Giang, "Sớm loại bỏ bè lũ thần phục Bắc Kinh" [Get
Rid of the Clique Submitting to Beijing], April 24, 2016, 1 (on file with the author).

19. "Kiến nghị vì công lý cho các ngư dân vô tội ở Hòa Lộc" [Petition for Justice for
Innocent Fishers in Hòa Lộc], *Tuổi Trẻ* [Youth], January 20, 2005, 5.

20. "Sinh viên Sài Gòn căng biểu ngữ biểu tình chống Trung Cộng bị công an bắt"
[Police Arrest Sài Gòn Students Displaying Banners While Demonstrating against
Communist China], January 23, 2005, Greenspun, accessed June 21, 2016, http://www
.greenspun.com/bboard/q-and-a-fetch-msg.tcl?msg_id=00CiOX; Phạm Thanh Nghiên, "Uất ức"; Tuong Vu, "The Party v. the People: Anti-China Nationalism," *Journal*

of Vietnamese Studies 9 (Fall 2014): 41. I searched ten major party-state authorized newspapers published in early 2005 but found no stories about the January 23 demonstrations.

21. Cẩm Hà, "Cảnh sát biển Trung Quốc vi phạm nghiêm trọng luật pháp quốc tế" [Chinese Coast Guard Seriously Violate International Law], *Tuổi Trẻ*, January 21, 2005, 15.

22. In 2012 alone, Hà Nội had "dozens of marches and demonstrations" regarding China's actions in the East Sea, said Hồ Quang Lợi, head of the city's Propaganda and Education Committee. Đào Tuấn, "Tổ chức nhóm chuyên gia bút chiến trên Internet" [Organize a Group of Polemical Experts for the Internet], January 9, 2013, *Lao Động* [Labor], accessed May 11, 2015, http://laodong.com.vn/chinh-tri/to-chuc-nhom-chuyen-gia-but-chien-tren-internet-98582.bld.

23. "Lời kêu gọi biểu tình yêu nước của 20 tổ chức dân sự Việt Nam" [A Call from 20 Vietnamese Civic Organizations for Patriotic Demonstrations], May 7, 2014, Ba Sàm [Gossip], accessed May 7, 2014, http://www.basam.info/2014/05/07/loi-keu-goi-bieu-tinh-yeu-nuoc-cua-20-to-chuc-dan-su-viet-nam/#more-129987.

24. Thiên Duy, "Lời kể của sinh viên Sài Gòn" [A Sài Gòn Student's Report], December 10, 2007, BBC, accessed December 13, 2007, http://www.bbc.co.uk/vietnamese/forum/story/2007/12/071210_thienduyaboutprotest.shtml; Hoàng Xuân Ba, "Sự trỗi dậy của truyền thông phi chính thống" [Emergence of Unorthodox Communication], January 27, 2008, BBC, accessed February 11, 2008, http://www.bbc.co.uk/vietnamese/forum/story/2007/12/071210_thienduyaboutprotest.shtml. An account of the 2007 demonstrations is in Bill Hayton, *Vietnam: Rising Dragon* (New Haven, CT: Yale University Press, 2010), 192.

25. "Nhiều người hưởng ứng biểu tình chống Trung Quốc" [Many Responding to Anti-China Demonstration], June 2, 2011, Người Việt [Vietnamese People], accessed June 14, 2011, http://www.nguoi-viet.com/absolutenm2/templates/?a=132004; Thụ My, "Dân Việt Nam sẵn sàng chống xâm lược" [Vietnamese Are Ready to Oppose Aggression], December 8, 2012, Ba Sàm, accessed December 9, 2012, http://anhbasam.wordpress.com/2012/12/09/dan-viet-nam-san-sang-chong-xam-luoc-khong-de-trung-quoc-coi-khinh/#more-84697.

26. "Lời kêu gọi tổng biểu tình trên toàn quốc ngày chủ nhật 18.5.2014" [A Call for Nationwide Demonstrations on Sunday, May 18, 2014], Tễu, accessed May 16, 2014, http://xuandienhannom.blogspot.com/2014/05/loi-keu-goi-bieu-tinh-chong-trung-quoc.html#more.

27. Nearly all banners and placards at the demonstrations were in Vietnamese. Occasionally demonstrators had a few in foreign languages, usually English and Chinese.

28. Gia Minh, "Giới trẻ không cúi đầu trước Trung Quốc" [Youth Don't Bow to China], June 9, 2011, RFA, accessed June 21, 2011, http://www.rfa.org/vietnamese/in_depth/rally-against-china-tq-06082011162404.html; "Sẽ có biểu tình chống TQ vào Chủ nhật?" [Will There Be a Protest against China on Sunday?], December 6, 2012, BBC, accessed December 10, 2012, http://www.bbc.co.uk/vietnamese/vietnam/2012/12/121206_viet_protest_possible.shtml.

29. Trần Hiền Thảo, Hà Thị Đông Xuân, và nhóm sinh viên [group of students], "Hàng triệu người đã công khai 'chọn con đường'" [Millions of People Publicly "Chose

the Way"], December 12, 2007, *Thông Luận* [Thorough Discussion], accessed February 13, 2009, http://www.thongluan.org/vn/modules.php?name=News&file=article&sid=2351.

30. Phương Ngạn, "Biểu tình chống TQ và vai trò của trí thức" [Demonstration against China and the Role of Intellectuals], June 12, 2011, Người Việt, accessed June 14, 2011, http://www.nguoi-viet.com/absolutenm2/templates/default.aspx?a=132430&z=2.

31. "Hà Nội bùng nổ biểu tình" [Demonstrations Break Out in Hà Nội], November 5, 2015, Dân quyền [People's Rights], accessed November 5, 2015, http://danquyenvn.blogspot.com/2015/11/tin-cuc-nong-21h-ha-noi-bung-no-bieu.html#more.

32. Khánh An, "Họ đã vươn vai thành Thánh Gióng?" [Did Squaring Their Shoulders Make Them Heroes?], June 23, 2011, RFA, accessed September 14, 2011, http://www.rfa.org/vietnamese/in_depth/aross-street-like-another-part2-ka-06232011170148.html.

33. Khánh An, "Nên hay không tiếp tục biểu tình?" [Continue Demonstrations or Not?], June 8, 2011, RFA, accessed September 12, 2011, http://www.rfa.org/vietnamese/in_depth/demonstration-should-or-not-ka-06082011204548.html.

34. Lê Phú Khải, "Thấy gì qua cuộc biểu tình ngày 9/12/2012 tại Sài Gòn" [Things Seen at Sài Gòn's December 12, 2012 Demonstration], December 12, 2012, Bauxite Việt Nam, accessed December 17, 2012, http://boxitvn.blogspot.fr/2012/12/thay-gi-qua-cuoc-bieu-tinh-ngay-9122012.html#more.

35. Chapter 1 discusses those May 2014 workers' demonstrations.

36. "Chúng tôi phải nằm xuống để đất nước-dân tộc này phải đứng lên" [We Lie Down (in protest) in Order That the Country and Nation Stand Up], June 3, 2013, No-U, accessed January 23, 2015, http://thanhvdgt1.blogspot.com/2013/06/chung-toi-phai-nam-xuong-e-at-nuoc-nay.html#more.

37. The organizations' actual names are Đoàn Thanh Niên Cộng Sản and Mặt Trận Tổ Quốc.

38. See accounts by Nguyễn Tuấn and an unnamed writer in *Tổ Quốc*, May 15, 2014, 11 and 13–15. From time to time, individual officials said they unsuccessfully urged party-state leaders to support other demonstrations. An example is Hồ Ngọc Nhuận, deputy president of the Homeland Front in Hồ Chí Minh City; see Nguyễn Hùng and Hạnh Ly, "Vì sao chính quyền ngăn biểu tình?" [Why Do Authorities Prevent Demonstrations?], December 9, 2012, BBC, accessed April 1, 2014, http://www.bbc.co.uk/vietnamese/vietnam/2012/12/121209_tai_sao_chinh_quyen_ngan_bieu_tinh.shtml.

39. Quốc Triệu, "Người dân Cần Thơ tuần hành phản đối Trung Quốc" [Cần Thơ People March against China], May 13, 2014, VnExpress, accessed May 16, 2014, http://vnexpress.net/tin-tuc/thoi-su/nguoi-dan-can-tho-tuan-hanh-phan-doi-trung-quoc-2989745.html; "Người dân ba miền tuần hành phản đối Trung Quốc" [People in All Three Regions March against China], May 11, 2014, VnExpress, accessed May 16, 2014, http://vnexpress.net/tin-tuc/thoi-su/nguoi-dan-ba-mien-tuan-hanh-phan-doi-trung-quoc-2989072.html.

40. Accounts of Hà Nội police quickly dispersing demonstrators, detaining some, on December 6, 2008, and June 2, 2013, include Hiền Vy, "Sinh viên Việt Nam bị ngăn chặn biểu tình phản đối Trung Quốc" [Vietnamese Students Blocked from Demonstrating against China], December 9, 2008, RFA, accessed December 16, 2008, http://

www.rfa.org/vietnamese/in_depth/the-failed-China-protest-of-Students-in-Vietnam-
HVy-12092008110125.html; "Hàng chục người bị bắt hôm nay do biểu tình chống
Trung Quốc xâm lược" [Dozens Arrested for Demonstrating against China's Aggres-
sion], June 2, 2013, Quan Làm Báo [Public Servant Journalist], accessed June 4, 2013,
http://quanlambao.blogspot.com/2013/06/hang-chuc-nguoi-bi-bat-hom-nay-do-bieu
.html; "Chúng tôi phải nằm."

41. Thiên Duy, "Lời kể của sinh viên Sài Gòn"; reports in *Tự Do Ngôn Luận* [Free
Speech] December 15, 2007, 27–32, and January 1, 2008, 31–33; Grant McCool, "Na-
tionalist Vietnam Protests Draw Myriad Interests," January 11, 2008, Reuters, accessed
January 13, 2008, vnnews-l; Thiện Giao, "Công an thẩm vấn gắt gao những người
tham gia biểu tình chống Trung Quốc" [Security Police Severely Question Anti-China
Demonstrators], January 24, 2008, RFA, accessed February 22, 2008, http://www.rfa
.org/vietnamese/in_depth/2008/01/24/AntiChineseAgressionProtestersInterrogated-
ByVnAuthorities_TGiao/.

42. "Một ngày không thể quên" [An Unforgettable Day], December 10, 2012, Quê
Choa [My Country], accessed December 11, 2012, http://quechoa.vn/2012/12/10/mot
-ngay-khong-the-quen/; Ngô Thị Hồng Lâm, "Chúng ta cần sức mạnh" [We Must
Be Strong], December 19, 2012, Bauxite Việt Nam, accessed December 19, 2012,
http://www.boxitvn.net/bai/43684; "Thú bông và đồ chơi biểu tình chống Trung
Quốc" [Toys Demonstrate against China], December 16, 2012, No-U, accessed December 23, 2012, http://thanhvdgt1.blogspot.com/2012/12/thu-bong-va-o-choi-bieu
-tinh-chong.html.

43. "Chính quyền VN giải tán biểu tình" [Vietnam's Government Breaks Up
Demonstration], May 18, 2014, BBC, accessed May 18, 2014, http://www.bbc.co.uk/viet-
namese/vietnam/2014/05/140518_anti_china_protests_dispersed.shtml; Hà Sĩ Phu,
"Đấu tranh cứu nước cần muôn vẻ linh hoạt!" [Struggle to Save the Nation Needs
Countless Forms of Action], May 18, 2014, Ba Sàm, accessed May 18, 2014, https://
anhbasam.wordpress.com/2014/05/18/2238-dau-tranh-cuu-nuoc-can-muon-ve-linh
-hoat/#more-131271; "Hình ảnh cuộc biểu tình của Sài Gòn yêu nước sáng ngày
18.5.2014" [Photos of Patriots Demonstrating in Sài Gòn on the Morning of May 18, 2014],
May 18, 2014, Tễu, accessed May 18, 2014, http://xuandienhannom.blogspot.com/2014
/05/hinh-anh-sai-gon-bieu-tinh-sang-ngay.html.

44. See, for instance, Tạ Phong Tần, "Báo Việt Nam và biểu tình chống Trung Quốc"
[Vietnamese News and the Demonstrations against China], June 9, 2011, Người Việt, ac-
cessed June 14, 2011, http://www.nguoi-viet.com/absolutenm2/templates/?a=132298;
Phương Ngạn, "Biểu tình chống Trung Quốc ở Việt Nam" [Demonstrations in Vietnam
against China], June 5, 2011, Người Việt, accessed June 14, 2011, http://www.nguoi-viet.
com/absolutenm2/templates/default.aspx?a=132125&z=1; *Thế hệ f* [The f (Facebook)
Generation] (Vietnam: Nxb Liên Mạng, 2011), a compilation of the writings of young
Vietnamese about the protests on June 5 and 12, 2011.

45. "VN, China Vow to Resolve East Sea Issue Peacefully," June 27, 2011, Vietnam
News Service, accessed January 20, 2016, http://vietnamnews.vn/society/212725/vn
-china-vow-to-resolve-east-sea-issue-peacefully.html.

46. From the dozens of accounts about the June-August 2011 demonstrations,
here are a few: "Biểu tình chống TQ lại tiếp diễn ở Sài Gòn, Hà Nội" [Demonstrations

against China Continue in Sài Gòn and Hà Nội], June 12, 2011, Diễn Đàn Thế Kỷ [Century Forum], accessed June 14, 2011, http://www.diendantheky.net/2011/06/bieu-tinh-chong-tq-lai-tiep-dien-o-sai.html; Vũ Danh Phóng, "Lại đi biểu tình chống Trung Quốc xâm lược" [Demonstrating Again against Chinese Aggression], June 13, 2011, Bauxite Việt Nam, accessed June 15, 2011, http://boxitvn.wordpress.com/2011/06/13/l%E1%BA%A1i-di-bi%E1%BB%83u-tnh-ch%E1%BB%91ng-trung-qu%E1%BB%91c-xm-l%C6%B0%E1%BB%A3c/; Phương Ngạn, "Biểu tình chống TQ và vai trò của trí thức"; Khối Tự do Dân chủ 8406 [Bloc 8406 for Freedom and Democracy] and Nhóm Linh mục Nguyễn Kim Điền, "Tuyên bố chung nhân các cuộc biểu tình chống Trung Cộng" [Announcement Regarding Demonstrations against Communist China], June 25, 2011, *Tự Do Ngôn Luận*, July 1, 2011, 3; "Yêu nước như thế nào mới là đúng cách?" [What's the Correct Way to Be Patriotic?], August 28, 2011, BlogAnhVu, accessed September 1, 2011, http://bloganhvu.blogspot.com/2011/08/yeu-nuoc-nhu-nao-moi-la-ung-cach-1.html, http://bloganhvu.blogspot.com/2011/08/yeu-nuoc-nhu-nao-moi-la-ung-cach-2.html, http://bloganhvu.blogspot.com/2011/08/yeu-nuoc-nhu-nao-moi-la-ung-cach-3.html.

47. Phan Nguyễn Việt Đăng, "Sài Gòn: sáng 19/6, từ cuộc biểu tình không thành, chợt hiểu!" [Sài Gòn: June 19, a.m., a Revelation from a Failed Demonstration!], June 19, 2011, RFA, accessed September 14, 2011, http://www.rfa.org/vietnamese/HumanRights/3rd-anticn-protest-pnvd-06192011203322.html. For a similar assessment, see Tạ Phong Tần, "Báo Việt Nam."

48. Phan Nguyễn Việt Đăng, "Sài Gòn: sáng 19/6"; Ian Timberlake, "Vietnamese Hold Anti-China Protest after Crackdown," Agence France Presse (AFP), accessed August 11, 2011, http://sg.news.yahoo.com/vietnamese-hold-anti-china-protest-crackdown-060610756.html; Phạm Xuân Nguyên, "Người mọc đuôi" [A Person Growing a Tail], August 8, 2011, Ba Sàm, accessed August 24, 2011, http://anhbasam.wordpress.com/2011/08/14/262-ng%C6%B0%E1%BB%9Di-m%E1%BB%8Dc-duoi/.

49. "Kiến nghị của công dân (về việc Phản đối Thông báo trái pháp luật của UBNDTP Hà Nội cấm thực hiện Quyền biểu tình theo Hiến pháp)" [Citizen's Petition: Regarding the Hà Nội People's Committee's Unlawful Announcement against Exercising the Constitutional Right to Demonstrate], August 18, 2011, Ba Sàm, accessed August 21, 2011, http://anhbasam.wordpress.com/2011/08/19/275-ki%E1%BA%BFn-ngh%E1%BB%8B-v%E1%BB%81-b%E1%BA%A3n-thong-bao-c%E1%BA%A5m-bi%E1%BB%83u-tinh.

50. John Ruwitch, "Vietnam Stops Anti-China Protest, Detains Many," August 21, 2011, Reuters, accessed August 24, 2011, http://www.reuters.com/article/2011/08/21/us-vietnam-protest-idUSTRE77K0FF20110821.

51. Nguyễn Thanh Giang, "Cần dựng tượng Lê Thị Tuyết Mai" [Erect a Statue of Lê Thị Tuyết Mai], May 28, 2014, Đàn chim Việt, accessed January 31, 2016, http://www.danchimviet.info/archives/87560/can-dung-tuong-le-thi-tuyet-mai/2014/05; Tân Tiến, "Tự thiêu phản đối Trung Quốc xâm phạm chủ quyền" [Immolation to Oppose China's Violation of Sovereignty], May 23, 2014, *Người Lao Động*, accessed January 31, 2016, http://nld.com.vn/thoi-su-trong-nuoc/tu-thieu-phan-doi-trung-quoc-xam-pham-chu-quyen-20140523174918338.htm.

52. Phạm Đình Trọng, "Thông báo về việc từ bỏ đảng tịch đảng viên đảng Cộng sản" [Announcing a Member's Withdrawal from the Communist Party], November 20, 2009, *Tổ Quốc*, December 15, 2009, 6.

53. Marianne Brown, "In Vietnam, Anti-China Protests Get Creative," January 25, 2013, Voice of America (VOA), accessed January 26, 2013, http://www.voanews.com/content/in-vietnam-protest-against-china-get-creative/1590665.html.

54. "Tiểu sử của blogger Điếu Cày" [Biography of Blogger Điếu Cày], October 10, 2014, Tễu, accessed January 23, 2017, https://xuandienhannom.blogspot.com/2014/10/tin-nong-vn-phong-thich-blogger-ieu-cay.html; "Biography," Facebook Blogger Điếu Cày, accessed January 23, 2017, https://www.facebook.com/Blogger-%C4%90i%E1%BA%BFu-C%C3%A0y-Nguy%E1%BB%85n-V%C4%83n-H%E1%BA%A3i-16721195335255/about/.

55. Phạm Thanh Nghiên, "Đôi nét về Blogger Nguyễn Ngọc Như Quỳnh" [A Few Remarks about Blogger Nguyễn Ngọc Như Quỳnh], October 14, 2016, Dân Làm Báo [Citizen Journalist], accessed January 23, 2017, http://danlambaovn.blogspot.com/2016/10/oi-net-vebloggernguyen-ngoc-nhu-quynh.html.

56. Tương Lai, "Suy ngẫm dưới chân tượng Đức Thánh Trần" [Meditating at the Foot of Trần Hưng Đạo's Statue], February 22, 2013, para. 3, Ba Sàm, accessed February 27, 2013, http://anhbasam.wordpress.com/2013/02/22/1633-suy-ngam-duoi-chan-tuong-duc-thanh-tran/. Also see comments by retired colonel Nguyễn Đăng Quang in "Kiến nghị đầu tiên của các thành viên lực lượng vũ trang" [First Petition by Members of the Armed Forces], September 6, 2014, Radio France International (RFI), accessed December 30, 2015, http://vi.rfi.fr/viet-nam/20140906-viet-nam-cuu-si-quan-kien-nghi-chinh-quyen-minh-bach-quan-he-voi-trung-quoc.

57. Materials on which this paragraph is based include Tương Lai interview, "Đảng 'nên đặt Tổ quốc lên trên hết'" [The Party "Should Put the Homeland above Everything Else"], December 6, 2012, BBC, accessed December 9, 2012, http://anhbasam.wordpress.com/2012/12/07/1445-gs-tuong-lai-dang-nen-dat-to-quoc-len-tren-het/#more-84462; Tương Lai interview, "Tại sao tôi ủng hộ Thủ tướng" [Why I Support the Prime Minister], February 28, 2014, RFA, accessed August 8, 2015, https://vi-vn.facebook.com/chepsuviet/posts/257646544416621; Tương Lai, "Nước xa & Lửa gần" [Distant Water and Nearby Fire], July 1, 2014, Diễn Đàn [Forum], accessed July 13, 2014, http://www.diendan.org/viet-nam/nuoc-xa-lua-gan (a modified version in English is his "An Overdue Vietnam-U.S. Alliance," *International New York Times*, July 14, 2012, 6).

58. For an analysis of other Vietnamese during the 2010s who also contended that VCP leaders were putting communist ideology and their hold on power ahead of nationalism, see Tuong Vu, "The Party v. the People," 44–55. Elsewhere, Tuong Vu argues that VCP leaders have long been more committed to communism than to nationalism and have sought to fold the latter into the former: Tuong Vu, *Vietnam's Communist Revolution: The Power and Limits of Ideology* (New York: Cambridge University Press, 2017).

59. In the 361 names there were 115, nearly one-third, who signed more than one statement and accounted for 61 percent of all signatures. Of the 115, 53 people signed two statements, 20 signed three, 16 signed four, 10 signed five, 9 signed six, 6 signed seven, and 1 signed eight. The signatures of the 62 people signing three or more statements

numbered 278, equaling 44 percent of the 630 signatures of people in Vietnam on the eleven statements.

60. Huỳnh Tấn Mẫm, "Thông báo số 2 của tập thể 42 công dân" [Announcement Number 2 from the Group of 42 Citizens], August 15, 2012, Quan Làm Báo, accessed April 1, 2014, http://quanlambao-vn.com/article.php?id=1775&cat_id=6. Some additional sources about and by him are Mặc Lâm, "Phỏng vấn BS Huỳnh Tấn Mẫm sau cuộc biểu tình 9/12/2012" [Interview with Dr. Huỳnh Tấn Mẫm Following the December 9, 2012 Demonstration], RFA, accessed April 1, 2014, http://www.rfa.org/vietnamese/in_depth/interview-huynh-tan-mam-mlam-12092012123502.html; Thượng Tùng, "Bác sĩ Huỳnh Tấn Mẫm: Tôi may mắn được nhiều người yêu thương" [Doctor Huỳnh Tấn Mẫm: I'm Lucky That Many People Care about Me], August 30, 2008, *Tuổi Trẻ*, accessed April 1, 2014, http://tuoitre.vn/Chinh-tri-Xa-hoi/276145/bac-si-huynh-tan-mam-toi-may-man-duoc-nhieu-nguoi-yeu-thuong.html.

61. Nguyễn Trọng Vĩnh, "Từ Đảng Cộng sản ban đầu đến Đảng Cộng sản hiện nay" [From the Communist Party's Beginning until Today], December 27, 2012, Bauxite Việt Nam, accessed January 3, 2013, http://boxitvn.blogspot.fr/2012/12/tu-ang-cong-san-ban-au-en-ang-cong-san.html.

62. For detailed analyses of the controversial bauxite deal with China and the origins and consequences of the petition, see Jason Morris-Jung, "The Vietnamese Bauxite Controversy: Towards a More Oppositional Politics," *Journal of Vietnamese Studies* 10 (Winter 2015): 63–109, and Morris-Jung, "Vietnamese Bauxite Mining Controversy: The Emergence of a New Oppositional Politics" (PhD diss., University of California, Berkeley, 2013).

63. "Kính gửi Ông Trương Tấn Sang, Chủ tích nước . . ." [Respectfully Sending to Mr. Trương Tấn Sang, President . . . (and several more national leaders)], May 14, 2014, accessed March 17, 2015, https://docs.google.com/document/d/1RSjufZiPBIn4c-mnWvVgMKOz_zLB7mfXc1uWxvbmRuYM/edit?pref=2&pli=1. The list of signers as of late May 2014 is at Qũy Nghiên cứu Biển Đông [East Sea Research Foundation], accessed September 15, 2016, https://qncbd.wordpress.com/2014/05/27/danh-sach-nguoi-ky-ten-thu-yeu-cau-lanh-dao-viet-nam-dua-trung-quoc-ra-toa-den-het-ngay-2452014/.

64. As a sign of unity with other Southeast Asian countries, suggested the August 6, 2012 letter, call the East Sea the Southeast Asia Sea.

65. Conversations I had in Hà Nội, October–November 2016.

66. Gia Minh, "Về 'Thư ngỏ gửi cho BCH Trung Ương và toàn thể đảng viên ĐCSVN'" [Regarding the "Open Letter to the Central Executive Committee and All VCP members"], July 29, 2014, RFA, accessed July 30, 2014, http://www.rfa.org/vietnamese/in_depth/party-mem-speak-up-07292014052726.html.

67. "Quốc hội không dám bạch hóa Mật nghị Thành Đô 1990" [National Assembly Doesn't Dare Clarify the 1990 Chengdu Secret Meeting], October 15, 2014, Dân Làm Báo, accessed February 13, 2016, https://groups.yahoo.com/neo/groups/quanxuacva/conversations/messages/33109; Minh Trí, "Hội nghị Thành Đô: đâu là sự thật?" [Chengdu Conference: Where's the Truth?], October 23, 2014, Dân Làm Báo, accessed February 11, 2016, https://www.facebook.com/danlambaovn/posts/761700527218601.

68. Gia Minh, "Ban Tuyên giáo TW phổ biến tài liệu Hội nghị Thành Đô" [Central Propaganda and Education Board Circulates Material about the Chengdu Conference],

October 13, 2014, RFA, accessed February 11, 2016, http://www.rfa.org/vietnamese/in_depth/thanh-do-agree-declassi-10132014065248.html. For a scholarly analysis of the Chengdu meeting and its importance, see David W. P. Elliott, *Changing Worlds: Vietnam's Transition from Cold War to Globalization* (New York: Oxford University Press, 2012), 112–16.

69. "Những kẻ phá hoại đội lốt nhà dân chủ sẽ sa lưới pháp luật!" [Saboteurs Masquerading as Democrats Will Fall into the Net of the Law], December 13, 2014, Nguyễn Tấn Dũng, accessed September 16, 2015, http://nguyentandung.org/nhung-ke-pha-hoai-doi-lot-nha-dan-chu-se-sa-luoi-phap-luat.html.

70. For examples, see "Thứ trưởng ngoại giao Vũ Dũng" [Deputy Foreign Minister Vũ Dũng], January 4, 2008, *Tuổi Trẻ*, accessed January 7, 2008, http://www.tuoitre.com.vn/Tianyon/Index.aspx?ArticleID=237188&ChannelID=3; "Rare Protest in Vietnam over China Claims to Offshore Oil Blocks," July 1, 2012, Reuters, accessed July 2, 2012, http://in.reuters.com/article/2012/07/01/vietnam-china-oil-idINL3E8I106L20120701; "Phát biểu của Thủ tướng Nguyễn Tấn Dũng tại Diễn đàn Kinh tế Thế giới" [Speech by Prime Minister Nguyễn Tấn Dũng to the World Economic Forum], May 22, 2014, *Tiền Phong*, accessed January 8, 2017, http://www.tienphong.vn/xa-hoi/phat-bieu-cua-thu-tuong-nguyen-tan-dung-tai-dien-dan-kinh-te-the-gioi-708208.tpo.

71. One analysis of this diplomacy is Ramses Amer, "China, Vietnam, and the South China Sea: Disputes and Dispute Management," *Ocean Development and International Law* 45, no. 1 (2015): 17–40.

72. Carlyle A. Thayer, "Vietnam's Strategy of 'Cooperating and Struggling' with China over Maritime Disputes in the South China Sea," *Journal of Asian Security and International Affairs* 3, no. 2 (2016): 200–240; Alexander L. Vuving, "Vietnam, the US, and Japan in the South China Sea," November 26, 2014, *The Diplomat*, accessed November 27, 2014, http://thediplomat.com/2014/11/vietnam-the-us-and-japan-in-the-south-china-sea/.

73. This objective is an important aspect of normalizing the asymmetry between the two countries that Brantly Womack analyzed in *China and Vietnam: The Politics of Asymmetry* (New York: Cambridge University Press, 2006), 212–37.

74. Mặc Lâm, "Biểu tình chống Trung Quốc tại sao lại không nên?" [Why Are Demonstrations against China Unnecessary?], January 4, 2013, RFA, accessed January 5, 2013, http://www.rfa.org/vietnamese/vietnam/xa-hoi/anti-cn-emonstrate-wh-not-vh-01042013134655.html. Also see "Biểu tình chống TQ 'gây bất ổn'" [Demonstrations against China "Provoke instability"], January 1, 2013, BBC, accessed January 11, 2017, http://www.bbc.com/vietnamese/vietnam/2013/01/130101_nguyen_chi_vinh_iv_tuoi_tre.shtml.

75. Hà Giang, "Hoàng Sa và Trường Sa có còn là của Việt Nam?" [Are the Paracel and Spratly Islands Still Vietnam's?], September 16, 2009, RFA, accessed October 27, 2009, http://www.rfa.org/vietnamese/programs/OneStoryaWeek/Do-Paracel-Spratly-Islands-still-belong-to-VietNam-09162009121804.html. Nguyễn Ngọc Như Quỳnh, also known by her blog name Mẹ Nấm, continued to criticize China and the Vietnam party-state while also advocating democratization. Authorities often badgered her; then in 2016 police arrested her on charges of spreading propaganda against the state. See "Bắt tạm giam blogger Mẹ Nấm" [Mẹ Nấm Arrested and Detained"], October 10, 2016,

Vietnam.net, accessed October 11, 2016, http://vietnamnet.vn/vn/thoi-su/chinh-tri /333295/bat-tam-giam-blogger-me-nam.html.

76. "VN xử nặng Điếu Cày và Tạ Phong Tần" [Vietnam Makes Heavy Judgment against Điếu Cày and Tạ Phong Tần], September 24, 2012, BBC, accessed January 11, 2017, http://www.bbc.com/vietnamese/mobile/vietnam/2012/09/120924_bloggers_verdict. shtml. Điếu Cày, a.k.a. Nguyễn Văn Hải, was sentenced to twelve years' imprisonment. After serving two years, however, he was released on condition that he leave Vietnam and was sent to the United States in October 2014.

77. An admirer of the No-U wrote about such abuses: Nguyễn Khắc Mai, "Chính quyền Hà Nội nên cám ơn và xin lỗi No-U" [Hà Nội Officials Should Thank and Apologize to No-U], July 16, 2016, Ba Sàm, accessed January 31, 2017, http://basamnews .info/2016/07/16/9174-chinh-quyen-ha-noi-nen-cam-on-va-xin-loi-no-u/#more-150126.

78. My informants in Hà Nội, September 2012, were one petition signer who was at the session and two people who heard accounts from other participants. The petition itself is "Kiến nghị của công dân."

79. TS-BS Huỳnh Tấn Mẫm, "Thông báo số 2 của tập thể 42 công dân" [Second Announcement from Group of 42 Citizens], August 15, 2012, Quan Làm Báo, accessed April 1, 2014, http://quanlambao-vn.com/article.php?id=1775&cat_id=6.

80. Morris-Jung, "The Vietnamese Bauxite Controversy," 87; "Đại biểu quốc hội 'chiếm diễn đàn,' kêu gọi ra nghị quyết về Biển Đông" [National Assembly Delegates "Seize the Forum," Urge a Resolution Regarding the East Sea], June 19, 2014, Dân Làm Báo, accessed January 31, 2017, http://danlambaovn.blogspot.com/2014/06/ai-bieu-quoc -hoi-chiem-dien-keu-goi-ra.html; Nguyễn Thanh Giang, "Sớm loại bỏ bè lũ"; Carlyle A. Thayer, "Political Legitimacy of Vietnam's One Party-State: Challenges and Responses," *Journal of Current Southeast Asian Affairs* 28, no. 4 (2009): 51.

81. Hà Giang, "Hoàng Sa và Trường Sa"; "Cách chức Tổng biên tập báo điện tử Đảng CSVN" [Editor of Online VCP Paper Dismissed], September 23, 2009, RFA, accessed September 30, 2009, http://www.rfa.org/vietnamese/VietnameseNews/vietnam-news/VCP-website-editor-in-chief-gets-fired-and-fined-09232009111536.html.

82. Trong Nghĩa, "Lần đầu tiên, lãnh đạo Việt Nam công khai xác định: Trung Quốc dùng võ lực chiếm Hoàng Sa" [For the First Time a Vietnamese Leader Publicly Affirms that China Forcefully Took the Paracels], November 27, 2011, RFI, accessed November 28, 2011, http://www.viet.rfi.fr/viet-nam/20111127-lan-dau-tien-lanh-dao-viet-nam-cong-khai-xac-dinh-trung-quocdung-vo-luc-chiem-hoa.

83. Carl Thayer, "4 Reasons Why China Removed Oil Rig HYSY-981 Sooner Than Planned," *The Diplomat*, July 22, 2014, 4; Rosemarie Francisco and Manuel Mogato, "Vietnam PM Says Considering Legal Action against China over Disputed Waters," May 22, 2014, Reuters, accessed January 8, 2017, http://www.reuters.com/article/us-vietnam-china-idUSBREA4K1AK20140522.

4. Democratization

1. Nguyễn Thanh Giang, "Kính thưa đồng bào Việt Nam trong và ngoài nước" [Letter to Compatriots at Home and Abroad], February 3, 2010, DânTộc [Nation], ac-

cessed March 19, 2010, http://dantoc.net/?p=26521. His self-published autobiography details his background, family, work, relations with contemporaries, and political actions: Nguyễn Thanh Giang, *Người Đội Số Phận* [Carrying One's Fate] (Hà Nội, 2016).

2. Nguyễn Thanh Giang, "Thư ngỏ Bộ Chính trị Đảng Cộng sản Việt Nam" [Open Letter to the VCP's Political Bureau], July 17, 2003, *Điện Thư* [Electronic Letter], no. 6 (August 2003): 13.

3. Nguyễn Thanh Giang, *Đêm dày Lấp lánh* [Twinkling Dense Night] (n.p., 2012).

4. Related descriptions by participants included "*phong trào đấu tranh dân chủ*" [movement fighting for democracy] and "*phong trào bất đồng chính kiến và tranh đấu cho tự do dân chủ*" [political dissent movement fighting for freedom and democracy].

5. The quotation is from Stein Tønnesson, "The 'Vietnam Peace': How Priorities in Vietnam's Internal and External Policies Changed after 1987" (paper presented at 50th International Studies Association Convention, New York City, 2009), 15. It is a succinct version of the definition of dissident often used in analyses of political dissent in other communist-ruled countries. See, for example, Roy Medvedev, *On Soviet Dissent* (London: Constable, 1980), 1. This definition excludes from consideration private criticism and other everyday resistance to the political system, which also exists in Vietnam and likely feeds into public criticism. Such privately expressed criticism typically "breaks the surface of public life when authoritarian regimes take small steps toward liberalization" (Hank Johnston, "Talking the Walk: Speech Acts and Resistance in Authoritarian Regimes," in *Repression and Mobilization*, ed. Christian Davenport, Hank Johnston, and Carol Mueller [Minneapolis: University of Minnesota Press, 2005], 120).

6. In Vietnamese the first three are "*người phản kháng*"; "*nhà hoạt động dân chủ nhân quyền*"; and "*nhà đấu tranh dân chủ.*" "Dissident" is "*nhà bất đồng chính kiến*" or "*người bất đồng chính kiến,*" which literally means "a person with different political views," similar to "people who think differently," a translation of the Russian term dissidents in the Soviet Union reportedly preferred in the 1960s to1980s. They disliked the term "dissident" because that was the regime's label for them (Philip Boobbyer, *Conscience, Dissent, and Reform in Soviet Russia* [New York: Routledge, 2005], 74). Vietnamese officials often apply more pernicious descriptions such as "political opportunists," "regime malcontents," and "transgressors of criminal law, criminals" ("*kẻ cơ hội chính trị,*" "*kẻ bất mãn chế độ,*" and "*đối tượng vi phạm luật pháp hình sự*").

7. I use the dissidents' terminology "democratization movement" as a summary description for the intensified demand for regime change. Whether the phenomenon fulfills social science definitions for a political or social movement is a question for others to address.

8. For an approximate number of these critics and some of their names, see Nguyễn Vũ Bình, "Phong trào dân chủ Việt Nam trước vận hội lớn" [Vietnam's Democracy Movement Facing Large Opportunity], *Tự Do Ngôn Luận* [Free Speech], April 1, 2014, 10; and VNN, "Phỏng vấn đặc biệt chiến sĩ dân chủ, nhà báo Nguyễn Khắc Toàn" [Special Interview with Journalist and Fighter for Democracy Nguyễn Khắc Toàn], August 8, 2006, Mạng Ý Kiến [Opinion Net], accessed October 20, 2006, http://www.ykien.net/.

9. Phạm Quế Dương and Trần Văn Khuê, "Hội Nhân dân Việt Nam chống tham nhũng" [Vietnamese People's Association against Corruption], September 2, 2001,

Mạng Ý Kiến, accessed December 17, 2003, http://www.ykien.net/vdhchongtn.html; Nguyễn Vũ Bình, "Bản điều trần về tình trạng nhân quyền tại Việt Nam" [Testimony Regarding Human Rights Conditions in Vietnam], July 19, 2002, *Điện Thư*, no. 14 (December 2003): 2; Phạm Quế Dương and Trần Khuê, "Kỷ niệm một năm ngày thành lập Hội Nhân dân Việt Nam chống Tham nhũng, 02.9.01-02.9.02" [First Anniversary of the Vietnamese People's Association against Corruption], Mạng Ý Kiến, accessed January 5, 2005, http://www.ykien.net/clbdt018.html. Trần Khuê, also known as Trần Văn Khuê, is a military veteran and a scholar. Phạm Quế Dương, a retired military colonel, was a VCP member from 1948 until 1999, when he quit in protest because the party ejected retired general Trần Độ, another dissident.

10. The Club's Vietnamese name is Câu Lạc Bộ Dân Chủ. The sixty-fifth and final issue of *Điện Thư* was July 2007.

11. *Người Sài Gòn* [Saigonese] started in early 1996 and ended April 1997 in the face of imminent detection by security police. The cover page for a compilation of articles from several issues indicates the publication was circulated mainly by fax machines. Accessed September 2001 at http://www.lmvntd.org/ngsaigon/ngsaigon_vsc.htm.

12. The actual names are, respectively, Liên Minh Dân Chủ Nhân Quyền Việt Nam; Hội Cựu Tù Nhân Chính Trị và Tôn Giáo; and Ủy Ban Nhân Quyền Việt Nam.

13. The actual names are Đảng Thăng Tiến Việt Nam, Đảng Dân Chủ Việt Nam (also called Đảng Dân Chủ Việt Nam Thế kỷ 21) and Đảng Dân Chủ Nhân Dân.

14. The actual titles are, respectively, *Tổ Quốc, Tự Do Ngôn Luận, Tự Do Dân Chủ*, and *Dân Chủ*. A key initiator of *Tổ Quốc* was Nguyễn Thanh Giang, who is discussed in the opening paragraphs of this chapter.

15. In Vietnamese, Bloc 8406 is Khối 8406. The "8406" in its name comes from the date sequence as often written in Vietnamese materials—8/4/06—meaning 8 April 2006, the date of that Declaration. The Declaration is "Tuyên ngôn Tự do Dân chủ cho Việt Nam." It came more than eighteen months earlier than a similar one in China, called Charter 08, issued by Chinese political dissidents in December 2008.

16. Tabulated from the list attached to "Tuyên Ngôn 8406 Tự do Dân chủ cho Việt Nam 2006" [Declaration 8406: Freedom and Democracy for Vietnam in 2006], May 9, 2006, Lên đường [Start a Journey], accessed May 11, 2006, http://www.lenduong.net/article.php3?id_article=17063.

17. The seventeen people are Bạch Ngọc Dương, Chân Tín, Đỗ Nam Hải, Hoàng Minh Chính, Hoàng Tiến, Lê Thị Công Nhân, Nguyễn Chính Kết, Nguyễn Khắc Toàn, Nguyễn Phòng, Nguyễn Phương Anh, Nguyễn Thanh Giang, Nguyễn Văn Đài, Nguyễn Văn Lý, Phan Văn Lợi, Trần Anh Kim, Trần Khải Thanh Thủy, and Trần Khuê. My information about them and their public political activities comes from numerous Internet materials, primarily interviews with and essays by the individuals themselves and documents from the organizations in which they were involved. There was an eighteenth person, Dương Văn Dương, prominent in more than one organization but the only additional information I could find is that he lived in Thái Bình province.

18. Information about Nguyễn Chính Kết comes from his writings and interviews, especially his "Tại sao có quá ít người dám tranh đấu?" [Why So Few People Dare to

Struggle?], June 10, 2005, Phong trào dân chủ Việt Nam [Vietnam's Democracy Movement], accessed June 22, 2006, http://www.ptdcvn.org/TACGIA_TAVCPHAM/NguyenChinhKet/NCK-TaiSaoItDT.htm; and "Vì dân chủ tôi sẵn sàng đổi cả mạng sống" [For Democracy I'm Willing to Sacrifice My Life], November 29, 2006, *Thông Luận* [Thorough Discussion], accessed December 1, 2006, http://www.thongluan.org/vn/modules.php?name=News&file=article&sid=1296.

19. This paragraph draws on Trần Bình Nam, "Chào Mừng người em gái Lê Thị Công Nhân" [Welcome Sister Lê Thị Công Nhân], *Tự Do Dân Chủ* [Freedom and Democracy], April 7, 2010, 28–29; "Lời Kêu Gọi Dân Chủ cho Việt Nam: Thư Ngỏ gửi Tổng Thống Hoa Kỳ George W. Bush" [Calling for Democracy in Vietnam: An Open Letter Sent to President George W. Bush], *Tự Do Dân Chủ*, December 14, 2006, 8–9.

20. Khối 8406, "Quyết định bổ nhiệm đại diện Khối 8406 tại hải ngoại [Appointing a Bloc 8406 Overseas Representative], October 18, 2007, *Tự Do Ngôn Luận* [Free Speech], accessed February 22, 2008, http://www.tdngonluan.com/tailieu/tl_khoi8406_quyetdinhbonhiemdaidienhaingoai.htm.

21. Issues of each publication can be found at their websites: www.tdngonluan.com and https:/vi-vn.facebook.com/Tự-Do-Ngôn-Luận-238293869580176/timeline/ for *Tự Do Ngôn Luận* and www.to-quoc.blogspot.com for *Tổ Quốc* (although the latter stopped in late November 2016).

22. Among them were Anh Ba Sàm, AnhbaSG, Nhà Báo Tự Do, Trần Đông Chấn, and Osin.

23. See chapter 3.

24. David Uy, "Lược Sử Blog Việt" [Brief History of Vietnamese Blogging], June 24, 2012, Hãy Dành Thời Gian [Let's Make Time], accessed July 11, 2012, http://haydanhthoigian.net/2012/06/24/luoc-su-blog-viet-a-brief-history-of-blogs-in-vietnam/; Đoan Trang, "Chronology of the Blogging Movement in Vietnam," December 31, 2013, Đoan Trang, accessed March 14, 2014, http://www.phamdoantrang.com/2013/12/chronology-of-blogging-movement-in.html. (I am grateful to Duyên Bùi and David Brown for the second of these two.)

25. The name Anh Ba Sàm later became Ba Sàm [Gossip].

26. "Tuyên bố của Mạng Lưới Blogger Việt Nam" [Pronouncement of the Vietnamese Blogger Network], July 20, 2013, Mạng Lưới Blogger [Blogger Network], accessed July 4, 2014, http://tuyenbo258.blogspot.com/2013_07_01_archive.html; Mạng lưới Blogger Việt Nam, "Danh sách blogger ký tuyên bố 258" [List of Bloggers Signing Pronouncement 258], July 2013, Mạng Lưới Blogger, accessed August 4, 2014, http://tuyenbo258.blogspot.com/2013/07/tuyen-bo-cua-mang-luoi-blogger-viet-nam.html.

27. TechinAsia, "In Vietnam, for Every 100 People There Are 145 Mobile Phones," December 5, 2012, TechinAsia, accessed March 5, 2015, https://www.techinasia.com/vietnam-100-people-145-mobile-phones. For Internet statistics, see "Viet Nam Internet Users," Internet Live Stats, accessed March 5, 2015, http://www.internetlivestats.com/internet-users/viet-nam.

28. For some elaboration, see David G. Marr, "A Passion for Modernity: Intellectuals and the Media," in *Postwar Vietnam: Dynamics of a Transforming Society*, ed. Hy V. Luong (Boulder, CO: Rowman & Littlefield, 2003), 289–95; Catherine McKinley and

Anya Schiffrin, "Leninist Lapdogs to Bothersome Bloggers in Vietnam," in *State Power 2.0: Authoritarian Entrenchment and Political Engagement Worldwide*, ed. Muzammil M. Hussaid and Philip N. Howard (Burlington, VT: Ashgate, 2013), 125–38.

29. Russell Hiang-Khng Heng, "Of the State, For the State, Yet against the State: The Struggle Paradigm in Vietnam's Media Politics" (PhD diss., Australian National University, 1999), 231–33, 242–45. Also see Carlyle A. Thayer, "Political Reform in Vietnam: Doi Moi and the Emergence of Civil Society," in *Development of Civil Society in Communist Systems*, ed. Robert F. Miller (North Sydney, NSW: Allen & Unwin, 1992), 123.

30. Regarding the circulation of political statements to seek signatures from fellow citizens, see Jason Morris-Jung, "Vietnam's Online Petition Movement," in *Southeast Asian Affairs 2015*, ed. Daljit Singh (Singapore: Institute of Southeast Asian Studies, 2015), 402–15.

31. Chapter 5 elaborates.

32. Nguyễn Hải Sơn, "Dấu hỏi chấm than" [Question and Exclamation Marks], *Điện Thư*, no. 32 (December 2004): 22.

33. Nguyễn Xuân Nghĩa, interview by RFA, September 27, 2005, Mạng Ý Kiến, accessed October 30, 2005, http://www.ykien.net/tl_viettrung91.html#dhX050928a; Đặng Văn Việt, "Thư Góp Ý" [letter to national authorities], September 10, 2006, *Tổ Quốc* [Homeland], October 1, 2006, 5; Phạm Quế Dương, interview by RFA, November 25, 2004, Le Phai, accessed January 7, 2005, http://www.lephai.com/dt20041203d. html; Lê Chí Quang, "Muốn chống tham nhũng, phải chống cái cơ chế để ra tham nhũng" [To Fight Corruption One Needs to Fight the Structure That Produces It], August 19, 2001, *Điện Thư*, no. 22 (June 2004): 3–4; Tống Văn Công, "Đổi mới đảng, tránh nguy cơ sup đổ" [Renovate the Party, Avoid Danger of Being Overthrown], September 23, 2009, Diễn Đàn [Forum], accessed October 2, 2009, http://www.diendan.org/viet-nam/111oi-moi-111ang-tranh-nguy-co-sup-11o/. At the time of their comments, Nguyễn Xuân Nghĩa was a journalist and writer in the city of Hải Phòng, and Đặng Văn Việt, a veteran of revolutions against France and long-time VCP member, lived in Hà Nội. Tống Văn Công, a former editor of the newspaper *Lao Động* [Labor] and VCP member for over fifty-five years, said in 2014 he was leaving the party in disgust. Tống Văn Công, "Lời từ biệt đảng Cộng sản VN của nguyên Tổng Biên Tập báo Lao động" [Former General Editor of the Newspaper Labor says Goodbye to the VCP], February 25, 2014, *Tổ Quốc*, March 1, 2014, 13–21.

34. Phạm Hồng Sơn and Thư Lê, Foreword to translation of "What Is Democracy?," January 2002, Mạng Ý Kiến, accessed October 10, 2003, http://www.ykien.net/bnphsthenaodc.html; Trần Độ, "Nhật ký rồng rắn" [Diary of a Dragon Snake], part 1, *Điện Thư*, no. 29 (November 2004): 6, and part 3, *Điện Thư*, no. 31 (November 2004): 3 and 5; Nguyễn Khắc Toàn, "Khát vọng tự do" [Craving Freedom], April 25, 2006, Mạng Ý Kiến, accessed June 20, 2006, http://www.ykien.net/. Phạm Hồng Sơn, a medical doctor, resides in Hà Nội. Nguyễn Khắc Toàn once owned and operated an electronics shop and a real estate office in Hà Nội.

35. For example, see Vi Đức Hồi, "Đối mặt" [Facing Up], November 25, 2008, *Thông Luận*, accessed November 26, 2008, http://www.thongluan.org/vn/modules .php?name=News&file=article&sid=3301. The relevant passages are on pages 19 and 21

(printed on 8½ × 11 inch paper) in this lengthy account about how the author, a provincial official and VCP member, decided to join the pro-democracy movement.

36. For instance, see Lê Hồng Hà, "Tiền đồ phát triển của đất nước và trách nhiệm của giới trí thức" [The Country's Development Prospects and Intellectuals' Responsibilities], 2004, section 2, Mạng Ý Kiến, accessed March 3, 2004, http://www.ykien.net/bnlhhtrithuc.html; Lê Hồng Hà, interview by RFA, February 1, 2007, *Thông Luận*, accessed February 2, 2007, http://www.thongluan.org/vn/modules.php?name=Content&pa=showpage&pid=493.

37. Hoàng Tiến, "'Kẻ sĩ phải nói những điều ích nước lợi dân'" ["Scholars Should Say Things Useful for the Country and People"], *Thông Luận*, March 2005, 8; Bạch Ngọc Dương, "Những suy nghĩ về dân chủ đích thực cho Việt Nam" [Thoughts about Real Democracy for Vietnam], October 20, 2007, *Thông Luận*, accessed October 26, 2007, http://www.thongluan.org/vn/modules.php?name= News&file=article&sid=2196; Trần Lâm, "Sự thay đổi đã đến gần" [Change Is Near], November 30, 2009, *Thông Luận*, accessed January 29, 2010, http://www.thongluan.org/vn/modules.php?name= News&file=article&sid=4377. Hoàng Tiến, a writer in Hà Nội, participated in the revolution for independence; Bạch Ngọc Dương is an engineer in Hải Phòng.

38. Nguyễn Chính Kết, "Nguy cơ mất nước đã đến rất gần" [Threat of National Destruction Is Near], April 5, 2009, Đối Thoại [Dialogue], accessed April 17, 2009, http://www.doi-thoai.com/baimoi0409_126. html. Also see Trần Khuê, interview by *Công Lý*, 2001, Mạng Ý Kiến, accessed December 4, 2003, http://www.ykien.net/dttkphongvan.html; Nguyễn Thanh Giang, "Bộ Quốc Phòng rời bỏ nhiệm vụ chính của mình" [Ministry of Defense Has Abandoned Its Primary Responsibility], *Điện Thư*, no. 33 (December 2004): 3–6; Trần Lâm, "Sự thay đổi"; Phạm Đình Trọng, "Thông báo về việc từ bỏ đảng tịch đảng viên Đảng Cộng Sản" [Announcing a Member's Withdrawal from the Communist Party], November 20, 2009, *Tổ Quốc*, December 15, 2009, 6–7; and numerous materials on the Bauxite Viet Nam website http://boxitvn.wordpress.com. Phạm Đình Trọng, a writer in Hồ Chí Minh City, quit the VCP in 2009 out of disgust with the regime's policies on China and several other matters.

39. "Tuyên ngôn Tự do"; Đỗ Nam Hải, "Phát biểu trong hội ngộ các thành viên của Phong trào yểm trợ Khối 8406" [Speech to Participants in Movement Helping Bloc 8406], March 2008, Đối Thoại, accessed April 4, 2008, http://www.doi-thoai.com/baimoi0308_288.html; Phạm Hồng Sơn, "Ngày Độc Lập, nghĩ về độc lập tư duy" [Reflections on Independence Day about Independence], *Thông Luận*, September 2009, 8–10; Trần Lâm, "Phong trào dân chủ Việt Nam" [Vietnam's Democracy Movement], December 2005, Mạng Ý Kiến, accessed May 19, 2006, http://www.ykien.net/. Trần Lâm, a Hải Phòng resident, a lawyer, and former judge in Vietnam's supreme court, died in November 2014 at the age of ninety.

40. For example, see Nguyễn Thanh Giang, "Bàn về dân chủ" [On Democracy], *Điện Thư*, no. 56 (March 2006): 22–23; Nguyễn Vũ Bình, interview by BBC, June 15, 2002, Mạng Ý Kiến, accessed February 4, 2004, http://www.ykien.net/ mykbdv45.html; "Lời kêu gọi cho quyền thành lập và hoạt động đảng phái tại Việt Nam" [Calling for the Right to Establish and Operate Political Parties in Vietnam], April 6, 2006, Le Phai, accessed April 7, 2006, http://lephai.com/uni/n2006/dt20060406a.htm, which was

signed by 116 advocates for democracy. Nguyễn Vũ Bình was an editor for a VCP journal in Hà Nội but was fired after he requested permission to establish an opposition party in 2000 and later imprisoned.

41. The name comes from two of the journals published by participants: *Nhân Văn* [Humanity] and *Giai Phẩm* [Masterworks]. My discussion is based on Georges Boudarel, "The Nhân-Văn Giai-Phẩm Affair," *Vietnam Forum* 13 (1990): 154–74; Hoa Mai, ed., *The "Nhan-Van" Affair* (Saigon(?): Vietnam Chapter of the Asian People's Anti-Communist League, n.d. [circa 1958]); Heng, "Of the State, For the State," 78–110; Huy Đức, *Bên Thắng Cuộc* [The Winning Side], vol. 2 (Saigon: OsinBook, 2012), 13–24; Hirohide Kurihara, "Changes in the Literary Policy of the Vietnamese Workers' Party, 1956–1958," in *Indochina in the 1940s and 1950s*, ed. Takashi Shiraishi and Motoo Furuta (Ithaca, NY: Southeast Asia Program, Cornell University, 1992), 165–96; Kim N. B. Ninh, *A World Transformed: The Politics of Culture in Revolutionary Vietnam, 1945–1965* (Ann Arbor: University of Michigan Press, 2002), 121–63; Peter Zinoman, "Nhân Văn-Giai Phẩm and Vietnamese 'Reform Communism' in the 1950s," *Journal of Cold War Studies* 13 (Winter 2011): 60–100.

42. The club's actual name is Câu Lạc Bộ Những Người Kháng Chiến Cũ Thành Phố Hồ Chí Minh. My discussion of it relies primarily on Heng, "Of the State, For the State," 219–49.

43. See chapter 5.

44. Reported dates of his birth range between 1922 and 1924. For an informed account of Trần Độ's background and political views, see Ken MacLean, "A 'Biography Not' of General Trần Độ: His Dissident Writings, Elite Politics, and Death in Retrospect," *Journal of Vietnamese Studies* 8 (Winter 2013): 34–79.

45. Trần Độ wrote about his experience then and the people he met: *Kể chuyện Điện Biên: Bút ký* [Recounting Điện Biên: Notes] (Hanoi: Nxb Văn Nghệ, 1955).

46. Trần Độ, "Một cái nhìn trở lại" [A Retrospection], part 1, September 23, 1998, *Diễn Đàn* [Forum], no. 81 (January 1999): 12. Also see Trần Độ, "Một chiến lược dân chủ hóa để chống tham nhũng" [A Democratization Strategy to Fight Corruption], April 2000, Mạng Ý Kiến, accessed January 5, 2005, http://www.ykien.net/vdtd3.html.

47. Trần Độ, "Nhật ký rồng rắn," part 1, 3, 6; part 3, 4.

48. Trần Độ, "Nhật ký rồng rắn," part 1, 3–5; part 3, 5.

49. Trần Độ, "Đảng Cộng Sản và dân chủ ở Việt Nam" [The Communist Party and Democracy in Vietnam], November 20, 2001, 13, Mạng Ý Kiến, accessed November 20, 2003, http://www.ykien.net/bntddcsdc.html.

50. After being expelled, Trần Độ wrote that he had no regrets about being a VCP member for fifty-eight years and urged party members to renovate it because, as one VCP motto says, "renovate or die." Trần Độ, "Mấy lời" [A Few Words], January 8, 1999, *Thông Luận*, accessed January 8, 1999, http://www.thongluan.org/VN/NS/TL123-tudo.html.

51. The argument is scattered across several writings; see particularly Trần Độ, "Đảng Cộng Sản và dân chủ," and Trần Độ, "Con đường dân chủ hóa ở Việt Nam" [Democratization Road in Vietnam], circa mid-2001, 1–17, Mạng Ý Kiến, accessed December 4, 2003, http://www.ykien.net/bntddh9danchu.html.

52. In 2001 he expressed some doubts about the VCP's ability to renovate itself [*tự đổi mới*] but concluded it could do it—and must. Trần Độ, "Con đường dân chủ," 6–7, 16–17.

53. His many writings about corruption include letters sent to high-level government authorities; for instance, Trần Huỳnh Duy Thức, Kính gửi Bí thư Thành ủy Tp HCM Nguyễn Minh Triết [Letter to Nguyễn Minh Triết, Communist Party Secretary, Hồ Chí Minh City], January 7, 2004, Mediafire, accessed March 30, 2012, http://www.mediafire.com/view/02d8pxccbmy728e/Thu+gui+Bi+Thu+Thanh+Uy+HCM.pdf. For an account of Trần Huỳnh Duy Thức's upbringing, youth, schooling, and business endeavors, see Phong trào Con đường Việt Nam (Biên soạn) [Vietnam Way Movement (compiler)], *Trần Huỳnh Duy Thức & Con đường nào cho Việt Nam* [Trần Huỳnh Duy Thức and What Is the Road for Vietnam] (n.p.: Phong trào Con đường Việt Nam, May 2013), 17–64.

54. Trần Huỳnh Duy Thức và những người bạn [Trần Huỳnh Duy Thức and friends], "Con đường Việt Nam: Con đường phát triển đất nước trên nền tảng quyền con người" [Vietnam Way: Road for Developing the Country Based on People's Rights] (written 2008–11), in Phong trào Con đường Việt Nam, *Trần Huỳnh Duy Thức*, 218, and see 192–93, 211–12. The discussion here also draws on the following by Trần Huỳnh Duy Thức: "Động lực cho thay đổi" [Impetus for Change], September 2008, written under pen name Trần Đông Chấn, accessed June 22, 2012, http://trandongchan.blogspot.com/2008/09/ong-luc-cho-thay-oi.html; and "Tự do và sự sợ hãi" [Freedom and Terror], November 2008, written under pen name Trần Đông Chấn, accessed June 11, 2012, http://trandongchan.blogspot.com/2008/11/tu-do-va-su-so-hai_08.html.

55. See the following by Trần Huỳnh Duy Thức: "Góp ý cho bộ chính trị 150 ngày sau đại hội X" [Ideas for the Political Bureau 150 Days after the Tenth Party Congress], September 2006, written under pen name Trần Đông Chấn, Trần Đông Chấn, accessed May 3, 2012, http://trandongchan.blogspot.com/2007/05/gop-y-cho-bo-chinh-tri-150-ngay-sau-ai_1068.html; "Khủng hoảng và thời cơ" [Crisis and Opportunity], June 2008, written under pen name Dương Hữu Canh, Trần Đông Chấn, accessed June 22, 2012, http://trandongchan.blogspot.com/2008/06/khung-hoang-va-thoi-co.html; and "Đô-la ngoại sẽ đi tới đâu" [Where the U.S. Dollar Is Going], August 5, 2008, 12–13, 15, written under pen name Trần Đông Chấn, 360 Yahoo, accessed June 22, 2012, http://360.yahoo.com/trandongchan.

56. See these writings by Trần Huỳnh Duy Thức: "Góp ý cho bộ chính trị"; "Khủng hoảng"; "Đơn Kháng Cáo Bản Án Sơ Thẩm" [Appealing the Sentence by the Court of First Instance], February 1, 2010, 8–9, 11, 22–23, 25, Mediafire, accessed March 30, 2012, http://www.mediafire.com/?4jc1hi8hxh57akf" \o "Đơn kháng cáo" \t; "Một năm sau Đại hội X—cảnh báo những nguy cơ quốc gia" [One Year after Tenth Party Congress: Warnings about National Dangers], April 2007, written under pen name Trần Đông Chấn, Trần Đông Chấn, accessed May 3, 2012, http://trandongchan.blogspot.com/2007/05/mot-nam-sau-ai-hoi-x-canh-bao-nhung_02.html; "Việt Nam đồng đang ở đâu và sẽ đi về đâu" [Where the Vietnamese Currency Is Going and Where It Will End Up], March 2008, written under pen name Trần Đông Chấn, Trần Đông Chấn, accessed

May 3, 2012, http://trandongchan.blogspot.com/2007/05/mot-nam-sau-ai-hoi-x-canh
-bao-nhung_3804.html; "Con đường Việt Nam: Cách để mỗi người giàu có" [Vietnam
Road: Way for All To Be Wealthy], December 2008, written under pen name Trần
Đông Chấn, Tranfami, accessed March 30, 2012, http://tranfami.wordpress.com/2012
/02/25/the-path-of-vietnam/. The last is the précis for a planned book that became a
long essay written primarily, it seems, by Trần Huỳnh Duy Thức and his friends Lê
Công Định and Lê Thăng Long. That essay is Trần Huỳnh Duy Thức và những người
bạn, "Con đường Việt Nam"; pages 169–71 there explain its origins.

57. Trần Huỳnh Duy Thức và những người bạn, "Con đường Việt Nam," 235–
40; Trần Huỳnh Duy Thức, "Đơn Kháng Cáo," 6–13.

58. The quoted passage is from Trần Huỳnh Duy Thức, "Khủng hoảng." Additional sources for this discussion include his "Con Đường Việt Nam: Cách để"; and
Trần Huỳnh Duy Thức và những người bạn, "Con Đường Việt Nam," 202, 203,
217, 222. One task for the state while guiding the market economy, he wrote on several occasions, is to guard against the rise of the "colossal enterprises" [*các doanh
nghiệp khổng lồ*] found in "capitalist market economies" [*các nền kinh tế thị trường tư
bản chủ nghĩa*]. Such enterprises, he said, obstruct and prevent new, smaller ones entering the market.

59. Trần Huỳnh Duy Thức, "Con Đường Việt Nam: Cách để" and "Đơn Kháng
Cáo," 17; Trần Huỳnh Duy Thức và những người bạn, "Con Đường Việt Nam,"
249–50.

60. Trần Huỳnh Duy Thức, "Chào 2009" [Greeting the Year 2009], January 2009,
written under pen name Trần Đông Chấn, Trần Đông Chấn, accessed June 11, 2002,
http://trandongchan.blogspot.com/2008_12_01_archive.html.

61. The quoted passage and some other aspects of Trần Huỳnh Duy Thức's assessment are in his "Đơn Kháng Cáo," 16. Additional sources for my discussion here are his
"Khủng hoảng"; "Con Đường Việt Nam: Cách để"; and "Động lực."

62. For that appeal, see Trần Huỳnh Duy Thức, "Đơn Kháng Cáo." Additional
sources for this paragraph include Viện Kiểm Sát Nhân Dân Tối Cao [The People's
Supreme Prosecutor General], "Cáo Trạng" [Indictment], November 23, 2009, 3–4,
6–7, 9–11, 15, Tiếng nói Dân chủ [Voice of Democracy], accessed July 11, 2012, http://
tiengnoidanchu.wordpress.com/2009/12/24/bản-cáo-trạng-của-vksn; "Trần Huỳnh
Duy Thức và đồng phạm lĩnh án từ 5 đến 16 năm tù" [Trần Huỳnh Duy Thức and
Accomplices Sentenced 5 to 16 Years], January 21, 2010, *Nhân Dân* [People], accessed
January 22, 2010, http://www.nhandan.com.vn/tinbai/?top=40&sub=67&article=166410;
"Vụ án 'hoạt động nhằm lật đổ chính quyền nhân dân'" [Trial for "Acting to Overthrow People's Authority"], January 21, 2010, *Tuổi Trẻ* [Youth], accessed January 25,
2010, http://www.tuoitre.com.vn/Tianyon/Index.aspx?ArticleID=359734&Channe
lID=6.

63. See, for instance, Đảng Dân Chủ Nhân Dân [People's Democratic Party],
"Tuyên Ngôn" [Declaration], January 1, 2005, *Điện Thư*, no. 48 (July 2005): 1, 5–6;
Đảng Thăng Tiến Việt Nam [Vietnamese Progressive Party], "Cương lĩnh tạm thời"
[Provisional Policy Outline], September 8, 2006, parts I and II, *Tự Do Ngôn Luận*, ac-
cessed September 29, 2006, http://www.tdngonluan.com/tailieu/tl_dangthangtienvietnam
_sept8.htm; Đặng Văn Việt, Kính gửi: Đại Hội X và Ban Chấp Hành Trung ương

khóa IX [Letter to the Tenth Party Congress and Ninth Plenum of its Central Executive Committee], February 12, 2006, *Điện Thư*, no. 55 (February 2006): 15; Trần Anh Kim, "Lời Cảnh Báo" [Sounding an Alarm], March 3, 2006, Mạng Ý Kiến, accessed April 7, 2006, http://www.ykien.net.

64. "Tuyên ngôn Tự do," part III.

65. Huỳnh Việt Lang, "Dân chủ và văn hóa tổ chức" [Democracy and Organization Culture], *Điện Thư*, no. 58 (May 2006): 39–40; Lê Quang Liêm, "Làm thế nào tiến đến dân chủ hóa Việt Nam?" [How to Progress to Democratizing Vietnam], *Tự Do Ngôn Luận*, May 15, 2006, 10; Nguyễn Vũ Bình, "Tương lai nào cho phong trào dân chủ Việt Nam?" [What Is the Future of Vietnam's Democracy Movement?], February 28, 2008, part 3, point 3, Mạng Ý Kiến, accessed March 6, 2008, http://ykien0711.blogvis.com/2008 /02/29/t%c6%b0%c6%a1ng-lai-nao-cho-phong-trao-dan-ch%e1%bb%a7 -vi%e1%bb%87t-nam/. Huỳnh Việt Lang, a Hồ Chí Minh City resident and member of the People's Democratic Party, was arrested in August 2006; Lê Quang Liêm is a Hòa Hảo Buddhist.

66. Phạm Quế Dương, "Một bài viết có tầm chiến lược cho phong trào dân chủ" [An Article of Strategic Relevance to a Democracy Movement], *Thông Luận*, September 2007, 15.

67. "Tuyên ngôn Tự do," part III.

68. For a chronicle of the declaration's creation, see Nguyễn Khắc Toàn, "Bạo quyền không thể đập tắt được sức mạnh của lương tri" [Tyrannical Power Can't Disrupt the Power of Conscience], April 10, 2006, Diễn đàn Tự do Dân chủ [Freedom and Democracy Forum], accessed May 11, 2006, http://diendantudodanchu.net/vn/modules .php?name=News&file=print&sid=1094.

69. Writings by Đỗ Nam Hải: "Thư ngỏ" [Public letter], December 10, 2004, *Điện Thư*, no. 34 (December 2004): 1–4; "Những tiếng nói dân chủ Việt Nam" [Voices of Vietnamese Democracy], December 14, 2004, *Điện Thư*, no. 35 (December 2004): 1–4; and "Quyết định của tổng giám đốc Ngân hàng Thương mại Cổ phần" [Decision of the Commercial Holding Bank's General Director], February 22, 2005, *Điện Thư*, no. 43 (April 2005): 3–5.

70. Mạng lưới Dân chủ [Democracy Network], "Phỏng vấn Phương Nam" [Phương Nam (a.k.a. Đỗ Nam Hải) Interview], *Điện Thư*, no. 34 (December 2004): 5–7; Phạm Điền, "Nhà Dân chủ Phương Nam" [Democracy Advocate Phương Nam (a.k.a. Đỗ Nam Hải)], May 11, 2005, RFA, accessed September 8, 2005, http://www .ykien.net/pn16.html.

71. Đỗ Nam Hải, "Thư ngỏ," 3.

72. Đỗ Nam Hải, "Những tiếng nói." For his disquisition on Vietnam's numerous domestic problems, including the inappropriateness of Marxist theory and of a market economy with socialist orientations, see "Việt Nam Đất nước tôi" [Vietnam, My Country], June 2000, *Điện Thư*, no. 28 (October 2004): 15–48.

73. Đỗ Nam Hải, "Phát biểu," 3.

74. Đỗ Nam Hải, "Quyết định," 4, and "Phát biểu," 3.

75. He hoped Vietnamese authorities would surrender early enough to avoid what happened in Romania in December 1989 when angry crowds stormed Ceauşescu's residence and executed him and his wife. Đỗ Nam Hải, "Thư ngỏ," 3.

76. Khối 8406 [Bloc 8406], "Cương lĩnh Khối 8406 hay Khối 8406 là gì" [Bloc 8406's Program or What Is Bloc 8406], October 8, 2006, article 2.1, Khối 8406, accessed December 1, 2014, http://khoi8406vn.blogspot.com.au/2014/06/cuong-linh.html.

77. See the following by Khối 8406: "Kêu gọi tẩy chay bầu cử Quốc hội 2007" [Call to Boycott National Assembly Elections in 2007], January 24, 2007, Đàn Chim Việt [Việt Flock], accessed April 19, 2007, http://www.danchimviet.com/php/modules.php?name=News&file=article&sid=2881; "Lời kêu gọi tẩy chay cuộc bầu cử Quốc hội khóa 13" [Call to Boycott Elections for the National Assembly's Thirteenth Session], February 1, 2011, Tự Do Ngôn Luận, February 1, 2011, 6–7; and "Lời tuyên bố nhân kỷ niệm 3 năm Tuyên ngôn Tự do Dân chủ 2006" [Announcement on the Occasion of the Third Anniversary of the 2006 Declaration on Freedom and Democracy], April 8, 2009, Tự Do Ngôn Luận, accessed June 23, 2009, http://www.tdngonluan.com/tailieu/tl_loituyenbon-hankyniem3nam_khoi8406.htm.

78. Đỗ Nam Hải, "Lượng định về phong trào đấu tranh giành lại tự do dân chủ cho VN trong thời gian qua" [Evaluating the Struggle Thus Far to Regain Freedom and Democracy for Vietnam], October 17, 2007, ViệtBáo [Việt News], accessed November 21, 2007, http://www.vietbao.com/?ppid=45&pid=114&nid=116821; Đỗ Nam Hải, "Phát biểu"; and these by Khối 8406: "Lời tuyên bố," and "Tuyên bố nhân kỷ niệm lần thứ 8 ngày thành lập" [Announcement on Occasion of Eighth Anniversary], April 8, 2014, Tự Do Ngôn Luận, April 15, 2014, 3–4.

79. Examples of accounts about the harassment: Ủy ban Nhân quyền Việt Nam [Vietnam Human Rights Committee], "Bản Lên án số 1" [Sentence, No. 1], December 10, 2006, Tự Do Ngôn Luận, December 15, 2006, 6; commentaries by Đỗ Nam Hải: "Lượng định"; "CSVN xông vào nhà lục soát, tịch thu tài sản Đỗ Nam Hải" [Vietnamese Communists Raid and Search Đỗ Nam Hải's House, Confiscate Possessions], March 26, 2009, ViệtBáo, accessed March 29, 2009, http://www.vietbao.com/?ppid=45&pid=4&nid=142578; "Luật pháp CSVN áp dụng tùy tiện cho nhà tranh đấu dân chủ" [Arbitrary Application of Vietnamese Communist Law against Fighters for Democracy], Tự Do Dân Chủ, April 7, 2010, 31–32.

80. Nguyễn Khanh, "Công an dùng áp lực gia đình buộc anh Đỗ Nam Hải phải ngưng tất cả hoạt động tranh đấu cho dân chủ" [Security Police Force Family to Require Đỗ Nam Hải to Stop All Pro-Democracy Activities], March 19, 2007, RFA, accessed March 29, 2007, http://www.rfa.org/vietnamese/in_depth/2007/03/19/Interview-DoNamHaiAndHoangHa_Khanh/.

81. Nguyễn Văn Đài, "Quyền Tự do Thành lập Đảng ở Việt Nam" [Freedom to Establish a Party in Vietnam], May 14, 2006, BBC, accessed June 22, 2006, http://www.bbc.co.uk/vietnamese/forum/story/2006/04/060425_quyenlapdang.shtml; Bá Tuấn, "Luật pháp có cấm?" [Prohibited by Law?], Pháp Luật [Law], May 10, 2004, 3; "'Thay đổi phải đến từ tư tưởng'" ["Change Must Come from Thought"], April 27, 2006, BBC, accessed May 25, 2006, http://www.bbc.co.uk/vietnamese/vietnam/story/2006/04/060427_nguyenvandai_interview.shtml; "BBC Phỏng vấn LS Nguyễn Văn Đài" [BBC Interviews Attorney Nguyễn Văn Đài], August 24, 2006, Le Phai, accessed September 4, 2006, http://lephai.com/uni/n2006/dt20060824k.htm; Bill Hayton, Vietnam: Rising Dragon (New Haven, CT: Yale University Press, 2010), 118–19, 122, 127. Regarding For Justice [Vì Công Lý], see Mark Sidel, Law and Society in Vietnam: The Transition from

Socialism in a Comparative Perspective (Cambridge: Cambridge University Press, 2008), 183–88.

82. Nguyễn Văn Đài, "Quyền Tự do," and his "Dân trí và chế độ dân chủ ở Việt Nam" [People's Intelligence and a Democratic System in Vietnam], June 3, 2006, BBC, accessed August 4, 2006, http://www.bbc.co.uk/vietnamese/vietnam/story/2006/05/060523 _dantri_danchu.shtml.

83. Viện Kiểm Sát Nhân Dân Thành Phố Hà Nội [The People's Prosecutor General of Hà Nội], "Cáo Trạng số 238. Vụ Án: Nguyễn Văn Đài—Lê Thị Công Nhân" [Indictment 238. Case: Nguyễn Văn Đài—Lê Thị Công Nhân], April 24, 2007, Mạng Ý Kiến, accessed May 28, 2007, http://ykien.net/blog/?p=1439.

84. Nguyễn Văn Đài, "Nhìn Miến Điện nghĩ về Việt Nam" [Look at Myanmar, Think about Vietnam], October 17, 2011, *Tự Do Ngôn Luận*, November 1, 2011, 14–15. In this article, he also celebrates the success of the Myanmar's democracy movement and the international community in pressuring that country's leaders to allow multiple political parties and embark on democratization.

85. Nguyễn Văn Đài's prescription is quoted in Gia Minh, "Vì sao vẫn chưa có những thay đổi cần thiết ở Việt Nam" [Why Necessary Changes in Vietnam Have Yet to Come], October 30, 2014, RFA, accessed November 19, 2014, http://www.rfa.org/viet-namese/in_depth/necessi-for-chng-vn-10302014064720.html?searchterm:utf8:ustring= Gia+Minh.

86. Tri Mi, "Activists: Arrest of Vietnam Rights Lawyer a Misstep," December 17, 2015, VOA, accessed December 18, 2015, http://www.voanews.com/content/activists-arrest-vietnam-rights-lawyer-misstep/3107724.html.

87. Lữ Phương, "Về vấn đề dân chủ hóa ở Việt Nam" [Democratization in Vietnam], June 2007, beginning "Tôi là người đang," Diễn Đàn, accessed August 31, 2007, http://www.diendan.org/viet-nam/noi-chuyen-voi-lu-phuong/. Also see Lê Hồng Hà, "Đấu tranh vì phát triển và dân chủ hóa đất nước" [Struggle for the Country's Development and Democratization], March 10, 2007, section "Gọi tên," Diễn Đàn, accessed July 11, 2007, http://www.diendan.org/viet-nam/le-hong-ha-111au-tranh-vi-phat-trien-va-dan-chu-hoa-111at-nuoc/. Lữ Phương, a Hồ Chí Minh City resident, was a VCP member in the pre-1975 underground Provisional Revolutionary Government in southern Vietnam.

88. See, for instance, Trần Bảo Lộc, "Góp ý với tác giả Nguyễn Gia Kiểng về bài viết 'Thời điểm của một xét lại bắt buộc'" [Suggestions for Nguyễn Gia Kiểng Regarding His Article "Timing for a Required Revision"], July 14, 2007, Đối Thoại, accessed August 2, 2007, http://www.doi-thoai.com/baimoi0707_332.html; Hà Sĩ Phu, "Thư ngỏ gửi ông Chủ tịch nước Nguyễn Minh Triết và Thủ tướng Nguyễn Tấn Dũng" [Open Letter to President Nguyễn Minh Triết and Prime Minister Nguyễn Tấn Dũng], September 9, 2008, Talawas, accessed October 29, 2008, http://www.talawas.org/ta-laDB/showFile.php?res=14174&rb=0401; Lữ Phương, "Về vấn đề dân chủ," beginning "Điều đặc biệt." Hà Sĩ Phu, a biologist, started to publicly criticize the government in the late 1980s. He lives in Đà Lạt, as does Trần Bảo Lộc.

89. Hà Sĩ Phu, "Cuộc giằng co về dân chủ còn kéo dài" [Wrangle for Democracy Continues], August 22, 2007, BBC, accessed August 24, 2007, http://www.bbc.co.uk/ vietnamese/vietnam/story/2007/08/070822_hasiphu_interview.shtml.

90. Trần Bảo Lộc, "Góp ý với tác giả"; Đoàn Giao Thủy, "Gặp Hà Sĩ Phu ở Đà Lạt" [Meeting Hà Sĩ Phu in Đà Lạt], July 10, 2007, Diễn Đàn, accessed July 11, 2007, http://www.diendan.org/viet-nam/gap-ha-si-phu-o-111a-lat; Lữ Phương, "Về vấn đề Dân chủ," beginning "Cách đây không lâu."

91. Lê Hồng Hà, "Đấu tranh," section "Gọi tên," and "Mấy suy nghĩ về tiến độ phát triển đất nước Việt Nam trong đầu thế kỷ XXI" [Thoughts on Vietnam's Development Progress at the Beginning of the 21st Century], December 2005, points 3–6, Le Phai, accessed December 19, 2005, http://lephai.com/uni/n2005/dt20051213f.htm; Trần Lâm, "Phải chăng đã đến hồi bĩ cực?" [Is the Age of Affliction Coming?], *Tổ Quốc*, May 1, 2009, 6.

92. Lê Hồng Hà, "Đấu tranh," section "Gọi tên."

93. For material about Lê Hồng Hà's life, see Lê Hồng Hà, Kính gửi Ban chấp hành Trung Ương Đảng Khóa VII [Letter to the Party's Central Executive Committee, Seventh Plenum], July 18, 1995, appended to Trần Thư, *Tử tù tự Xử lí Nội bộ* [Internally Settled Death Sentence] (Westminister, CA: Văn Nghệ, 1996), 255–66; Lê Hồng Hà, "Mấy suy nghĩ tiến độ"; Bùi Tín, "Về ông Lê Hồng Hà" [About Lê Hồng Hà], October 24, 2014, Trần Hoàng, accessed January 21, 2015, https://hoangtran204.wordpress.com/2014/10/24/27454; Carlyle A. Thayer, "Political Dissent and Political Reform in Vietnam 1997–2002," in *The Power of Ideas*, ed. Claudia Derichs and Thomas Heberer (Copenhagen: NIAS Press, 2006), 119–20. Some accounts have other dates for his imprisonment.

94. For one of his early critical commentaries, see Lê Hồng Hà, "Chủ nghĩa Xã hội Dân chủ" [Democratic Socialism], December 14, 1991, Le Phai, accessed December 19, 2005, http://lephai.com/uni/n2005/dt20051114a.htm. His study included the demise of the Soviet Union and Eastern European political systems.

95. Lê Hồng Hà, "Đấu tranh." "Self-disintegrate" is my gloss on three terms he uses: *tự tan rã, tự tan vỡ*, and *tự vỡ*, each with slightly different meanings.

96. Lê Hồng Hà, "Đấu tranh."

97. Ban biên tập [Editorial Board], "Đàn áp đã có một chân dung" [Portrait of Repression], *Tổ Quốc*, August 15, 2011, 1; Human Rights Watch, *Vietnam: The Party vs. Legal Activist Cu Huy Ha Vu* (New York: Human Rights Watch, 2011), 15.

98. This paragraph is based on several sources, including Human Rights Watch, *Vietnam*, 9–10; and VOA, "TS Cù Huy Hà Vũ, từ khởi kiện Thủ tướng đến yêu cầu xóa bỏ điều 4 Hiến Pháp" [Dr. Cù Huy Hà Vũ, from Suing the Prime Minister to Demanding the Removal of Article 4 from the Constitution], June 20, 2010, *Tự Do Dân Chủ*, June 30, 2010, 29.

99. "Một họa sĩ kiện UBND Thừa Thiên Huế vì đồi Vọng Cảnh" [Artist Sues Thừa Thiên Huế People's Committee regarding Vọng Cảnh Hill], April 23, 2005, *Tuổi Trẻ*, accessed January 23, 2015, http://tuoitre.vn/tin/chinh-tri-xa-hoi/20050423/mot-hoa-si-kien-ubnd-thua-thien-hue-vi-doi-vong-canh/75670.html; Hẩy Lý, "Cù Huy Hà Vũ chính thức khởi kiện UBND Thừa Thiên-Huế" [Cù Huy Hà Vũ Files Suit against Thừa Thiên-Huế People's Committee], May 20, 2005, ViệtBáo, accessed January 23, 2015, http://vietbao.vn/Van-hoa/Cu-Huy-Ha-Vu-chinh-thuc-khoi-kien-UBND-Thua-Thien-Hue/20436589/181/. Later others also sued authorities over the project, which ended up being suspended.

100. Cù Huy Hà Vũ, "Chủ nhiệm Ủy ban Kiểm tra trung ương Nguyễn Văn Chi bảo kê bỏ tù những người tố cáo Bí thư Thành ủy Đà Nẵng Nguyễn Bá Thanh tham nhũng hay Đảng lệ đè pháp luật?" [What Is Nguyễn Văn Chi, Chair of the Central Inspectorate, Protecting: The Imprisonment of Those Accusing Đà Nẵng Party Secretary Nguyễn Bá Thanh of Corruption or (Communist) Party Rules Suppressing the Law?], May 23, 2010, Bauxite Việt Nam, accessed October 14, 2011, http://boxitvn.wordpress.com /2010/05/24/ch%e1%bb%a7-nhi%e1%bb%87m-%e1%bb%a7y-ban-ki%e1%bb%83m-tra -trung-%c6%b0%c6%a1ng-nguy%e1%bb%85n-van-chi-b%e1%ba%a3o-k -b%e1%bb%8f-t-nh%e1%bb%afng-ng%c6%b0%e1%bb%9di-t%e1%bb%91-co-b/. Also see "Bắt nhà báo Dương Ngọc Tiến là thái độ nghiêm khắc của lực lượng CAND" [Arresting Journalist Dương Ngọc Tiến Is a Severe Measure by the People's Security Police], March 4, 2008, *An Ninh Thủ Đô* [Security in the Capital], accessed June 17, 2011, http://www.baomoi.com/Home/PhapLuat/www.anninhthudo.vn/Bat-nha-bao-Duong-Ngoc-Tien-la-thai-do-nghiem-khac-cua-luc-luong-CAND/1429130.epi; Thanh Trúc, "Chánh Án Tòa Đà Nẵng học luật ở đâu?" [Where Did Đà Nẵng's Presiding Judge Study Law?], August 3, 2009, RFA, accessed October 14, 2011, http://www .rfa.org/vietnamese/in_depth/Attornet-at-law-explains-why-judge-seriously-violated -indictee-rights-08032009171446.html. Cù Huy Hà Vũ's wife, Nguyễn Thị Dương Hà, was Dương Tiến's attorney.

101. Phương Loan, "Ghi nhận từ một buổi lấy phiếu tín nhiệm ứng viên ĐBQH" [Notes on Vote of Confidence for National Assembly Candidates], April 3, 2007, ViệtBáo, accessed January 28, 2015, http://vietbao.vn/Chinh-Tri/Ghi-nhan-tu-mot-buoi-lay-phieu -tin-nhiem-ung-vien-DBQH/20680608/96/; VOA, "TS Cù Huy Hà Vũ," 30.

102. Thiện Giao, "Trả đơn kiện Thủ tướng về vụ bauxite" [Papers Suing Prime Minister in Bauxite Case Returned], June 25, 2009, RFA, accessed November 17, 2010, http://www.rfa.org/vietnamese/in_depth/Hanoi-court-rejects-a-lawsuit-aimed-at-Viet-PM-TGiao-06252009115848.html; Hà Giang, "Ở Việt Nam, không ai có quyền kiện Thủ tướng" [In Vietnam No One Has a Right to Sue the Prime Minister], September 24, 2009, RFA, accessed November 17, 2010, http://www.rfa.org/vietnamese/ in_depth/In-vietnam-no-one-can-sue-the-prime-minister-hgiang-09242009095817. html.

103. Cù Huy Hà Vũ, "Đơn khởi kiện Thủ tướng chính phủ Nguyễn Tấn Dũng về hành vi ban hành nghị định cấm công dân khiếu nại tập thể trái hiến pháp và pháp luật" [Suit against prime minister Nguyễn Tấn Dũng for Issuing an Illegal and Unconstitutional Directive Prohibiting Citizens from Making Collective Complaints], October 21, 2010, Bauxite Việt Nam, accessed January 28, 2015, https://boxitvn.wordpress.com/2010/10 /28/d%C6%A1n-kh%E1%BB%9Fi-ki%E1%BB%87n-th%E1%BB%A7 -t%C6%B0%E1%BB%9Bng-chnh-ph%E1%BB%A7-nguy%E1%BB%85n-t%E1 %BA%A5n-dung-v%E1%BB%81-hnh-vi-ban-hnh-ngh%E1%BB%8B-d%E1%BB %8Bnh-c/.

104. See the discussion in Human Rights Watch, *Vietnam*, 6–23.

105. See, for example, Nguyễn Xuân Diện, "Thông tin về cuộc gặp của vợ chồng TS Cù Huy Hà Vũ" [News of Dr. Cù Huy Hà Vũ and Wife Meeting], June 16, 2013, Bauxite Việt Nam, accessed June 17, 2013, http://www.boxitvn.net/bai/16834; Mike Ives, "Prison Hunger Strike by Vietnam Revolutionary's Son Tests Government's Culture of

Intimidation," June 18, 2013, *Washington Post*, accessed June 19, 2013, http://www.washingtonpost.com/world/asia_pacific/prison-hunger-strike-by-vietnam-revolutionaryss-son-tests-governments-culture-of-intimidation/2013/06/19/9299ac1c-d8b7-11e2-b418-9dfa095e125d_story.html.

106. Tòa Án Nhân Dân Tỉnh Thanh Hóa [People's Court, Thanh Hóa province], "Quyết định tạm đình chỉ chấp hành án phạt tù" [Decision to Temporarily Suspend Prison Sentence], April 6, 2014 (on file with author). Some independent journalists in Vietnam reported that pressure from several members of the United States Congress influenced Vietnamese authorities to release Cù Huy Hà Vũ; see Mặc Lâm, "Phạm Chí Dũng cây viết đầy hoài bão" [Phạm Chí Dũng's Aspirational Pen], April 18, 2013, RFA, accessed May 5, 2014, http://www.rfa.org/vietnamese/in_depth/phm-c-dung-tal-wri-04182013070833.html.

107. This paragraph and the next draw on several sources, especially Lê Hiếu Đằng, "Dân chủ là giải pháp cho các vấn đề của đất nước" [Democracy Is the Solution to the Country's Problems], November 15, 2010, Bauxite Việt Nam, accessed November 24, 2010, http://boxitvn.blogspot.com/2010/11/dan-chu-la-giai-phap-cho-cac-van-e-cua.html; Nguyễn Quang A, "Xã hội dân sự đâu có đáng sợ" [There's Nothing to Fear about Civil Society], April 12, 2009, *Lao Động*, accessed April 13, 2009, http://www.laodong.com.vn/Utilities/PrintView.aspx?ID=133512; Trần Bảo Lộc, "Dân chủ phải được học" [Democracy Needs Study], *Thông Luận*, September 2007, 13–14; Tương Lai, "Tiến trình dân chủ hóa xã hội" [Process of Democratizing Society], February 10, 2007, *Thanh Niên* [Young People], accessed March 8, 2007, http://www3.thanhnien.com.vn/Chaobuoisang/2007/2/11/181500.tno; two statements from Diễn đàn Xã hội Dân sự [Civil Society Forum]: "Tuyên bố về thực thi quyền dân sự và chính trị" [Announcement Regarding Realizing Civil and Political Rights], September 23, 2013, Diễn đàn Xã hội Dân sự, accessed October 3, 2013, http://diendanxahoidansu.wordpress.com/2013/09/23/tuyen-bo-ve-thuc-thi-quyen-dan-su-va-chinh-tri-2/, and "Một số nguyên tắc hoạt động của Diễn đàn Xã hội Dân sự" [Some Principles of the Civil Society Forum], November 23, 2013, Diễn đàn Xã hội Dân sự, accessed January 25, 2014, http://diendanxahoidansu.wordpress.com/2013/11/23/mot-so-nguyen-tac-hoat-dong-cua-dien-dan-xa-hoi-dan-su/. Lê Hiếu Đằng opposed the pre-1975 Sài Gòn government, held prominent positions in Hồ Chí Minh City before retiring in 2009, and was a VCP member for over forty years before quitting in disgust in 2013. Tương Lai's background is discussed in chapter 3.

108. The VCP also endorses this goal, an important convergence, said Nguyễn Quang A, between the regime and those like himself who seek to change the political system peacefully and nonviolently. Nguyễn Quang A, "Dân chủ chứ đâu chỉ là đa nguyên" [Democracy Is Not Just Pluralism], March 8, 2006, Talawas, accessed April 6, 2006, http://www.talawas.org/talaDB/showFile.php?res=6659&rb=0403.

109. Nguyễn Quang A, "Dân chủ chứ đâu," 2, 5.

110. Nguyễn Quang A, correspondence with author, January 24, 2014.

111. Nguyễn Quang A, correspondence with author, January 24, 2014; Nguyễn Quang A, "Mở rộng Thủ đô và quyền được thông tin" [The Capital's Expansion and the Right to Information], May 9, 2008, *Tiền Phong* [Vanguard], accessed July 2, 2008, http://www.tienphong.vn/Tianyon/Index.aspx?ArticleID=121838&ChannelID=19.

112. Nguyễn Quang A, "Dân chủ chứ đâu," 6.

113. Information about his background comes mainly from David W. P. Elliott, *Changing Worlds: Vietnam's Transition from Cold War to Globalization* (New York: Oxford University Press, 2012), 303–4, 307; Nguyễn Quang A, "Sự thay đổi lớn trong tư duy của Đảng" [Huge Change in the (Communist) Party's Thinking], February 28, 2006, ViệtBáo, accessed February 23, 2013, http://vietbao.vn/Xa-hoi/Su-thay-doi-lon -trong-tu-duy-cua-Dang/40124990/157/; Nguyễn Quang A, correspondence with author, April 11, 2015.

114. Nguyễn Quang A, "Trí thức là ai?" [Who Is an Intellectual?], January 30, 2007, *Thông Luận*, accessed February 2, 2007, http://www.thongluan.org/vn/modules.php?na me=News&file=article&sid=1488; Nam Nguyên, "TS Nguyễn Quang A: Xu hướng thời đại cần ý kiến đa chiều" [Dr. Nguyễn Quang A: Toward an Era Requiring Diverse Ideas], October 22, 2008, RFA, accessed October 28, 2008, http://www.rfa.org/vietnam-ese/in_depth/policy-makers-had-better-consult-independent-researchs-NNguyen -10222008155252.html.

115. Thủ tướng Chính phủ [Prime Minister], "Quyết định của Thủ tướng Chính phủ số 97/2009/QĐ-TTg ngày 24 tháng 07 năm 2009" [Prime Ministerial Directive 97/2009/QĐ-TTg, 24 July 2009], Vietlaw, accessed September 15, 2009, http://www .vietlaw.gov.vn/LAWNET/docView.do?docid=23551&type=html&search.

116. Hội đồng Viện Nghiên cứu Phát triển IDS [Council, Institute for Development Studies], Kính gửi Thủ tướng Nguyễn Tấn Dũng [Letter to Prime Minister Nguyễn Tấn Dũng], August 6, 2009 (copy in author's files); "Tuyên bố của Viện Nghiên cứu Phát triển IDS" [Announcement from the Institute for Development Studies], September 14, 2009, Diễn Đàn, accessed September 16, 2009, http://www.diendan.org/viet-nam/tuyen-bo-ids-giai-the; "Quyết định khó khăn" [Tough Decision], September 16, 2009, BBC, accessed September 16, 2009, http://bauxitevietnam.info/c/9087.html.

117. "Kiến Nghị về sửa đổi Hiến Pháp 1992" [Petition Regarding Revising the 1992 Constitution], January 19, 2013, 1, Bauxite Việt Nam, accessed January 24, 2013, http:// www.boxitvn.net/bai/44588. This document has the critique, names of initial signers, and a possible alternative constitution. Additional sources for my account here include Nguyễn Quang A, "Lấy ý kiến nhân dân và trưng cầu dân ý" [Referendum and Getting People's Views], *Tổ Quốc*, January 15, 2013, 5–6; Nguyễn Đắc Kiên, "Trách Nhiệm với chữ ký" [Responsibility with Signature], March 27, 2013, Bauxite Việt Nam, accessed May 21, 2014, http://boxitvn.blogspot.com/2013/03/trach-nhiem-voi-chu-ky.html; Andrew Wells-Dang, "The Political Influence of Civil Society in Vietnam," in *Politics in Contemporary Vietnam*, ed. Jonathan D. London (New York: Palgrave Macmillan, 2014), 176–79; Nguyễn Quang A, correspondence with author, January 24, 2014.

118. Nguyễn Quang A, correspondence with author, January 24, 2014.

119. Diễn đàn Xã hội Dân sự, "Tuyên bố về thực thi." Over eight hundred Vietnam-ese, mostly in Vietnam, endorsed the Civil Society Forum when it began in Septem-ber 2013.

120. 20 tổ chức dân sự [20 Civic Organizations], "Tuyên bố số 2" [Announcement Number 2], *Tổ Quốc*, May 15, 2014, 5–6; 21 tổ chức xã hội dân sự [21 Civil Society Organizations], "Tuyên bố của các tổ chức xã hội dân sự độc lập tại VN về vụ án bà Bùi Minh Hằng, cô Nguyễn Thị Thúy Quỳnh và ông Nguyễn Văn Minh" [Announcement

from Independent Civil Society Organizations in Vietnam Regarding the Case of Bùi Minh Hằng, Nguyễn Thị Thúy Quỳnh, and Nguyễn Văn Minh], August 21, 2014, *Tự Do Ngôn Luận*, September 1, 2014, 3–4.

121. Diễn đàn Xã hội Dân sự, "Một số nguyên tắc," 2.

122. Vũ Đông Hà, "Sự thật vụ bắt giữ Phạm Chí Dũng" [Truth Regarding Phạm Chí Dũng's Arrest], July 25, 2012, Quan Làm Báo [Public Servant Journalist], accessed May 5, 2014, http://quanlambao.blogspot.com/2012/07/su-that-ang-sau-pham -chi-dung-bi-bat_25.html?utm_source=BP_recent; Mặc Lâm, "TS Phạm Chí Dũng bị cấm đi Genève" [Dr. Phạm Chí Dũng Forbidden to Go to Geneva], February 1, 2013, RFA, accessed November 19, 2014, http://www.rfa.org/vietnamese/in_depth/ pham-chi-dung-baaned-to-geneva-02012014084854.html; Mặc Lâm, "Phạm Chí Dũng cây viết."

123. Phạm Chí Dũng, quoted by Nguyễn Thanh Giang, "Mà lòng đã chắc những ngày một hai" [Heart Felt Feeling from the Start], *Tổ Quốc*, July 15, 2014, 7.

124. Phạm Chí Dũng, "Thách thức của xã hội dân sự VN" [Civil Society's Challenges in Vietnam], *Tự Do Ngôn Luận*, April 1, 2014, 14–15.

125. Charter 77 refers to both a pro-democracy group in Czechoslovakia and the document its members issued in January 1977 that advocated a range of human rights and criticized the country's authoritarian regime at that time.

126. The Vietnamese name is Hội Cựu tù nhân Lương tâm Việt Nam.

127. Hội Nhà báo độc lập Việt Nam, "Tuyên bố thành lập Hội Nhà báo độc lập Việt Nam" [Announcing the Formation of the Independent Journalists Association of Vietnam], July 4, 2014, Ba Sàm, accessed February 24, 2015, https://anhbasam.word press.com/2014/07/04/2734-tuyen-bo-thanh-lap-hoi-nha-bao-doc-lap-viet-nam/. This announcement includes the names of the association's initial members.

128. 21 tổ chức, "Tuyên bố"; 25 tổ chức xã hội dân sự tại Việt Nam [25 Civil Society Organizations in Vietnam], "Bản lên tiếng về các vụ bạo hành tra tấn gần đây của công an VN" [Statement to Speak Out about the Security Police's Recent Violence and Torture], November 6, 2014, *Tự Do Ngôn Luận*, November 15, 2014, 3–4.

129. Nguyễn Vũ Bình, "Tương lai nào," point 1; and my discussions with three regime critics, Hà Nội, October–November 2016.

130. See passage in chapter 1 about repression against a few workers and regime critics attempting to establish independent labor unions.

131. Nguyễn Vũ Bình, "Tương lai nào," points 3 and 4.

132. Nguyễn Vũ Bình, "Phong trào dân chủ Việt Nam trước vận hội lớn" [Vietnam's Democracy Movement Facing Large Opportunity], March 17, 2014, *Tự Do Ngôn Luận*, April 1, 2014, 12.

133. Interview with Lê Hồng Hà, "Đảng Cộng Sản chỉ còn vai trò kìm hãm xã hội" [The Communist Party's Only Role Is to Impede Society], *Tổ Quốc*, March 15, 2012, 14.

134. "Ngày 30/4 khởi đầu một trào lưu bất đồng" [April 30 (1975) Started a Different Trend], April 30, 2013, BBC, accessed May 9, 2013, http://www.bbc.co.uk/vietnam ese/vietnam/2013/04/130430_vn_luphuong_30april.shtml.

135. Lê Hồng Hà, "Mấy suy nghĩ về tình hình, nhiệm vụ hiện nay" [Thoughts about the Present Situation and Tasks], *Tổ Quốc*, April 1, 2014, 21.

136. "Tuyên bố Nghị định số 72/2013/NĐ-CP vi phạm Hiến pháp, pháp luật Việt Nam và các công ước quốc tế mà Việt Nam tham gia" [Proclamation: Government Decree 72/2013 Violates Vietnam's Constitution and Laws as well as International Conventions That Vietnam Has Joined], August 8, 2013, Tễu, accessed April 5, 2014, http://xuandienhannom.blogspot.com/2013/08/toan-van-ban-tuyen-bo-phan-oi-nghi -inh.html); 25 tổ chức xã hội dân sự, "Bản lên tiếng."

5. Party-State Authorities

1. As of early May 2006, 424 Vietnamese in Vietnam had signed online the April 8, 2006 statement "Tuyên ngôn Tự do Dân chủ cho Việt Nam" [Declaration on Freedom and Democracy]. Hundreds more signed later that year, although many were Vietnamese living abroad. In early March 2013, nearly three hundred Vietnamese in Vietnam were among the first five hundred signers online of an open letter itemizing key features of democratization needed for their country. An additional 2,800 Vietnamese subsequently signed the letter, but a large majority were Vietnamese living abroad. "Tuyên Ngôn 8406 Tự do Dân chủ cho Việt Nam 2006" [Declaration 8406: Freedom and Democracy for Vietnam in 2006], May 9, 2006, Lên đường [Start a Journey], accessed May 11, 2006, http://www.lenduong.net/article.php3?id_article=17063); "Thư ngỏ của Nhà báo Nguyễn Đắc Kiên gửi bạn đọc" [Open Letter from Journalist Nguyễn Đắc Kiên to Readers], March 4, 2013; attached to the letter are signers' names and locations (in author's files).

2. See especially articles 24 and 25 of Vietnam's constitution, Hiến Pháp Nước Cộng Hòa Xã Hội Chủ Nghĩa Việt Nam (2013).

3. Học Viện Chính Trị [Political Institute], *Sự Thật Vấn đề Dân chủ và Nhân quyền trong Chiến lược "Diễn biến Hòa bình" ở Việt Nam* [Realities of Democracy and Human Rights in the "Peaceful Evolution" Strategy in Vietnam] (Hà Nội: Nxb Chính trị Quốc gia-Sự thật, 2011), 11–15. This book by a team of researchers in the VCP's Political Institute lays out the party leadership's position on democracy and related topics.

4. Học Viện Chính Trị, *Sự Thật Vấn đề Dân chủ*, 16–28.

5. Article 4, paragraph 1 of Vietnam's constitution: Hiến Pháp (2013).

6. Peter Zinoman, "Nhân Văn-Giai Phẩm and Vietnamese 'Reform Communism' in the 1950s," *Journal of Cold War Studies* 13 (Winter 2011): 77.

7. Zinoman, "Nhân Văn-Giai Phẩm," 66–67; Russell Hiang-Khng Heng, "Of the State, For the State, Yet against the State: The Struggle Paradigm in Vietnam's Media Politics" (PhD diss., Australian National University), 83–85, 221–22, 236–37; Greg Lockhart, "Introduction: Nguyen Huy Thiep and the Faces of Vietnamese Literature," in *The General Retires and Other Stories*, by Nguyen Huy Thiep, trans. Greg Lockhart (New York: Oxford University Press, 1992), 3–12.

8. Heng, "Of the State," 92, 95, 229–30, 235, 240.

9. Heng, "Of the State," 90–91, 94; Zinoman, "Nhân Văn-Giai Phẩm," 77–79; Kim N. B. Ninh, *A World Transformed: The Politics of Culture in Revolutionary Vietnam, 1945–1965* (Ann Arbor: University of Michigan Press, 2002), 154–55, 158–59; *Bọn "Nhân Văn-Giai Phẩm" trước Tòa Án Dư Luận* [The "Nhân Văn-Giai Phẩm" Gang

Faces the Court of Public Opinion] (Hà Nội: Nxb Sự Thật, 1959), 156–77, 180–211, 212–26, 344–53, 362–64.

10. Heng, "Of the State," 236–44.

11. Ninh, *A World Transformed*, 142, 144, 154, 199–200; Heng, "Of the State," 99–100, 107–8.

12. Heng, "Of the State," 233, 242–44.

13. Zinoman, "Nhân Văn-Giai Phẩm," 81–82; Huy Đức, *Bên Thắng Cuộc* [The Winning Side], vol. 2 (Sài Gòn: Nxb OsinBook, 2012), 19–23.

14. Peter Zinoman, "Nhân Văn Giai Phẩm on Trial: The Prosecution of Nguyễn Hữu Đang and Thụy An," *Journal of Vietnamese Studies* 11 (Summer–Fall 2016): 189–93, 199–203.

15. Heng, "Of the State," 245–46.

16. As studies of authoritarian regimes have shown, when the state's reach is shortened or weakened, niches for criticism and resistance open and expand. See, for instance, Vincent Boudreau, *Resisting Dictatorship: Repression and Protests in Southeast Asia* (Cambridge: Cambridge University Press, 2004), 33–35; Christian Joppke, "Revisionism, Dissidence, Nationalism: Opposition in Leninist Regimes," *British Journal of Sociology* 45 (December 1994): 546–48; Oldrich Tuma, "Czechoslovakia," in *Dissent and Opposition in Communist Eastern Europe*, ed. Detlef Pollack and Jan Wielgohs (Burlington, VT: Ashgate, 2004), 29–49.

17. An Duc Nguyen, "Citizen Journalism in Vietnam: Technologies, Democracy and the Nation-State in a Globalised News Environment," undated, circa 2009, Academia, accessed July 23, 2015, http://www.academia.edu/1883946/citizen_journalism_in_vietnam_technologies_democracy_and_the_nation-state_in_a_globalised_news_environment. Also see Michael Gray, "Control and Dissent in Vietnam's Online World," January 2015, 2–12, Tia Sang, accessed March 12, 2015, http://www.tiasangvietnam.org/wp-content/uploads/2015/02/TSVN.Backgrounder.Social.Media_.Jan15.pdf.

18. This paragraph draws on Thiem Hai Bui, "The Influence of Social Media in Vietnam's Elite Politics," *Journal of Current Southeast Asian Affairs* 35, no. 2 (2016): 89–112; David W. P. Elliott, *Changing Worlds: Vietnam's Transition from Cold War to Globalization* (New York: Oxford University Press, 2012); Martin Gainsborough, *Vietnam: Rethinking the State* (London: Zed Books, 2010), 157–331; John Stanley Gillespie, *Transplanting Commercial Law Reform: Developing a "Rule of Law" in Vietnam* (Burlington, VT: Ashgate, 2010), 223–59; Tuong Vu, "Persistence amid Decay: The Communist Party of Vietnam at 83," in *Politics in Contemporary Vietnam*, ed. Jonathan D. London (New York: Palgrave Macmillan, 2014), 21–41; Alexander L. Vuving, "Vietnam: A Tale of Four Players," in *Southeast Asian Affairs 2010*, ed. Daljit Singh (Singapore: Institute of Southeast Asian Studies, 2010), 367–91; Andrew Wells-Dang, *Civil Society Networks in China and Vietnam* (New York: Palgrave Macmillan, 2012), 1–84, 106–35, 169–87.

19. Alexander L. Vuving, "Vietnam in 2012: A Rent-Seeking State on the Verge of a Crisis," in *Southeast Asian Affairs 2013*, ed. Daljit Singh (Singapore: Institute of Southeast Asian Studies, 2014), 325–47; Vuving, "Vietnam: A Tale"; Carlyle A. Thayer, "The Trial of Lê Công Định: New Challenges to the Legitimacy of Vietnam's Party-State,"

Journal of Vietnamese Studies 5 (Fall 2010): 199–202. For an analysis skeptical of seeing party-state internal politics in terms of reformers, conservatives, and other such factions, see Martin Gainsborough, "From Patronage to 'Outcomes': Vietnam's Communist Party Congresses Revisited," *Journal of Vietnamese Studies* 2 (Winter 2007): 3–26.

20. Interview with Võ Văn Kiệt, May 7, 2007, BBC, accessed May 15, 2007, http://www.bbc.co.uk/vietnamese/vietnam/story/2007/05/070504_vo_van_kiet_part_two.shtml.

21. My conversations with VCP members, 2012 and 2016. Occasionally such views are expressed publicly. In a BBC interview on April 4, 2014, the former National Assembly delegate Nguyễn Minh Thuyết said that so long as critics are nonviolent, government leaders should be more relaxed about people who disagree with them. (The interview is reproduced in *Tổ Quốc* [Homeland], April 15, 2014, 12–13.)

22. My discussions with democratization advocates in 2016.

23. Nguyễn Khắc Toàn, "Trao đổi trong buổi làm việc với các sĩ quan an ninh của sở công an Hà Nội tại quán trà ngay sau Tết Nguyên Đán Mậu-Tý năm 2008" [Exchanges with Local Security Police Officials at a Tea Shop Immediately after the New Year], March 5–6, 2008, Đối Thoại [Dialogue], accessed March 19, 2008, http://www.doi-thoai.com/baimoi0308_174.html and http://www.doi-thoai.com/baimoi0308_208.html, and accessed April 4, 2008, http://www.doi-thoai.com/baimoi0308_323.html.

24. In Vietnamese, political activist is *nhà hoạt động chính trị*, and the other cited terms are *kẻ cơ hội chính trị, kẻ bất mãn chế độ*, and *đối tượng vi phạm luật pháp hình sự*.

25. This paragraph is based on "Trao bản Kiến nghị về sửa đổi Hiến pháp 1992" [Presenting a Petition about Revising the 1992 Constitution], Ba Sàm [Gossip], accessed February 11, 2013, http://anhbasam.wordpress.com/2013/02/05/1594-trao-ban-kien-nghi-ve-sua-doi-hien-phap-1994/; Phan Trung Lý, Uỷ ban Dự thảo Sửa đổi Hiến Pháp năm 1992 [Committee for Drafting Revisions to the 1992 Constitution], số 227 UBDTSĐHP, to Nguyễn Đình Lộc, February 7, 2013; "Thông Báo của Nhóm 'Kiến nghị 72'" [Announcement from the "Petition 72" Group], February 18, 2013, Ba Sàm, accessed February 19, 2013, http://anhbasam.wordpress.com/2013/02/18/1621-thong-bao-cua-nhom-kien-nghi-72/#more-93536. The letter from Phan Trung Lý is attached to the "Thông Báo" document.

26. One delegation member was Nguyễn Quang A, a regime critic discussed in chapter 4, which also has material about the petition.

27. For an overview of the agencies, see Carlyle A. Thayer, "The Apparatus of Authoritarian Rule in Vietnam," in *Politics in Contemporary Vietnam*, ed. London, 135–61. Bill Hayton has an informative account of what the agencies did against several dissidents during 2006–7: *Vietnam: Rising Dragon* (New Haven, CT: Yale University Press, 2010), 122–34.

28. An example is a commentary by an unidentified writer posted December 13, 2014 on Nguyễn Tấn Dũng, accessed September 16, 2015, http://nguyentandung.org/nhung-ke-pha-hoai-doi-lot-nha-dan-chu-se-sa-luoi-phap-luat.html.

29. Examples: "Câu kết trong-ngoài và mưu đồ chính trị nham hiểm" [Internal-External Collusion and Insidious Political Plots], September 5, 2007, *Quân Đội Nhân*

Dân [People's Army], accessed September 7, 2007, http://www.qdnd.vn/qdnd/baongay. quocphong.anninh.22783.qdnd; Lệ Chi, "Đa đảng hay một đảng lãnh đạo cầm quyền—Đâu là chân lý?" [Multiple Parties or One Ruling Party—Where Is the Truth?], May 31, 2010, *Quân Đội Nhân Dân*, accessed June 28, 2010, http://www.qdnd.vn/QDND-Site/vi-VN/61/43/5/5/5/113727/Default.aspx; Tuấn Hưng, "Bi hài chiêu trò của mấy 'nhà dân chủ'!" [Ridiculous Comedy by Several "Democrats"], September 18, 2014, *Nhân Dân* [People], accessed September 16, 2015, http://www.nhandan.org.vn/chinhtri/binh-luan-phe-phan/item/24344202-bi-hai-chieu-tro-cua-may-nha-dan-chu.html.

30. For instance, "Sự thật về 'tờ báo lậu' Tổ Quốc" [The Truth about the "Underground Newspaper" *Tổ Quốc*], December 7, 2008, *Công An Nhân Dân* [People's Public Security], accessed December 15, 2008, http://www.congan.com.vn/phong_su_dieu_tra/2008/12/20081205.55165.ca; Nguyễn Văn Minh, "Cảnh giác với liều thuốc dân chủ 'hội, đoàn độc lập'" [Vigilance toward the Democracy Remedy from an "Independent Association or Organization"], June 23, 2014, *Quân Đội Nhân Dân*, accessed September 16, 2015, http://www.qdnd.vn/qdndsite/vi-vn/61/43/chong-dien-bien-hoa-binh/canh-giac-voi-lieu-thuoc-dan-chu-hoi-doan-doc-lap/307756.html; "Ngụy dân chủ bi thảm dưới mắt các nhà tự xưng là dân chủ" [A Tragic Puppet Democracy under the Very Eyes of Those Calling Themselves Democrats], August 12, 2015, *Tuần Báo Văn Nghệ* [Arts and Literature Weekly], accessed September 16, 2015, http://tuanbaovannghetphcm.vn/nguy-dan-chu-bi-tham-duoi-mat-cac-nha-tu-xung-la-dan-chu/.

31. An example is the article "Nguyễn Khắc Toàn, kẻ vụ lợi bằng việc làm phản dân hại nước" [Nguyễn Khắc Toàn, a Mercenary Who Betrays the People and Damages the Country], June 8, 2009, *Công An Nhân Dân*, accessed July 2, 2009, http://www.cand.com.vn/vi-VN/binhluan/2009/6/114397.cand.

32. Jason Morris-Jung's dissertation has a rich discussion of website owners in 2009–10, especially Bauxite Việt Nam people, contending with government-instigated hacking, counterfeit e-mails, firewalls, and other cyber attacks. "The Vietnamese Bauxite Mining Controversy: The Emergence of a New Oppositional Politics" (PhD diss., University of California, Berkeley, 2013), 156–62. For earlier efforts of the party-state to control the Internet, see Björn Surborg, "On-line with the People in Line: Internet Development and Flexible Control of the Net in Vietnam," *Geoforum* 39 (2008): 351–55, accessed May 19, 2015, doi:10.1016/j.geoforum.2007.07.008.

33. "Tổ chức nhóm chuyên gia bút chiến trên Internet" [Organized Group Specialized in Internet Polemics], January 9, 2013, *Lao Động* [Labor], accessed May 11, 2015, http://laodong.com.vn/chinh-tri/to-chuc-nhom-chuyen-gia-but-chien-tren-internet-98582.bld; "Vietnam's Propaganda Agents Battle Bloggers On-line," January 19, 2013, *Bangkok Post*, accessed January 25, 2013, http://www.bangkokpost.com/tech/computer/331539/vietnam-propaganda-agents-battle-bloggers-online. Other accounts of authorities' use of the Internet to track and oppose critics include Gray, "Control and Dissent in Vietnam's Online World," 4–12; Catherine McKinley and Anya Schiffrin, "Leninist Lapdogs to Bothersome Bloggers in Vietnam," in *State Power 2.0: Authoritarian Entrenchment and Political Engagement Worldwide*, ed. Muzammil M. Hussaid and Philip N. Howard (Burlington, VT: Ashgate, 2013), 125–38.

34. Nguyễn Vũ Bình, "Tương lai nào cho phong trào dân chủ Việt Nam?" [What's the Future for Vietnam's Democracy Movement?], February 28, 2008, Mạng Ý Kiến [Opinion Net], accessed March 6, 2008, http://ykien0711.blogvis.com/2008/02/29 /t%c6%b0%c6%a1ng-lai-nao-cho-phong-trao-dan-ch%e1%bb%a7-vi%e1%bb%87t -nam/; Nghiêm Văn Thạch, "Tại sao có thể nhẹ dạ đến như thế?" [How Is Such Thoughtlessness Possible?], *Tổ Quốc*, November 1, 2014, 12–14.

35. Nhóm phóng viên Phong trào tranh đấu vì Dân chủ, Hà Nội [Democracy Movement Journalists in Hà Nội], "Hà Nội: công an tiếp tục sách nhiễu các nhà dân chủ" [Security Police Continue to Harass Democracy Activists], June 4, 2008, Mạng Ý Kiến, accessed June 18, 2008, http://ykienblog.wordpress.com/2008/06/05/ha-noi-cong-an -ti%e1%ba%bfp-t%e1%bb%a5c-sach-nhi%e1%bb%85u-cac-nha-dan-ch%e1%bb%a7/; "Nhìn lại nhân quyền Việt Nam năm 2014" [Looking Back at Human Rights in Vietnam in 2014], January 2015, Dân Làm Báo [Citizen Journalist], accessed August 31, 2015, http://danlambaovn.blogspot.com/2015/01/nhin-lai-nhan-quyen-viet-nam-2014 .html.

36. "Công An CS Hà Nội tiếp tục đàn áp dã man, khốc liệt gia đình nữ nhà báo tranh đấu Dương Thị Xuân" [Communist Security Police in Hà Nội Continue Ruthless Repression against Family of Dương Thị Xuân, an Activist Journalist], January 15, 2009, Đối Thoại, accessed January 16, 2009, http://www.doi-thoai.com/baimoi 0109_196.html; Vietnam Sydney Radio's interview with Dương Thị Xuân, January 14–15, 2009, Tiếng Nói Tự Do Dân Chủ [Voice of Freedom and Democracy], accessed January 29, 2009, http://tiengnoitudodanchu.org/modules.php?name=News&file =article&sid=6923.

37. "Công an Quảng Nam lại tiếp tục sách nhiễu gia đình nhà văn Huỳnh Ngọc Tuấn" [Quảng Nam Security Police Continue to Abuse Writer Huỳnh Ngọc Tuấn's Family], November 9, 2011, Dân Luận [People Discuss], accessed August 29, 2015, https:// www.danluan.org/tin-tuc/20111108/cap-nhat-cong-an-quang-nam-lai-tiep-tuc-sach -nhieu-gia-dinh-nha-van-huynh-ngoc-tuan; Huỳnh Ngọc Tuấn, "Thư tố cáo" [Denunciation], February 12, 2014, Dân Luận, accessed August 29, 2015, https://www.danluan .org/tin-tuc/20140212/huynh-ngoc-tuan-thu-to-cao; Huỳnh Ngọc Tuấn and Huỳnh Trọng Hiếu, "Thư kêu cứu" [Plea for Help], February 20, 2014, FVPOC (Former Vietnamese Prisoners of Conscience), accessed August 29, 2015, http://fvpoc.org/2014/02/20 /thu-keu-cuu-cua-nha-van-huynh-ngoc-tuan-va-huynh-trong-hieu/; Huỳnh Thục Vy, "Lại những trò bẩn của an ninh cộng sản [More Filthy Tricks by Communist Security], April 4, 2013, Quê Choa [My Country], accessed April 11, 2013, http://quechoa.vn/2013 /04/10/truy-buc-den-ba-doi/#more-35823.

38. Open letter from Vũ Hoàng Hải, August 9, 2006, Mạng Ý Kiến, accessed August 11, 2006, http://www.ykien.net/; interview with Nguyễn Ngọc Quang, August 9, 2006, RFA, accessed August 11, 2006, http://www.rfa.org/vietnamese/in_depth /2006/08/09/Interview_NNQ_member_of_democracy_group_TMi/.

39. Letter from Đỗ Bá Tân, husband of Trần Khải Thanh Thủy, to Hà Nội city officials, October 15, 2009, vnnews-l, accessed November 13, 2009, vnnews-l@anu.edu.au.

40. Phạm Bá Hải, "Nhận diện chủ trương bạo hành, tra tấn, hãm hại giới bảo vệ nhân quyền" [Identifying the Policy to Assault, Torture, and Use Violence against

Human Rights Defenders], November 11, 2014, *Tự Do Ngôn Luận* [Free Speech], November 15, 2014, 26; "Nhìn lại nhân quyền," section IV.

41. Human Rights Watch, *No Country for Human Rights Activists: Assaults on Bloggers and Democracy Campaigners in Vietnam* (New York: Human Rights Watch, 2017). My conversations in Hà Nội and other sources indicate that the regime has not killed dissidents. The only possible case I am aware of concerns Lê Trí Tuệ, a regime critic who, after fleeing to Cambodia in 2007 to escape arrest, is rumored to have been murdered by Vietnamese security police. Lê Minh, "Lê Trí Tuệ: Anh còn sống hay đã chết?" [Lê Trí Tuệ: Are You Alive or Dead?], May 4, 2009, VietLand, accessed January 7, 2010, http://www.vietland.net/main/showthread.php?t=9808.

42. One of Trần Đại Sơn's early public criticisms was "Cần phải cân nhắc thiệt hơn" [Need a Franker Assessment of Pros and Cons], *Điện Thư* [Electronic Letter], no. 8 (October 2003): 8–9.

43. Đặng Văn Việt's name disappeared from the editorial board list in *Tổ Quốc*'s third issue, October 15, 2006. Perhaps because of age (by 2006 he was about eighty-six), his activism lessened, but he was still producing political commentary in 2015. See interview in Gia Minh, "Đề nghị mới nhất cho sửa đổi hiến pháp" [Newest Suggestion for Revising the Constitution], July 15, 2015, RFA, accessed November 15, 2015, http://www.rfa.org/vietnamese/in_depth/latest-propo-contitu-amen-0715201 3074807.html.

44. An early public statement of Trần Lâm's views on the human rights situation in Vietnam is "Tủi hổ quá Việt Nam ơi!" [Vietnam, How Shameful!], June 16, 2005, Mạng Ý Kiến, accessed May 19, 2006, http://www.ykien.net/.

45. Lữ Phương, "Những chuyến ra đi" [Departures], 2008, Viet Studies, accessed January 12, 2010, http://www.viet-studies.info/LuPhuong/LuPhuong_NhungChuyenRaDi.htm; interview with Lữ Phương by Diễn đàn [Forum], July 1995, Mạng Ý Kiến, accessed January 14, 2004, http://www.ykien.net/luphuong04.html.

46. For an overview of these interrogations, see "Trò phân mảnh và tung hỏa mù của an ninh Cộng sản" [Divisive Tricks and Smokescreens of Communist Security], July 18, 2013, Viet Studies, accessed September 16, 2015, http://viet-studies.info/kinhte /TroPhanManh_RFA.htm. For specific examples, see Vi Đức Hồi's descriptions of interrogations he endured in 2007: "Đối Mặt: Đường đến với phong trào dân chủ" [Opposite Side: Road to Being with the Democratization Movement], July 20, 2009, parts 11–14 and 19–21. The thirty-five parts of this memoir were posted one by one on the *Thông Luận* [Thorough Discussion] website, beginning November 2008 and ending July 2009.

47. "Kỹ Sư Bạch Ngọc Dương đào thoát qua Cam Bốt" [Engineer Bạch Ngọc Dương Flees to Cambodia], May 15, 2007, Vietnam Exodus, accessed December 27, 2009, http://www.vietnamexodus.org/vne/modules.php?name=News&file=article& sid=1812; Lê Minh, "Bài viết về Lê Trí Tuệ" [About Lê Trí Tuệ], May 4, 2009, VietLand, accessed January 7, 2010, http://www.vietland.net/main/showthread. php?t=9808.

48. Khối 8406, "Quyết định bổ nhiệm Đại diện Khối 8406 tại Hải ngoại" [Resolution Appointing a Bloc 8406 Overseas Representative], October 18, 2007, *Tự Do Ngôn*

Luận, February 22, 2008, http://www.tdngonluan.com/tailieu/tl_khoi8406_quyetdinh-
bonhiem daidienhaingoai.htm.

49. "Internet Writer Bui Kim Thanh Released," August 13, 2008, International
Pen, accessed May 3, 2010, http://www.internationalpen.org.uk/go/news/vietnam-
internet-writer-bui-kim-th-nh-f-released; "Bóc trần dã tâm của bọn khủng bố" [Ter-
rorists' Evil Intentions Exposed], April 21, 2009, *Công An Nhân Dân*, accessed May 3,
2010, http://www.cand.com.vn/vi-VN/binhluan/2008/9/112115.cand. Unlike in China,
and before it the Soviet Union, authorities in Vietnam have not made a habit of treating
dissidents as mentally deranged. For China, see Robin Munro, *China's Psychiatric Inqui-
sition: Dissent, Psychiatry and the Law in Post-1949 China* (London: Wildy, Simmonds &
Hill, 2006).

50. For some of Bùi Minh Quốc and Vũ Cao Quận's backgrounds and views, see Bùi
Minh Quốc, "Đảng ta, Nhân dân ta, và đồng chí ta" [Our Party, Our People, and Our
Comrades], February 3, 2015, *Tổ Quốc*, March 15, 2015, 5–7; Vũ Cao Quận, "Mấy giọt
chữ năm gà" [A Few Words in the Year of the Rooster], *Điện Thư*, no. 43 (April 2005):
19–20; interview with Vũ Cao Quận, October 2, 2009, Đối Thoại, accessed October 6,
2009, http://www.doi-thoai.com/baimoi1009_024.html. Chapter 4 has material about
Nguyễn Quang A, Phạm Chí Dũng, and Trần Độ.

51. Chapter 4 has material about Đỗ Nam Hải and Nguyễn Thanh Giang. Informa-
tion about the others named here comes from numerous sources, such as Hoàng Tiến,
"Tại sao tôi bỏ đảng Mác-Lê để đi tìm Phật" [Why I Abandoned the Party of Marx and
Lenin to Look for Buddhism], December 31, 1992, Mạng Ý kiến, accessed February 19,
2004, http://www.ykien.net/bnhttaisao.html; Dương Thị Xuân, Kính gửi: ông Nguyễn
Tấn Dũng Thủ tướng chính phủ nước [Letter to Prime Minister Nguyễn Tấn Dũng],
February 8, 2007, Người Việt [Vietnamese People], accessed December 15, 2009, http://
nguoi-viet.com/absolutenm/anmviewer.asp?a=55526&z=12; Nguyễn Văn May and Lê
Thị Thúy Minh (parents of Nguyễn Phương Anh), Kính gửi: ông Nguyễn Văn
Hưởng, Thứ trưởng Bộ Công An [Letter to Nguyễn Văn Hưởng, Deputy Minister,
Ministry of Public Safety], December 22, 2007, ViệtBáo [Việt News], accessed March 15,
2010, http://www.vietbao.com/?ppid=45&pid=45&nid=120781; Nguyễn Thanh Giang,
Người Đội Số Phận [Carrying One's Fate] (Hà Nội, 2016), chaps. 5, 6, 10, 11, and 13.

52. Gainsborough, *Vietnam*, 177–90.

53. Interview with Đỗ Nam Hải, *Tự Do Dân Chủ*, April 7, 2010, 31–32.

54. Conversations with VCP members, 2012, 2015, and 2016.

55. Indicative of Nguyễn Quang A's popularity within Vietnam is the large number
of people, including many peasants and workers, who converged on Hà Nội's international airport to demand his release when security agents detained and interrogated him
for fifteen hours at the airport upon his return on September 1, 2015 from an overseas
trip. He later wrote about the ordeal: "Cám ơn tất cả anh chị em" [Thank You
Brothers and Sisters] on his Facebook page, accessed November 5, 2015, https://www
.facebook.com/a.nguyenquang.16/posts/1713257205568981.

56. I have found no reliable figures for how many Vietnamese have been imprisoned for criticizing particular policies or aspects of the party-state government or for
opposing the entire system and advocating democratization. Party-state authorities

insist Vietnam has no political prisoners, only people who have committed crimes. The typical criminal charges against regime critics are spreading propaganda against the state, abusing freedoms in order to jeopardize the state, undermining unity, disrupting security, and trying to overthrow the government. For these sorts of crimes, the International Society for Human Rights reported, 263 Vietnamese were imprisoned between 2005 and 2013 (cited in Phạm Đoan Trang, "Blogging Has Replaced Journalism as the Most Dangerous Job in Vietnam," November 23, 2013, Southeast Asia Press Alliance, accessed October 16, 2015, www.seapa.org/the-law-of-state-impunity/). (I am grateful to Bùi Duyên for bringing this essay to my attention.) As of January 2014, Human Rights Watch estimated, 150–200 Vietnamese were in prison for such violations; most had been convicted in 2010–12 (Human Rights Watch, "Vietnam: Country Summary," January 2014, 3, Human Rights Watch, accessed July 2, 2014, https://www.hrw.org/sites/default/files/related_material/vietnam_8.pdf).

57. The two are Nguyễn Mạnh Sơn, aged sixty-five when jailed in 2012, and Nguyễn Văn Tính, aged sixty-seven when imprisoned a second time in 2009.

58. "Tin Ghi Nhận" [News Notes], *Điện Thư*, June 2004, 1; Ban biên tập [Editorial Board], *Tổ Quốc*, January 15 and April 1, 2009; Nguyễn Văn Túc, "Chuyện ở ngày nay về những ông chủ và những người tự xưng là đầy tớ" [Story of Masters and People Calling Themselves Servants], *Tự Do Ngôn Luận*, August 15, 2007, 29–30; Trần Đức Tường, "Khi bọn phản quốc kết tội những người yêu nước" [When a Gang of Traitors Indict Patriots], *Tự Do Ngôn Luận*, October 15, 2009, 13.

59. Chapter 4 has some background about Lê Thị Công Nhân. Also, for her and Lê Công Định, see "Vietnamese Rights Activists Hold Out Hope for Democracy," February 18, 2015, RFA, accessed February 19, 2015, http://www.rfa.org/english/news/vietnam/vietnames-rights-activists-hope-for-democracy-02182015163742.html; Trần Ngọc Thành, "TPP & 'Công đoàn Độc lập Việt Nam'" [TPP (Trans-Pacific Partnership) and the "Independent Trade Union of Vietnam"], June 14, 2015, *Tự Do Ngôn Luận*, July 1, 2015, 28; Lê Công Định, "Việt Nam cần cộng đồng dân sự" [Vietnam Needs Civil Community], April 11, 2014, *Tự Do Ngôn Luận*, April 15, 2014, 11–13. Nguyễn Vũ Bình's views are discussed in chapter 4.

60. Hoàng Minh Chính interview on Đài Việt Nam California Radio, *Người Dân* [The People], no. 71 (July 1996): 12–15, 34–35; Hoàng Minh Chính, open letter, August 27, 1993, *Đối Thoại*, no. 3 (July–August, 1994): 11–23.

61. Đảng Dân Chủ Việt Nam in Vietnamese; also known as Đảng Dân Chủ Việt Nam XXI [Twenty-First Century Vietnamese Democratic Party].

62. "Cựu trung tá Trần Anh Kim, nhà tranh đấu và bất đồng chính kiến, bị công an bắt giữ 3 giờ đồng tại Hà Nội" [Hà Nội Security Police Detain for Three Hours Former Lieutenant Colonel Trần Anh Kim, Dissident and Fighter], April 30, 2006, Mạng Ý Kiến, accessed July 19, 2006, http://www.ykien.net/; Việt Hà, "Ông Trần Anh Kim bị tuyên án 5 năm rưỡi tù giam" [Trần Anh Kim Sentenced to Five and a Half Years' Imprisonment], December 29, 2009, RFA, accessed December 29, 2009, http://tiengnoitudodanchu.org/modules.php?name=News&file=article&sid=8516.

63. Liên hội Nhân quyền Việt Nam ở Thụy Sĩ [Swiss Federation for Vietnamese Human Rights], "Văn bút" [Pen Pal], September 29, 2009, *Tự Do Ngôn Luận*, October 1, 2009, 6; "Thêm người bất đồng chính kiến bị bắt tại Hải Phòng" [More Dissidents Arrested in Hải Phòng], May 9, 2009, Đàn Chim Việt [Việt Flock], accessed May 14, 2009, http://danchimviet.com/articles/1108/1/Them-ngi-bt-ng-chinh -kin-b-bt-ti-Hi-Phong/Page1.html; Gia Minh, "2 tù chính trị được ân xá" [Two Political Prisoners Pardoned], August 30, 2011, RFA, accessed August 18, 2015, http:// www.rfa.org/vietnamese/in_depth/vn-pardons-10-thous-pris-08302011063244.html.

64. "Vụ án Nguyễn Đan Quế" [Nguyễn Đan Quế's case], July, 29, 2004, Mạng Ý Kiến, accessed September 24, 2004, http://www.ykien.net/tl_ndq.html; "High Cost of Lifelong Commitment to Human Rights," August 18, 2004, Amnesty International, accessed January 14, 2005, http://news.amnesty.org/index/ENGASA418182004; interview with Nguyễn Đan Quế, February 4, 2004, VOA, accessed February 7, 2006, http://www.voanews.com/uspolicy/Ontheline/2006-02-03-voa3.cfm?renderfor-print=1.

65. Công An tỉnh Thừa Thiên Huế [Security Police, Thừa Thiên Huế Province], "Bản Kết Luận Điều Tra—Vụ án: Nguyễn Văn Lý và đồng bọn" [Investigation Report Regarding Nguyễn Văn Lý and Accomplices], March 13, 2007, *Thông Luận*, accessed March 23, 2007, http://www.thongluan.org/vn/modules.php?name=Content&pa=show page&pid=610; Cát Linh, "Thơ gởi Chủ tịch nước kêu gọi trả tự do cho LM Nguyễn Văn Lý" [Letter to Nation's President Calls for Father Nguyễn Văn Lý's Release], May 12, 2015, RFA, accessed July 30, 2015, http://www.rfa.org/vietnamese/in_depth/let-to-pres-sang-abt-lm-ly-05122015112216.html.

66. "'Xét xử' nữ tù nhân chính trị Hồ Thị Bích Khương 2 năm tù giam" [Political Prisoner Hồ Thị Bích Khương "Sentenced" to Two Years' Imprisonment], May 5, 2008, Đối Thoại, accessed May 8, 2008, http://www.doi-thoai.com/baimoi0508_096 .html; "Human Rights Defender Ho Thi Bich Khuong Beaten in Prison," December 3, 2012, Amnesty International, accessed December 4, 2012, http://www.isavelives.be/en/node/10299.

67. Cơ quan An ninh Điều tra, Bộ Công An, Hà Nội [Security Investigation Section, Ministry of Public Security, Hà Nội], "Vụ án: Nguyễn Xuân Nghĩa cùng đồng bọn tuyên truyền chống Nhà nước CHXHCN Việt Nam" [The Case of Nguyễn Xuân Nghĩa et al. Propagandizing against the State of the Socialist Republic of Vietnam], May 17, 2009, Dân Luận, accessed August 7, 2015, https://www.danluan.org/tin -tuc/20090714/ket-luan-dieu-tra-vu-an-nguyen-xuan-nghia-va-dong-bon; "Trong phiên tòa phúc thẩm ba nông dân" [Court of Appeal Hearing for Three Peasants], November 3, 2012, Dân Luận, accessed August 7, 2015, https://www.danluan.org/tin-tuc /20121102/trong-phien-toa-phuc-tham-ba-nong-dan-bac-giang-chi-co-cong-an-hoi -dong-xet-xu-va.

68. The actual name is Công Đoàn Độc Lập Việt Nam.

69. "Bà Trần Khải Thanh Thủy được thả" [Trần Khải Thanh Thủy Released], January 31, 2008, BBC, accessed February 11, 2008, http://www.bbc.co.uk/vietnamese/ vietnam/story/2008/01/080131_trankhaithanhthuyrelease.shtml; "Dissident Writer Tried

for Hooliganism," February 5, 2010, VietCatholic News, accessed February 6, 2010, http://vietcatholic.net/News/Html/76545.htm.

70. Gia Minh, "Phỏng vấn anh Nguyễn Ngọc Tường Thi về bản án 'rải truyền đơn'" [Interview with Nguyễn Ngọc Tường Thi about Sentence for "Distributing Leaflets"], December 22, 2012, RFA, accessed August 6, 2015, http://www.rfa.org/vietnamese/in_depth/former-political-prisoner-speaks-out-gmin-12222012123902.html.

71. Phạm Bá Hải, "Nhận diện chủ trương," 25, 27. In 2013 and 2014, this account says, authorities arrested only twelve people who had voiced political criticisms but does not say how many advocated democratization.

72. Nguyễn Xuân Nghĩa, "Muốn đi tù—chuyện thật như đùa" [Wanting Imprisonment—a True Story Similar to a Joke], July 18, 2015, Dân Làm Báo, accessed August 4, 2015, http://danlambaovn.blogspot.com/2015/07/muon-i-tu-chuyen-that-nhu-ua.html.

73. Đoàn Văn Diên told a reporter a year after completing his prison sentence that he was refraining from political activities because his son, Đoàn Huy Chương, was still in prison. Nevertheless, he was listed in 2015 as a member of the Hội cựu Tù nhân Lương Tâm Việt Nam [Association of Former Vietnamese Prisoners of Conscience (AFVPOC)]. Gia Minh, "Một cựu tù tiếp tục bị áp chế" [A Former Prisoner Still Being Oppressed], December 31, 2012, RFA, accessed July 31, 2015, http://www.rfa.org/vietnamese/in_depth/politic-prison-drive-t-blind-alley-gm-12312012134306.html; "Danh sách toàn bộ hội viên Hội CTNLTVN" [List of AFVPOC Members], FVPOC, accessed August 4, 2015, http://fvpoc.org/members-hoi-vien/.

74. The rest of this paragraph draws mainly on "Thả tù chính trị, Việt Nam muốn đổi gì?" [What Does Vietnam Want in Exchange for Releasing Political Prisoners?], a BBC report reprinted in *Tổ Quốc*, April 15, 2014, 12–14; and an interview with Phạm Chí Dũng, April 10, 2014, RFI, accessed May 5, 2014, http://www.viet.rfi.fr/vietnam/20140410-pham-chi-dung-hay-de-yen-cho-ong-cu-huy-ha-vu-song-nhu-mot-nguoi-binh-thuong.

75. Articles 79, 88, and 258, Vietnam's criminal code, Bộ Luật Hình Sự, 1999. Apparently courts can impose sentences less severe than the code stipulates. Hồ Thị Bích Khương, Lê Thị Lệ Hằng, Nguyễn Kim Nhàn, and Vũ Hoàng Hải were sentenced to two years' imprisonment for spreading propaganda against the state, one year less than the stated minimum.

76. My analysis of data for approach and sentences of sixty-eight regime critics.

77. My discussions with attorneys in Hà Nội, September 2012.

78. Phone interview with a Vietnamese political activist, June 2012; John Gillespie, "The Juridification of Cause Advocacy in Socialist Asia: Vietnam as a Case Study," conference paper, 2012, 13; interview with Đỗ Nam Hải, 30–31; "Gia đình Nguyễn Tiến Trung lên tiếng" [Nguyễn Tiến Trung's Family Speaks Out], January 20, 2010, VOA, accessed January 22, 2010, http://www.voanews.com/vietnamese/2010-01-20-voa42.cfm.

79. "Gia đình Nguyễn Tiến Trung"; phone interview with a Vietnamese political activist, June 2012; interview with Đỗ Nam Hải, 30.

80. Hồ Thị Bích Khương, "Bước đường đấu tranh cho công lý và dân chủ của tôi" [My Journey of Fighting for Justice and Democracy], 2009, parts 22 and 23, Người Việt, accessed August 19, 2009, http://www.nguoi-viet.com/absolutenm/anmviewer .asp?a=98561&z=2.

81. I have no evidence of party-state authorities putting critics in "tiger cages," in which critics of the Republic of Vietnam were often kept, or subjecting them to similar extreme physical hardship.

82. Several dissidents have recounted their prison experiences. See, for example, Hoàng Minh Chính, "Tố cáo khẩn cấp việc bị cáo nhà báo Vũ Bình bị ngược đãi tại nhà giam Hỏa Lò Mới" [Denouncing the Mistreatment of Journalist Defendant Vũ Bình in the Hỏa Lò Mới Prison], April 22, 2004, *Điện Thư*, no. 19 (April 2004): 2–7; VOA, interview with Lê Thị Công Nhân, March 12, 2010, Dân Luận, accessed April 13, 2010, http:// danluan.org/node/4397#comment-10309; interview with Nguyễn Văn Đài, March 6, 2011, RFA, accessed March 7, 2011, http://www.rfa.org/vietnamese/in_depth/After-4-years-in-prison-attorney-at-law-nguyen-van-dai-was-released-answer-the-interview-by-rfa-vhung-03062011095826.html; interview with Huỳnh Việt Lang, October 28, 2011, Đàn Chim Việt, accessed July 28, 2015, http://www.danchimviet.info/archives/44867/hu%E1%BB%B3nh-vi%E1%BB%87t-lang-tr%E1%BA%A3-l%E1%BB%9Di-ph%E1%BB%8Fng-v%E1%BA%A5n-dan-chim-vi%E1%BB%87t/2011/10.

6. Reprise and Prospects

1. See, for instance, Alexander Vuving, "Vietnam: A Tale of Four Players," in *Southeast Asian Affairs 2010*, ed. Daljit Singh (Singapore: Institute of Southeast Asian Studies, 2010), 367–91; Vuving, "Vietnam in 2012: A Rent-Seeking State on the Verge of a Crisis," in *Southeast Asian Affairs 2013*, ed. Daljit Singh (Singapore: Institute of Southeast Asian Studies, 2013), 325–47; Martin Gainsborough, "From Patronage to 'Outcomes': Vietnam's Communist Party Congresses Reconsidered," *Journal of Vietnamese Studies* 2 (Winter 2007): 3–26.

2. Martin Gainsborough, *Vietnam: Rethinking the State* (New York: Zed Books, 2010), 177–84.

3. Adam Fforde, "Vietnam in 2004: Popular Authority Seeking Power?" *Asian Survey* 45, no. 1 (2005): 146–52; Fforde, "Vietnam: A Note. Instability, the Causes of Development Success and the Need for Strategic Rethinking," 2005, Aduki, accessed November 21, 2010, http://www.aduki.com.au/Instability%202005%20-%20Adam %20Fforde.pdf#search=%22fforde%20note%20on%20instability%22; Fforde, "Vietnam in 2012: The End of the Party," *Asian Survey* 53, no. 1 (2013): 101–8.

4. Regina Abrami, Edmund Malesky, and Yu Zheng, "Vietnam through Chinese Eyes: Divergent Accountability in Single-Party Regimes," in *Why Communism Did Not Collapse: Understanding Authoritarian Regime Resilience in Asia and Europe*, ed. Martin K. Dimitrov (New York: Cambridge University Press, 2014), 237–75; Thomas Jandl, *Vietnam in the Global Economy: The Dynamics of Integration, Decentralization, and Contested Politics* (Lanham, MD: Lexington Books, 2013); Edmund Malesky, Regina Abrami, and Yu Zheng, "Institutions and Inequality in Single-Party Regimes:

A Comparative Analysis of Vietnam and China," *Comparative Politics* 43 (July 2011): 401–19.

5. The earliest depiction of this dialogue that I have located is in Ken Post, *Revolution, Socialism and Nationalism in Viet Nam*, vol. 3 (Aldershot, England: Dartmouth, 1989). Relations between national authorities and villagers in northern Vietnam in the 1960s, Post wrote, involved "a kind of dialogue in which ideas and the policies which seemed to follow from them would be enunciated from above and people would react below, not with public utterances nor with wide-scale collective action independent of the Party and the state, but in a multitude of acts of private comment and individual response" (14; also see 212). This dialogical conceptualization of state-society, authorities-citizens relations has been elaborated in other analyses, among them Kristin Pelzer, "Socio-cultural Dimensions of Renovation in Vietnam: *Doi Moi* as Dialogue and Transformation in Gender Relations," in *Reinventing Vietnamese Socialism*, ed. William S. Turley and Mark Selden (Boulder, CO: Westview Press, 1993), 309–36; Hy Van Luong, "The Marxist State and the Dialogic Restructuration of Culture in Rural Vietnam," in *Indochina: Social and Cultural Change*, ed. David Elliott et al. (Claremont, CA: Claremont-McKenna College, 1994), 79–117; Benedict J. Tria Kerkvliet, "An Approach for Analyzing State-Society Relations in Vietnam," *Sojourn: Journal of Social Issues in Southeast Asia* 16, no. 2 (2001): 238–78; Hy V. Luong, "Introduction: Postwar Vietnamese Society: An Overview of Transformational Dynamics," in *Postwar Vietnam: Dynamics of a Transforming Society*, ed. Hy V. Luong (Singapore: Institute of Southeast Asian Studies, 2003), 1–26; John Kleinen, *Vietnam: One-Party State and the Mimicry of Civil Society* (Bangkok: Research Institute on Contemporary Southeast Asia, 2015).

6. The dialogical interpretation of state-society relations in Vietnam is similar to but broader than the "consultative" and "deliberative" interpretations scholars have used when analyzing other one-party states. It is broader by including citizens conveying preferences and information to authorities without authorities first asking them (which consultative authoritarianism requires) and without authorities making space for them to do so (which deliberative authoritarian requires). Citizens can create those methods and means of communication themselves. Baogang He, "Participatory and Deliberative Institutions in China," in *The Search for Deliberative Democracy in China*, ed. Ethan J. Leib and Baogang He (New York: Palgrave Macmillan, 2006), 175–96; Baogang He and Mark E. Warren, "Authoritarian Deliberation: The Deliberative Turn in Chinese Political Development," *Perspectives on Politics* 9 (June 2011): 269–89.

7. Đặng Phong, *"Phá Rào" trong Kinh tế vào Đêm trước Đổi mới* ["Fence Breaking" in the Economy on the Eve of Renovation] (Hà Nội: Nxb Tri Thức, 2009); Adam Fforde and Stefan de Vylder, *From Plan to Market: The Economic Transition in Vietnam* (Boulder, CO: Westview Press, 1996); Benedict J. Tria Kerkvliet, *The Power of Everyday Politics: How Vietnamese Peasants Transformed National Policy* (Ithaca, NY: Cornell University Press, 2005); David W. H. Koh, *Wards of Hanoi* (Singapore: Institute of Southeast Asian Studies, 2006).

8. For instance, Thiem Hai Bui, "The Influence of Social Media in Vietnam's Elite Politics," *Journal of Current Southeast Asian Affairs* 35, no. 2 (2016): 89–112; David Koh,

"Political Reform and Democratization in Vietnam," in *East Asian Democracy and Political Changes in China: A New Goose Flying?*, ed. Zhengxu Wang and Colin Duerkop (Singapore: Konrad Adenauer Stiftung, 2008), 75–96; Jonathan London, "Viet Nam and the Making of Market-Leninism," *Pacific Review* 42 (July 2009): 375–99; Jason Morris-Jung, "Vietnam's Online Petition Movement," in *Southeast Asian Affairs 2015*, ed. Daljit Singh (Singapore: Institute of Southeast Asian Studies, 2015), 402–15; Jörg Wischermann, "Governance and Civil Society Action in Vietnam: Changing the Rules from Within—Potentials and Limits," *Asian Politics & Policy* 3, no. 3 (2011): 383–411.

9. Edmund Malesky and Paul Schuler, "Nodding or Needling: Analyzing Delegate Responsiveness in an Authoritarian Parliament," *American Political Science Review* 106 (August 2010): 19.

10. Thomas Sikor, "Local Government in the Exercise of State Power: The Politics of Land Allocation in Black Thai Villages," in *Beyond Hanoi: Local Government in Vietnam*, ed. Benedict J. Tria Kerkvliet and David G. Marr (Singapore: Institute of Southeast Asian Studies, 2004), 188–92; Sango Mahanty and Dang Dinh Trung, "Between 'State' and 'Society': Commune Authorities and the Environment in Vietnam's Craft Villages," *Asia Pacific Viewpoint* (2015): 13–14, accessed June 11, 2015, doi:10.1111/apv.12077.

11. Thiem H. Bui, "Development of Civil Society and Dynamics of Governance in Vietnam's One Party Rule," *Global Change, Peace & Security* 25, no. 1 (2013): 77–93; Bùi Hải Thiêm, "Pluralism Unleashed: The Politics of Reforming the Vietnamese Constitution," *Journal of Vietnamese Studies* 9 (Fall 2014): 1–32; Tuong Vu, "The Party v. the People: Anti-China Nationalism in Contemporary Vietnam," *Journal of Vietnamese Studies* 9 (Fall 2014): 33–66.

12. This paragraph and the next one draw on Martin Gainsborough, "Elites vs. Reform in Laos, Cambodia, and Vietnam," *Journal of Democracy* 23 (April 2012): 34–46; Le Hong Hiep, "The One Party-State and Prospects for Democratization in Vietnam," *ISEAS Perspective*, no. 63 (December 2013): 1–11; Benedict J. Tria Kerkvliet, "Democracy and Vietnam," in *Routledge Handbook of Southeast Asian Democratization*, ed. William Case (London: Routledge, 2015), 426–41.

13. "Lời bộc bạch của một đảng viên" [Frank Remarks of a Party Member], May 2, 2009, Psonkhanh blog, accessed July 11, 2012, http://vn.360plus.yahoo.com/psonkhanh; Đỗ Xuân Thọ, "Thư gửi Ban Chấp hành Trung ương Đảng Cộng sản Việt Nam" [Letter to the VCP's Central Executive Committee], March 16, 2010, *Tổ Quốc* [Homeland], April 1, 2010, 17–20.

14. See sample survey results reported in Russell J. Dalton and Nhu-Ngoc T. Ong, *The Vietnamese Public in Transition: The World Values Survey: Vietnam 2001* (Irvine, CA: Center for the Study of Democracy, University of California, 2001), 7; Yun-han Chu, Bridget Welsh, and Alex Chang, "Congruence and Variation in Sources of Regime Support in Asia" (Asian Barometer and Global Barometer Working Paper Series, No. 53, Taipei, 2012), 7.

15. Making a similar point are Tu Phuong Nguyen, "Rethinking State-Society Relations in Vietnam: The Case of Business Associations in Ho Chi Minh City," *Asian*

Studies Review 38, no. 1 (2014): 201; Wischermann, "Governance and Civil Society Action," 408.

16. For a thoughtful discussion of this possibility, see Brantly Womack, "Modernization and the Sino-Vietnamese Model," *International Journal of China Studies* 2 (August-September 2011): 157–75.

Index